Big Change

"With his route-map, Paul Taffinder achieves what in many other books remains an empty promise: he combines a brilliant insight into the complex mechanisms of change with an inspiring and practical guide on how to successfully drive corporate transformation. A real eye-opener."

Dr Siegfried Hoenle, Director, Warburg Dillon Read

"**Big Change** provides a comprehensive, clear and useful guide for all who confront the challenge of working in organizations facing transformation. Paul Taffinder has drawn together experiences with major organizations, current research and literature, and many practical and valuable resources and tips – all with a keen eye on raising the ambition for those who lead change. Rich with practical lessons, this is a *must read* for all within organizations who are facing the daunting challenge of riding the many waves of change."

*Scott G. Isaksen, President of the
Creative Problem Solving Group, Buffalo.
Former Director and Professor, The Center for Studies in
Creativity The State University of New York*

"A must for CEOs. This book contains many stimulating insights into the change issues relating to business transformation. A powerful journey providing detailed lessons written in a clear and easy, readable style."

Russell Evans, Group General Manager, GA Group

"As we approach the 21st century, this book – a timely and highly readable analysis of the essentials of successful corporate transformation – should be bought and studied by all CEOs and change agents, including those aspiring to such positions. It delivers fascinating insights into state-of-the-art 'big change' and as such is essential reading for managers in today's frenetic business world."

John Coleman, Director, The Change Partnership Ltd

"Great stories, great insights, great business psychology. A book that tells the whole story about why change works – or doesn't."

*Professor Mark Brown
Managing Director, Innovation Centre Europe Ltd
Visiting Professor of Innovation at Henley Management College*

"**Big Change** is an insightful book. It combines the big picture aspects of corporate transformation with useful case studies and action lists. It is an enlightening read for any senior manager working in today's changing business environment."

*Lynne Fisher, European Head of Training
and Development, Salomon Smith Barney*

Big Change

A Route-Map for Corporate Transformation

Paul Taffinder

JOHN WILEY & SONS

Chichester • New York • Weinheim • Brisbane • Singapore • Toronto

Copyright © 1998 by John Wiley & Sons Ltd,
Baffins Lane, Chichester,
West Sussex PO19 1UD, England

National   01243 779777
International (+44) 1243 779777
e-mail (for orders and customer service enquiries):
cs-books@wiley.co.uk
Visit our Home Page on http://www.wiley.co.uk
or http://www.wiley.com

Other Wiley Editorial Offices

John Wiley & Sons, Inc., 605 Third Avenue,
New York, NY 10158-0012, USA

WILEY-VCH Verlag GmbH, Pappelallee 3,
D-69469 Weinheim, Germany

Jacaranda Wiley Ltd, 33 Park Road, Milton,
Queensland 4064, Australia

John Wiley & Sons (Canada) Ltd, 22 Worcester Road,
Rexdale, Ontario M9W 1L1, Canada

John Wiley & Sons (Asia) Pte Ltd, 2 Clementi Loop #02-01,
Jin Xing Distripark, Singapore 129809

Library of Congress Cataloging-in-Publication Data

Taffinder, Paul.
    Big change : a route-map for corporate transformation / Paul
Taffinder.
        p.   cm.
    Includes index.
    ISBN 0-471-98288-1
    1. Organizational change. 2. Industrial management. I. Title.
HD58.8.T338   1988
658.4'06—dc21   97–47617
                                                                       CIP

British Library Cataloguing in Publication Data

A catalogue record for this book is available from the British Library

ISBN 0-471-98288-1

Typeset in 11/13pt Palatino by Mayhew Typesetting, Rhayader, Powys
Printed and bound in Great Britain by Bookcraft (Bath) Ltd, Midsomer Norton, Somerset

This book is printed on acid-free paper responsibly manufactured from sustainable
forestry, in which at least two trees are planted for each one used for paper production.

To my parents, Jack and Thelma, with love and thanks.

And to Nicholas, who arrived in the world when I started writing this book and, seven months later, showed a keen business appreciation by trying to eat the final manuscript

Contents

Foreword

The amount of information available to us doubles every five years. The power of the microchip doubles every eighteen months. We know from our own experience as business men and women that life is more complex, multi-faceted and faster moving than it has ever been.

In such circumstances there is the danger of dealing with the immediate and the urgent, to the detriment of the most important.

What strikes me forcefully in Paul Taffinder's excellent book is that the successful companies will be led by people who identify what is important and do something about it. The winning executives will be those who can step back and see the big picture; identify the need to improve, to change, to transform and, rather than simply plod on with incremental bits of change, will do those things in a radical way. They will be people who share their ideas and their vision, gain commitment and create excitement, and then work together to ensure that their vision becomes a winning reality.

Bookstore shelves these days groan under the weight of change theories and strategic models, but what is especially refreshing about this book is its pragmatism. It is an action-orientated manual, based on many organizations' hard-fought experience of how to go about the difficult process of change.

For me there were two powerful lessons that emerged as I read through the book. First, the criticality of knowing *when* to introduce big change and, second, the challenge of harnessing the diverse, so often untapped, skills of a company's workforce. As to timing, Paul Taffinder vividly demonstrates the unseen dangers of waiting until your company is showing signs of crisis before you start thinking about transforming it – by then it may be too late. The time to really worry is when you are successful, when you are making excellent profits, when the media say what a wonderful organization you are!

That is the time when it is so important to raise your sights to the future, anticipate what might happen and deal with it. That requires courage and tenacity of purpose. People will tell you 'don't fix it if it ain't broke'. The true art of leadership is to realize that it is broke – it just hasn't disintegrated in front of your eyes. I was struck by an analogy when I was looking at a very beautiful old house the other day. From the outside it looked in perfect condition. But in fact it was riddled with dry rot and was quite unsafe. Beware corporate dry rot. Business is not about looking at historic figures, not about taking comfort from an attractive profit and loss account or balance sheet – it is about identifying the sustainability of the revenue streams, it is about looking at the long-term competitiveness of products and services, it is about understanding where every penny of cost goes and making sure that it is really adding value.

So ask yourself: how successful is your company going to be in the future? What are your ambitions for the long-term future? And where is the dry rot that may not yet be visible – but is the more insidious for all that?

To be able to see the dry rot and raise corporate ambition means actively fighting any sense of complacency or arrogance. It requires restlessness, constant striving for perfection, an understanding of the fluidity of business, an appreciation that things are never permanent, never as good as they might look, that the company is always vulnerable. Invariably that under-standing and awareness lead to taking momentous decisions. It might mean changing a product range, creating a new distribu-tion channel, deciding not to operate in certain businesses or countries. Frequently these are decisions that cannot be enacted incrementally. You cannot leap a chasm in two bounds.

Another indisputable but too often neglected lesson, richly captured in the detailed business stories of this book, is about harnessing the creative energy of employees. I believe most of us running companies fail dismally to use all the talents of our people. Their ingenuity and their ability to innovate is sup-pressed either by the weight of bureaucracy and the narrow and rigid requirements we demand of them in a corporate structure, or is diminished because we executives, ourselves, have insuffi-cient imagination to identify ways of unleashing their innovative talent. Creativity and innovation, Paul Taffinder rightly admonishes us, begin at the top.

One of the big changes I have attempted in various companies, with varying degrees of success, is to introduce a total quality management process to encourage everyone to really participate in improving what they do in their own sphere of activity and in the company at large. It is about empowering staff to come up with ideas which mean we will do some things better, or stop doing some things altogether. At its best, the beauty of such a process is that we are asking everybody to help us manage the company more effectively. Nobody will do that better than the people who are closest to their own sphere of activity – something they will always know more about than anybody else. But this also means that everyone in the company must know where the company is going and how critical their role is in achieving corporate success.

The resounding theme of this book is about making *big* change and I am convinced that the way we manage our people offers one of the greatest change opportunities in commercial life. Like all big change it will not be without risk and will need courage and vision.

When all is said and done, big change requires time. Time to plan and time to drive through, but every minute of an executive's business life is precious. The demands on our time are high and clearly are unlikely to diminish.

How time is used becomes paramount. Spending some time reading this book could be one of the best investments you make.

Peter Ellwood

Peter Ellwood is Group Chief Executive of Lloyds TSB Group, an organization described by *The Economist* (17 January 1998) as 'the world's most valuable bank' with a market capitalization of some $70 billion and a staff of 85 000. Chief Executive of Barclaycard from 1985 until 1989, Peter Ellwood moved to TSB Bank where as CEO he set about successfully transforming its fortunes, culminating in the decisive merger with Lloyds Bank in 1995.

Acknowledgements

My thanks are due to a number of people around the world for their help in both the early thinking as well as the research and writing of this book.

First, my thanks to those people at the organizations included in the book who agreed to be interviewed or provide information during the course of research for the book. Their assistance has transformed what would otherwise be a story merely about organizational change to one about the people who make it happen. In most cases their experience and candid comments appear throughout the book – but I must especially thank those individuals who offered information and views but who wished to remain anonymous: I have respected their wish and I would like to thank them for helping to add depth to my interpretation of the often complex story of their organizations. They know who they are.

Moreover, several people in the various offices of Coopers & Lybrand provided background, facilitated introductions, worked hard to make arrangements for interviews or otherwise assisted in the innumerable tasks required in collecting information and helping me put one word behind another. In no particular order I should like to thank: Udo Leppin, Danilo Tondelli, Erik Rule, Michael Applin, Robin Tye, Ian Wilson, Harald Herrmann, Hansjoerg Dettwiler, John Dowson, Edgar Fluri, Keith Baldwin, Eric Milton, Paul Shelton, David Wells, Ed Horgan, Wood Parker, Mike Griffin, Gideon Bainton, Lucy Charles, Michelle Pieri, Sheila Small, Jonathan Brantigan, Claire Renn, Dawn Dobbins, Priti Vaghela, Trevor Norkett, Seema Rampersad, William Ristoff and there are no doubt several others I have neglected to mention. Special thanks to Barbara Shore for the artistic and graphics work.

My thanks also to Mike Lewis, now at Stanford Research Institute International, for some of the early thinking on corporate transformation.

In addition, my ideas have developed over time because of the thinking and experience of colleagues at Coopers & Lybrand in the Corporate Transformation team, in particular: Frank Milton, who listened and thought it was a good idea, Peter Williams, Peter Sedgwick, Ian Bradbury, Paul Gibbons, Peninah Thomson, Michael Thomas, Paul Oliver and Trevor Davis.

Thanks to the Sunday Times for permission to reprint the extract on p. 3, © Nicholas Fraser/*The Sunday Times*, London, 1995.

Finally, heartfelt thanks to Mandy for putting up with (and even showing interest in) yet another of my big ideas; and to Alan, for looking over my shoulder and offering me the uniqueness of a four-year-old's perspective on the whole endeavour.

1
Big Change? Change to What . . .?

I'M GETTING BETTER AND BETTER . . . AND BEING LEFT BEHIND

Big change is many things. It is scale. It is scope. It is effort. It is impact. You have picked up this book because you are affected by and wish to effect change. Change (and its puzzling sidekick transformation) are words people now use worldwide because we both fear big change and we desire it, because we observe the trauma of shocking upheavals (the collapse of the Soviet bloc) and demand it (the privatization of bloated state bureaucracies). In macrocosm, big change is easy to see: only consider the two examples above. In microcosm, also, it exists in as disturbing and as promising a form, only more personal.

On the one hand, via the Internet and amoeba-like groupware technology, the sum total of my electronic correspondence expands at exponential rates – each day. If I attempt to deal with all the implicit information and decisions in a habitual way (tried and tested over generations of management) that is systematic and all-inclusive, then I will run further and further behind and will eventually fail. The cost will be high: the loss of my job, possibly my career, certainly my self-esteem and my health. The organization I work for will also lose. By contrast, if I change the way I deal with incoming information, in a heuristic manner, if I scan, if I learn to decimate, to select the relevant from the rest, then the flood of information, cleverly handled, becomes an advantage. Three things have then happened: I have created for myself a new defence against overwhelming complexity and change, I have equipped myself with a new competence, and I have secured an advantage that most others may lack.

There is a simple message here and it is the essential message of this book, boiled down to that one sentence. However, for me as an individual and, by extension, for the organizations we all inhabit, the world is never still. No one seriously doubts that worldwide competition will not intensify, nor that scale advantages will not encourage many industries to condense still further, that international benchmarks of quality or performance will not ratchet up under relentless pressure and technology throw up bewildering and unimagined marvels, nor indeed that each new idea or transformation will not be disposed of when it has run its course.

Further still, all this complexity is yet one thin layer of multiple nets of complexity, coupled together by networked structures of global proportions – economic, political, commercial, market, professional and social. Even by themselves these structures produce change. Together, they feed off each other, producing fragmentation and dislocation in the selfsame structures and of an order and direction which is near impossible to foresee. Epithets such as revolutionary and transformational seem barely adequate.

Faced with the single difficulty of burgeoning Lotus notes on my laptop screen, my response is probably *not* to transform the way I work – no big change here . . . yet. Like most organizational denizens I continue to adjust incrementally and haphazardly. I focus on the regular messages I typically come across each day. I partially read most, delete some, and park those over which I cannot instantly make up my mind. In three weeks' time I still haven't read them properly and I convince myself they probably weren't important anyway. Like a paper in-tray, they accumulate in a growing pile. In the end, prodded to action by a tart reminder from the IT administrator that I am clogging system memory, I delete them.

Strangely (and deceptively), I am none the worse for this behaviour. No dark consequences befall me. I am as effective as my peers. In the main, they behave much like me. Moreover, I am not dissimilar to my competitors in benchmark firms. I know some of them: we chat over drinks from time to time. And yet I feel under pressure. I feel the need to improve, to be better at what I do. And I am nervous about being left behind. I put time into learning more about the software available. I ask colleagues for advice now and again. Frequently I ponder on the possibility of securing extra resource to plough through all the incoming data, but there is a financial cost attached. Would it be justified? And would it work effectively if I were not constantly on the case? Occasionally, I dream wishfully of a kind of Eureka moment when an idea leaps out at me and the solution materializes shortly thereafter.

Of course, there does come a moment when everything changes, when the next great advance comes – at least as far as my colleagues and I are concerned. Jane in Company XYZ has developed and implemented an on-line editor that gives her automatic scanning/sorting/prioritizing/deleting for all incoming electronic mail. I and my colleagues, who have all been adjusting our performance at roughly the same rate and in generally the same ways and by assiduous (if unconscious) benchmarking against each other, are left behind. As far as we're concerned, this change has happened overnight. It is a revolution. It is a catastrophe. Jane has an on-line editor! How will we keep up? For Jane, however, the change has not been instantaneous, though it is still transformational. Jane is in this happy position because either (a) she was in the right place at the right time (she was lucky) or (b) she was innovative (she was thinking and acting differently to the rest of us). If Jane triumphs again by developing or using something that gives her a second or subsequent distinctive edge, then we know she's not just lucky.

The Art of Decimation

There's too much of everything. In the end, the abundance of information can paralyse, just like the excess of food, sleep or love. . . . The future of education will consist in telling people how to select or reject information. I'm beginning to teach my students the art of decimation. How do you know something will be useful any more? How do you acquire enough information about information?

Umberto Eco

Interviewed by Nicholas Fraser, Eco's pendulum of opinion

© Nicholas Fraser/*The Sunday Times*, London, 1995.

A MAD RACE TO CONVERGE

Credit Foncier de France had, for 140 years, a government-backed monopoly on cheap home-building loans for low-income customers. Technically a private enterprise but traditionally run by government appointees, Credit Foncier had made huge losses in the 1980s chiefly through property speculation. In 1995 Alain Juppé's centre-right government started to allow market forces to exert pressure on the bank by abolishing its monopoly. The expected pattern soon followed: splitting the business and refocusing as part of two other institutions, with the threat of 1800 job losses. Employees promptly took the bank's governor and ten board members hostage in a doomed attempt to prevent the inevitable.

As a result of the market forces we all know so well, corporate executives worldwide probably 'invested' something in excess of $90 billion in downsizing between 1993 and 1997. It is hard, though not always impossible, to stand aloof from this, as we shall see. The spiral of decline feeds on itself (Figure 1.1). As it becomes more difficult for a firm to show top-line growth, so pressure mounts to reduce costs and utilize the asset base better. The two together are likely to attract shareholder pressure to improve returns, resulting in a shorter-term corporate focus and the search for solutions such as liquidating assets. This in itself might not undermine the capability of the business to innovate and to grow, but it typically goes hand-in-hand with a shift in the culture of the firm to one of cost-cutting, bearing down on employee rewards and driving out those employees who dislike the new culture, retaining those who do (who then reinforce the new cost culture), and making the organization relatively unattractive to new joiners (and therefore shutting out one source of new ideas). All these things, in the multiple layers we have just outlined, will certainly reduce competitiveness, contributing further to an acceptance of the cost-reduction strategy and culture as the best way forward. Moreover, this overall cycle creates signals in the market. Here is a company struggling to sustain longer-term value growth. Shareholders seek to protect their returns. Company executives strive to extract greater value through cost reduction but on a rapidly diminishing scale. The share price weakens. The company comes under increasing competitive pressure and an overwhelming focus on cost reduction has so eroded its strategic sense, operational manoeuvr-

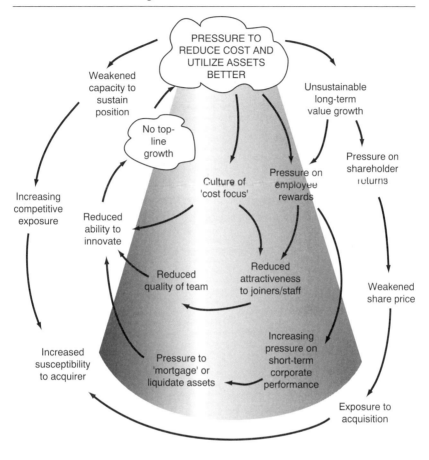

Figure 1.1 The spiral of decline.

ability and capacity to innovate that it is even less able to defend its position. The share price continues to weaken. It is therefore a prime target for acquisition or may indeed fail.

The concept of shareholder value, gaining in power now in countries beyond just the USA and Britain, has driven executives to demonstrate improved return on assets, usually in the manner described above by hammering down costs but also by continually adopting standards and ideas from other organizations and accordingly reshaping, piece by piece, their own firm. This process, viewed at a macro level, is nicely encapsulated in the 1996 Chatham House Forum Report, *Unsettled Times* (p.21):

> Managers set out to define their core business, selling non-core activities to third parties and buying-in ('out-sourcing') anything which they can

acquire from the open market that they cannot make more cheaply or reliably themselves. Having defined what it is that the firm is to do, the individual steps or processes by which this is achieved are scrutinised with a view to redesigning each in order to take account of information technology. This is often called *re-engineering*. Finally, each component of the re-engineered company is compared to that of other companies which carry out the same activity, a process called *benchmarking*, where the aim is both to achieve a parity of costs and also to 'borrow' useful ideas which others may have.

The result of all this, viewed industrywide and over longer timescales than many executives absorbed in corporate change choose to consider, is that organizations engaging in the same competitive war can end up looking like carbon copies. Moreover, a desperate spiral is created when, as shareholder pressure for capital to perform increases, firms adopt ever more defensive positions. The spiral becomes:

Refocus
Redesign
Benchmark
Converge

Convergence begins to happen at faster rates and the firms become even more similar, losing distinctiveness and any hope of differentiation. As the *Unsettled Times* report argues, an industry becomes both more competitive and less profitable. The despairing outcome is commoditization. We see it all around.

In the mid-1990s Europe's car-making industry reflected this. Overcapacity was the prime evil. Peugeot, Renault, Fiat, BMW, Volvo, Volkswagen and Mercedes were joined by General Motors and Ford as well as the Japanese auto companies in a scramble to survive. In spite of a growing market, profits were wafer-thin because of a bloody price war in many European countries – the surface manifestation of industry convergence.

Renault's case demonstrates the problems of convergence and commoditization. Louis Schweitzer, Renault's head, had been very successful in introducing new models but was rewarded with a staggering loss of a shade over $1 billion for the fiscal year ending 1997. What had he been doing wrong? Well, nothing obvious. Much of the loss was to cover downsizing (some 5500 job losses and more to come) and he aimed to get in excess of $3 billion per year savings out of the business by the year 2000. But, in a market crowded by me-too businesses, cost-competitiveness even of the most draconian sort is never going to be enough. Nor, strangely, is product innovation around new models and features, since these are things that are not easily defensible: the lifecycle of apparently innovative models or features in cars is very short, the risks of investment high. In such an industry, further cost-reduction, production streamlining and eventual consolidation is unavoidable. Gaining a defensible advantage will only occur through seizing the moment at the start of some kind of massive dislocation in the industry (which would have to be miraculously unanticipated by Renault's competitors) such as government policy intervention on car pollution, or by a technology-driven remaking of the industry's fundamental structure and character. In the first instance, Renault would have to be very lucky. In the second, Renault would have to be thinking and acting differently to all the other car-makers. And that would require a transformation.

Another example, but one where the chief executive took early action to pull his firm out of danger, is Schwab, the stockbrokers – a business that, with compound growth of 20% per annum since its founding in 1974, had no obvious reason to change. The firm and its competitors, known as 'discounters', grasped the new potential of on-line electronic share dealing via the Internet with some vigour and, being smaller, faster and more flexible than their bigger full-service rivals like Merrill Lynch, one might have expected Charles Schwab, founder of the firm, to intensively focus the firm's efforts on carving out the biggest share of this new electronic market. Far from it. Although Schwab launched e.Schwab as a new electronic service, he also began to shift strategic direction, away from what is essentially a straightforward transaction-based offering (and thus easily commoditized) towards other value-added services like performance analytics and investment advice. The knowledge 'bought' by investors is harder to specify and therefore to replicate – such things strengthen defensive capability against encroaching change.

The convergence pattern (refocus–redesign–benchmark–converge) might be considered to be confined to just the old industries. Much is made of the market capitalization of the new high-tech elite – Silicon Valley companies and their ilk worldwide – in contrast to the old guard of Ford, General Motors, Chrysler and the like. *The Economist* points to the premium that

Table 1.1 High-tech Premium

	Sales 1996 ($bn)	Employees 1996 (000)	Market capitalization mid-March ($bn)
General Motors	164.1	647	43
Ford	147.0	345	38
Chrysler	61.4	114	22
Total	372.5	1106	103
Intel	20.8	49	116
Microsoft	8.7	21	120
Cisco	4.1	10	34
Total	33.6	80	270

© *The Economist,* London (29 March 1997, p.31)

the high-technology giants Intel, Microsoft and Cisco Systems command over the long-established Detroit big three. In spite of sales ten times greater than those of the high-tech firms, the car-makers attract a market capitalization only one-third that of the new kids (Table 1.1). Even Jack Welch's General Electric, topping *Business Week*'s 1996 league of the global 1000 most valuable corporations with a market capitalization of $137 billion on sales of $70 billion, has fallen short of their premium.

This is remarkable, but not any guarantee for the future. In the decade between the mid-1950s and the 1960s, it is as well to remember, the chemicals industry surged along on a tidal wave of growth and profitability not dissimilar to the high-tech eruption of the late 1980s and 1990s.

A 'paradigm shift', to use Silicon Valley parlance, has clearly occurred in the high-tech industry. It will bring winners and losers. Even Microsoft, with undisputed dominance in the personal computer software market worldwide, found itself in 1995 somewhat on the back foot, forced to re-evaluate the popularity and influence of the Internet and therefore to swing the rudder of the Microsoft supertanker hard over for a 180-degree change in strategic direction. Until then Microsoft employees who publicly attached importance to the Internet were rumoured to be risking censure from on high. In fact, until 1995 the software giant's strategy was based on conventional windows-based computing. What changed all this was indeed a paradigm shift, what Gates himself called the 'Internet Tidal Wave' in a memo to Microsoft executives in May 1995 – a dramatic surge in the market for electronic information sharing via the Internet. As a result, Microsoft was then faced foursquare with the challenge of shaping the future of the Internet, in practice (through Microsoft's usual approach) by striving to become the industry's technical standard for consumers and flattening the competition.

Not a few in the industry could be declared unhappy at Microsoft's discomfort. There are many whose teeth gnash at the mere mention of Bill Gates and who have stood in active opposition to his ambition to monopolize, in effect, any markets he touches – not least upstart browser company Netscape, database software supplier Oracle and workstation maker Sun Microsystems.

But for all the rumour and criticism about Gates, what is really interesting about the (continuing) Microsoft story is the fact that, with all its achievements, its executives had not fallen asleep at the wheel. And, given the success and undoubted arrogance of the company, that might well have happened. Corporate history is littered with the bones of dinosaurs that had become complacent while grazing in their lush, fruitful valleys. IBM was nearly a case in point, crumbling from $6 billion profits in 1990 to a whopping $5 billion loss in 1992 but, more importantly, letting slip its global pre-eminence despite the harshest of cost reduction exercises. 'Trimming' 140 000 IBMers from its ranks has not been enough to stop its losing a once impregnable high ground.

No, hats off to Gates and team for (a) being aware of the danger of the Internet at a still early stage and (b) being willing and able to turn the supertanker around as aggressively as they did. Critics will say that Microsoft had no choice. This is true. Any other move would have been to stand against the Internet tidal wave. Nonetheless, the true marvel is the size of the organizational transformation that Gates launched and his preparedness to see the opportunities as well as the dangers. Here was a $9 billion, 18 000-person business. Faced with the dawning realization of a huge shift in its market, Microsoft was prepared to commit (for commit read lose) the equivalent of 11% of annual sales – a massive $1 billion – in the quest to be a major player in the Internet game. Certainly, with cash reserves in 1995 of over $4 billion ($9 billion by 1997) burning a very large hole in his pocket, Gates' investment was not all risk. Beyond the staggering losses the firm was willing to accept, however, we must think of the marketing strategies retargeted, the projects and initiatives axed, the programmers and other employees redirected to new objectives, the overturning of investment plans, and not least the learning of new knowledge and skills.

Bill Gates and his team were engaged in not simply a readjustment of their operations and a fight for continued dominance but a defence against the sudden and rapid growth of the small, innovative companies like Sun Microsystems which did so much to develop the Internet and moved to consolidate their strengths before Microsoft, IBM and Intel might embrace them in an all-enveloping bearhug.

Survival, and for the few high returns and dominance, will be determined by the willingness and capability of such firms to avoid the short-term draw towards churning out cloned technology for countries racing to match America's huge high-tech consumption (for that way the dragons of commoditization lie) and push both their products/services and organizational capabilities to increasingly sophisticated levels in the developed markets.

Hooray for Bill Gates . . . I Guess

In which Mr Badger advises Mr Toad to light the candles and read books

It snowed almost 60 cm in upstate New York – wet, gluey snow, so weighty that it brought down trees across power lines and left our farmhouse in the dark and cold for three days and nights. We huddled under five blankets and an 18-kg dog and read by the light of oil lamps.

The computer, of course, was dead. The Internet, an entire universe (bright leaping data, shooting stars, comets of information, evanescent meteor showers) shut down. We fumbled in the dark for match and wick; we watched our shadows on the wall.

That was weeks ago. Before the lights went out, I had been reading a colleague's article in *Time* ('Can Thor Make a Comeback?' Dec. 16) that described how ancient religions have at last found their way to the Internet. There seemed something funny and very American about insisting that eternity must scramble to catch up with progress – God's obligation to gadgets. It is the stout Cortez syndrome, the New World habit of needing a procession of new worlds, transformative revelations following upon one another like new-model cars.

Dynamics of progress: the Pacific that John Keats' stout Cortez (actually, it was a fat Balboa) beheld has become the Pacific Rim, and out over the horizon the Sandwich Islands have turned into an American state, Hawaii, where men may marry each other now. American fast food will gobble up China. The planet contracts to the size of a grape.

In *The Wind in the Willows*, Mr Toad romances his gypsy cart until he is transformed by the sight of that splendid innovation, the motorcar. The gypsy cart is forgotten – is junk. We are all Toad. We need the sobering voice of Mr Badger to talk us down from our manias.

Hooray for Bill Gates, I guess. Hooray (long ago) for Marconi's gypsy cart, the telegraph. The railroad across the US was a marvellous new cart (though you get an argument on that from remnant buffalo and Sioux). The US interstate-highway system, brightest cultural blossom of the Eisenhower years, was a wonder. So were the electric carving knife, the fax machine and the splendid neckties and haircuts of the 1970s.

Overstimulation, hypergreed and a kind of idiocy – those three stooges – have a way of tumbling into the room along with technological progress, which gives them respectability and theological cover. Mr Badger, Toad's killjoy twin, makes these points: 1) each transformative moment will be superseded by another one, tomorrow or the next day – all marvels are disposable; 2) innovations are not always wonderful; 3) the world is round and time is circular; human nature is constant, but 4) may be damaged – or what is worse, humiliated – by novelties, which (like '70s neckties or television in any decade) may have about them an aura of imbecility, leading to 5) the Paradox of Retro-grade Progress. Television is a Faustian bargain (a dazzling technology that induces dullness and even moronism), and the Internet has the same ominous tendencies. It is not a bad idea to mistrust the omnivorous vulgarity of innovation, even its (paradoxical) death instinct. Novelty, in its pointless ingenuity, keeps slaying itself.

Not that Mr Badger is a Luddite. He merely points out that technology has a mixed record. Citizens-band radio was a Toad mania long ago. Technology is sometimes, in the end, a little stupid – as anything must be that was brilliant yesterday but was surpassed overnight – a monster that lives on a hungry, dynamic need for its own obsolescence. The universe of Gutenberg should no more be an abandoned graveyard than, say, the American city, which, a generation after World War II, seemed to be in decline and headed toward extinction. Why did we need the cities when we had the new paradise of the suburbs? Who could ask for anything more?

It is a sound rule of travel, and of intellectual delight, to go where the others are not. There-fore, plunge back into books – not texts read in pixels off the screen, but read, rather, with their sweet weight of thought held in the hand. Go where others are not – to wonderful unread writers like Seneca or Plutarch, for example, whom I read during our blackout. They under-stood certain essentials that we have misplaced.

After three days, my computer sprang back to life, chipper, as if nothing had happened. I found myself wishing that a hard snow would fall on Seattle. Bill Gates and his geek brigades, I thought, need to sit in the dark for a while, or to light oil lamps and catch up on their reading.

I thought it, and nature responded with such biblical overreaction (the heaviest weather in the Pacific Northwest in 70 years, days of snow, ice, thaw, rainstorms, flood, power failures) that I began to feel guilty.

Lance Morrow, Hooray for Bill Gates . . . I guess, *Time* (13 January 1997, p.64)

© 1997 *Time Inc.* Reprinted by permission.

CREATING THE FUTURE

In business you will become locked in the twilight endgame of convergence if you are unable or too slow to understand and react to the future. To sustain a dominant and successful industry or market position in some cases will require from firms responses that are moderate and adaptive. For others, already locked in the endgame, as in Renault's case, nothing short of transformation will do. In both instances – moderate, adaptive change and transformational (big) change – deep and painful questions need to be asked about the business and its future. Obviously the past is not the future – but so many executives treat it that way. Microsoft's about-turn on the Internet is a fine example of courage under the weight of all previous pronouncements – though many might call it breathtaking arrogance. The top team of Microsoft (known as the boop – Bill and the Office of the President) were prepared to challenge the company's existing thinking and strategy. About a year earlier Hamel and Prahalad had called for firms to do exactly this in their 1994 ground-breaking book *Competing for the Future*:

> To extend industry foresight and develop a supporting strategic architecture, companies need a new perspective on what it means to be 'strategic'. They need to ask new strategy questions: not just how to maximize share and profits in today's businesses, but who do we want to be as a corporation in ten years' time, how can we reshape this industry to our advantage, what new functionalities do we want to create for customers, and what new core competencies should we be building? They need a new process for strategy-making, one that is more exploratory and less ritualistic. They need to apply new and different resources to the task of strategy-making, relying on the creativity of hundreds of managers and not just on the wisdom of a few planners (p.282).

And that's just for starters. Asking questions inevitably means having to answer them. Answering them requires the biggest challenge of all: *implementation* of big change. And Microsoft made big gains in the new Internet market in only one year, moving from what was, in effect, a zero market share in Web browsers to around 20%, although the question yet remains whether the company, stuck in 1997 on around 30%, has not left it too late to secure a significant role in the future networked world.

And what might organizations expect from the future? In what world will we and others compete? What will be the structure and nature of industries and organizations?

These are not questions of mere passing interest, nor agenda items over which executive teams might quickly gloss, on the assumption that the future is unknowable. Executive teams have the power not simply to react to whatever the future might throw their way but to *create* it. Gary Hamel refers to three different types of companies in a Harvard Business Review article entitled 'Strategy as revolution' (1996). First, there are the rule makers, the creators and upholders of industrial orthodoxy, such as IBM, United Airlines, Shell, Daimler Benz, Coca-Cola. Then there are the rule takers, the firms that follow the lead of the dominant oligarchy and among these are Fujitsu to IBM, Avis to Hertz or US Air to United. Finally there are the rule breakers, intent on overturning the accepted industrial order, such as The Body Shop, Direct Line, Southwest Airlines, Easyjet, ABB and many others.

Executive teams that understand the market and industry fracture lines that are driving change (or at least have a sense of how these might play out) have the advantage over both rule makers and rule takers. Moreover, their psychological frame of reference is different: they are not shackled by beliefs about the way things must be, nor by a fear of what is different (which the rule makers and rule takers characterize as subversiveness and therefore avoid). They are, like Microsoft's 'boop', able and willing to do the unexpected or the unpredictable. The transformation of an organization depends on this psychological frame of reference.

Speed, Specificity and Individual Psychology

Let's pretend we are Mr Toad. We are fascinated by new things, by the promise of tomorrow's technology. Where would Mr Toad start if he were looking at the future? One place to begin is in the realm of the futurists, who make a good living guessing about things that may come to pass. Not bad, but not to Toad's liking. For him this is too general, or too much of a linear extrapolation from current trends. It lacks imagination. Imagination *can* create the future. And so Toad prefers to start with science fiction. Science fiction offers a window on the future refreshingly uncluttered by artifacts of the present or past – and so, in that sense, provokes myriad possibilities. For example, in *The Nano Flower* (1995) Peter Hamilton invents a future which is both alien and contains powerful, haunting echoes from business today. In an early passage, for example:

> . . . the nodes with their logic matrices and data storage space gave her an augmented mentality able to interpret reports in milliseconds and implement decisions instantaneously . . . Companies and kombinates gave their own premier-grade executives identical implants in the belief they could boost their own managerial control in the same fashion (pp.36–7).

Another writer, Dan Simmons, paints an even more jaw-dropping picture in his novels *Hyperion* and *The Fall of Hyperion* – here an all-pervading Web of artificial intelligence, a datasphere affecting all life, both human and machine, but which is only explicable by crude analogy, thus 'towers of corporate and government data, highways of process flow, broad avenues of datumplane interaction . . . entire microecologies of dataflow and subroutine AIs . . .'.

And so the worlds of both these books are those in which information is instant and its sources galactic-wide and networked. Electronic data is received, processed, stored and directed at the neural level. Terminals, keyboards, screens and the like are nowhere in evidence. But even these changes, startling as they are, are only superficial to the profound transformation that has occurred in terms of, first, the *speed* at which decisions and actions can be taken and, second, the extent to which those decisions and actions can either be *specified* (defined, programmed, engineered) or are reliant on *individual psychology* (judgement, experience, trust).

We are building this future world now, of course, and it is very hard to predict what its overall shape and feel might be, still less the challenges and characteristics of its businesses or the day-to-day lives of its workforce. For one thing we lack the vocabulary to do so (although Bill Gates of Microsoft, Andy Grove of Intel and their peers are helping to correct this). Nevertheless, Hamilton and Simmons (and authors like them) show us some of the key criteria with which organizations must grapple and to which we shall return time and again in succeeding chapters of this book: speed, specificity and individual psychology.

Taking a big step back from Toad's wild-eyed science fiction future, but holding its possibilities firmly in the back of our minds, we might now invite Badger to inhabit our soul, to speak with his sober voice of logic and reasonableness. What we desire is a clue to the world of business along some timespan that is not so distant that it is neither believable nor reachable, for we live in the present and change cannot happen unless people feel a future to be accessible. Many sources can help us with this, but I have emphasized Samuel Huntington's great work *The Clash of Civilizations and the Remaking of World Order* (1996) as the broad canvas of social, political and economic movement upon which to inscribe the detail of organizational life in the next millennium. The palette is Chatham House Forum's *Unsettled Times* scenarios up to 2015. With both these sources I have taken the liberty of making my own interpretations of the consequences and implications for organizational design, mode of business operation and corporate culture.

Huntington pursues a number of themes in his analysis of the direction of global forces. Chief among them is the observation that modernization, of the sort that the countries outside the West are, to varying levels, experiencing, need not mean Westernization. So, for example, an Islamic way of life need be no blockage to economic growth. There is no proscription (whether in Islamic, Confucian or any other society) against electronic communication, mass education, efficiency in factories and so forth. And so, Huntington contends, 'the world is becoming more modern and less Western' (p.78).

Second, he makes some predictions about the West's control of resources around the year 2020 in comparison to its peak in 1920:

	1920	2020
Control of world territory	49%	24%
Per cent of world population	48%	10%
World economic product	70%	30%
Manufacturing output	84%	25%
Global military power	45%	10%

In economic terms the decline in manufacturing output is relatively less important. The shift to service industries in the industrialized world will make up for some of that decline. Nevertheless, the decline is enormous. Just 20 years ago, for example, the G7 (the USA, Japan, Germany, France, Britain, Italy and Canada) made up nine-tenths of the GDP output of all capitalist economies. With the spread of capitalism to other countries, by 1997 this was 50%. And the implications for organizations which have long been accustomed to operate in a particular (Western) business milieu   with all the assumptions that accompany that – are likewise enormous.

In the Chatham House report the author, Oliver Sparrow, ponders the global conditions that might lead to either adaptive success or structureless failure in the industrialized world. One of the most significant points he makes in overview is a reinforcement of the concept of speed. A year's absolute economic growth in 1800 is the same as a day's growth in 2000. Everything happens much faster. Moreover, the scale is greater. He discovers three scenarios: a *Faster, Faster* world of rapid and widespread commoditization in which nations must run faster, and faster still, in order to keep up; the *Post-Industrial Revolution* where local, focused networks across industries and countries exploit the possibilities of exponential growth in scientific knowledge, technology, judgement and management ability, reaping rich rewards (at least in the industrialized world); and *Rough Neighbours*, an intolerable and socially unmanageable version of *Faster, Faster* in which firms are forced to concentrate exclusively on this day's problems.

For organizations each of these scenarios looks somewhat different, but there are similarities.

Faster, Faster

In *Faster, Faster* 2015 IT has provided the means to better integrate and to specify at a more and more minute level the knowledge required to perform the vast majority of organizational functions. 'Chunking' and 'modularizing' of what were once core work activities and processes allow firms to buy these from a highly integrated global market. Specialization therefore has advanced apace and is commonplace but everyone has the means to do the same thing – information is widespread, transnational, indeed transparent – so competitive advantage cannot be attained easily. Huntington, in his work, comments on the huge advantage that the West and Japan have enjoyed in advanced technology industries, but cautions that technologies are being disseminated through an 'interconnected world' which the West itself has created. Thus, for the world of *Faster, Faster* success and failure turns on marginal differences in competence, closely guarded by each organization. There has been, declares Sparrow:

> . . . a wave of mergers and acquisitions . . . Shareholder pressure is intense. Increasingly fixed assets are valued at less than their replacement costs. Analysts seem to know more about the firm and its operating environment than do the management. Innovations come faster and faster, yet the financial yield is seldom more than disappointing. The fashion is for what is known as 'pacing', of keeping exactly abreast of the competition, while keeping them ignorant of your intentions. The typical firm operates in an outsourced, diversified network in which it seeks the lowest-cost, quality-assured intermediates with the fervour of a hunting weasel. It is, however, careful to keep the core of the company distinct and isolated from this. Career paths are heavily modified to meet this two-ring model, with the former management cadre operating in the inner core and contractors and service providers in the outer loop. This makes innovation doubly difficult, as those with technical knowledge are often isolated from central concerns that they might help to solve. Firms attempt to evaluate and husband their intellectual capital, as well as deny it to their rivals. (p.121)

To get further behind the detail of the report, I spoke to Dr Oliver Sparrow at Chatham House in St James's Square, London, where the Royal Institute of International Affairs has been pursuing its research since 1920 when former delegates of the Paris Peace Conference of 1919 set up the Institute. '*Faster, Faster* is a time,' argues Sparrow, 'when it has become impossible to defend against commoditization – although it is possible to slow its pace for individual firms. The core of the organization is therefore held together primarily by "defence folk", by which I mean lawyers and accountants and the like, holding the ring against continuous predation of whatever corporate advantages or secrets you have managed to retain. Aimless M&A characterizes this scenario. Indeed, businesses are driven to acquisition by the need to import some kind of short-term advantage.'

One of the problems, of course, with the 'defence folk' is that they have a background and a culture of defending the status quo and extracting value from assets. This ethos is so intensely reinforced by the predatory nature of markets that the defence folk find it harder and harder to communicate with those who can make a contribution to innovation. Further, as Sparrow maintains, 'because of their background they don't really understand the fundamentals of their business. What they're good at is defence, acquisition, pouncing on the new start-ups, buying into little joint ventures – so they find it increasingly hard to define their business logic in terms that make sense to either employees in the core or the contractors beyond.'

The notion of 'self-help' is also the *sine qua non* of the times. The state and organizations have thrown back any paternalistic assistance onto the individual – the state because it can no longer afford to, the organization because it has few employees at the core and must operate in as flexible and cost-efficient a manner as possible to meet the speed of competitor action and reaction.

The gold-collar or knowledge workers have the best of employment but hyper-powerful communications technology has sucked them into direct competition with other knowledge workers all over the world. The stakes, therefore, are always being raised. Graduates, of many hues, populate the remaining core of organizations, sometimes making up as much as 80% and more of staff complement. To be excellent is an entry requirement to knowledge work. To be exceptional, however, means to be a 'star' – once the preserve of Hollywood actors and investment bank traders, advisors and analysts. Huge payouts and benefits accrue to those whose knowledge provides an edge or whose performance contributes significant gains in shareholder value, or whose loss to the company (straight to a competitor) would be damaging. Loyalty, in the sense in which it was once understood, has less value in those firms sliding down the slippery convergence slope. To the extent that it builds or sustains a personal or corporate network, it continues to be a valued commodity, but in the best organizations it remains a powerful social–psychological force that unifies networked employees, contractors and suppliers – a defensive capability not subject to simple replication by competitors.

Moreover, the number of people engaged (both as providers and recipients) in personal 'performance investment', once known as continuing education and self-development, has soared. Seeking and securing a personal advantage across a broad suite of competencies, whether in personal characteristics or skill or knowledge, has become the lifetime preoccupation of tens of millions of workers in the two-ring model of employees and contractors/providers. Educational courseware is bought and provided globally and in large part digested at home by an increasing number of people working in dispersed datasphere networks. Such multimedia, interactive educational software has sufficient artificial intelligence to be able to pace the recipient, broaden or narrow, make connections to related topics and answer questions at many levels of sophistication.

Of course, the more successful that individual workers are in their own performance investment (crucially dependent on their personal wealth to begin with, since investment of any kind is costly), the more they differentiate themselves from those who cannot or who fail to invest. Modest capability means intermittent work on contract, a wage squeeze in real terms and an unforgiving commoditization of personal competence. Social dislocation and its consequences (falling wages, unemployment, societal tensions) are thus everywhere felt, but most especially in those countries which, for one reason or another, have found themselves on the periphery of global commerce. Nonetheless, the pressure is on everyone.

The Post-Industrial Revolution

Is knowledge mere information? Can it be exploited by IT to the nth degree? That is, can we analyse it, deconstruct its constituent elements, engineer and program it? Will it be possible to do this for most rational chunks of organizations? If so, then *Faster, Faster* will probably be the world that we are rushing towards. If not, if knowledge is (at least in clusters) intangible, rich and too complex for specification and, moreover, the supporting knowledge-based infrastructure (in all its social–psychological complexity) hard to replicate, then the world will be somewhat different.

In the *Post-Industrial* world of commerce, although rapid convergence and commoditization are still facts of life for the firms of 2015, complex sources of high value-added innovation offer the solid defensible positions which the fortunate will fight to sustain and to which most organizations aspire – and these are frequently sited in either geographical centres of excellence or among local, focused networks. Overall there are three types of industry:

> There is a scattering of traditional activities, still unmerged into the integrated and networked complexity of the bulk of the overlapping national economies of the IW. There are highly integrated, intensely competitive and broadly commoditized industries. These are, for the most part, transnational. Many have the ambition of becoming international, in some sense or another. A few truly global industries exist, almost invariably calling upon focused local centres of excellence for specific services, such as research and new product development. Finally, and of dominant importance to national welfare, there are clusters of capability, trust, tacit understanding and capability which seem very difficult to duplicate quickly or to a high quality. These draw upon the sheer complexity and integration of the IW economies (p.126).

In the commoditized industries of this scenario, firms are subject to some of the same pressures described in *Faster, Faster*. However, the opportunity to exploit knowledge clusters to produce innovation of the sort that offers defensible barriers means that firms are less exclusionary, less prone to protect their intellectual capital from competitors at all costs. To the contrary, it is essential to pull in assistance at both the strategic and core level, to leverage the huge and growing repositories of knowledge worldwide and to come together, where each owns only a part of the solution to a problem or opportunity, in alliances and partnerships to create sustainable innovations.

This is most especially true where large organizations have dispersed resources in a wide network – both structurally and geographically. IT enables firms to seek out and collaborate with external sources of expertise, thus reducing costs and focusing the business. So, for example, in addition to outsourcing IT, distribution, property and plant management much of the legal, personnel, customer service, sales and finance processes could be bought-in. (By 1997 in the USA, outsourcing spending of this type had already exceeded some $100 billion.)

With only business strategy, IT strategy and product development left in the core, at first blush the relative benefits of having a core business with outsourced, networked services seem persuasive, but this evolution has brought with it the need to *manage* rich complexity without direct authority or control. Thus, for any given business a small group of full-time strategists directs an enormous variety of services bought-in from outside networks to deliver its own product or service. If the product or service is straightforward, then IT will handle the bulk of coordination and integration. But if it is not, then complexity itself will need to be managed.

Oliver Sparrow again: 'The first thing to say is that a network is a nightmarish way to work. Nobody chooses a network. Networks are thrust upon us. There is a great deal of noise made nowadays about the desirability of delayering and networks. But this is nonsense! Most people want to work in hierarchies – they are comfortable. They want to know what is expected of them.'

This is not to say that networks will be rejected. Vertically integrated organizations will not be able to survive. Their boundaries will blur, they will retreat to the core and networks will be thrust upon them. They will have to cope with these changes. But the organizational world will be very complex. 'The nature of the beast,' suggests Sparrow, 'is such that any one business unit needs to look six different ways at any one time, to different suppliers and different potential customers and partners and so on – taking all their views into account . . .'

As a result, an essential competency of the *Post-Industrial* world is delivering complexity management (as it is in *Faster, Faster* but to a lesser degree). Since defensive capability stems from harnessing knowledge to new ends, in vast knowledge pools which we must remember are growing exponentially, complexity management is itself layered and only partly subject to IT facilitation. This network complexity and the need for complexity management will therefore drive demand for information-intermediaries. Michael Dertouzos, who runs MIT's Laboratory for Computer Science, contends that the Worldwide Web will actually create large numbers of new jobs and organizations dedicated to the intermediary work of sorting through the burgeoning info-junk – the 'too much of everything' described by Umberto Eco. In an interview with *Forbes* (2 June 1997, p.178) Dertouzes envisages an explosion of jobs such as info-tailors, info-brokers, and info-navigators, reasoning that we do not yet have the capability to build smart machines or search engines even one-thousandth as intelligent and flexible as people. Info-brokers and their like will succeed or fail to the degree that they are able to help business people find each other across the Web and facilitate trusting relationships. By 1997, the first glimmerings of this were already evident. Responsive Database Services Inc. was abstracting IT and telecommunications publications on a daily basis for customers who had discovered that real-time updates from the avalanche of wire stories jamming up networks and e-mail boxes was more of a hassle than a competitive advantage – true info-junk, clogging executives' time use and slowing up digestion, analysis and decison making. Up to 2015 electronic search engines will remain too crude a device to be able to emulate the critical and discerning info-tailor.

Much, then, rests on the social–psychological: judgement, intellectual firepower at a level of critical mass, and relationships between people within which new technology is not able directly to mediate – electronic communication, even via video or three-dimensional hologram, is not sufficient to enable *trust* to be built. The social and the psychological will not be reducible to electronic bytes. 'In *Post-Industrial* 2015,' Oliver Sparrow goes on, 'your synchronizing forces can no longer be written down in three-ring binders, nor specified in the electronic equivalent. There have to be tacit rules about how we work together and trust each other in networks.' Furthermore, as Professor Huntington contends, trade has always followed the patterns of alliance among cultural groupings and nations. 'In the emerging world,' he argues, 'patterns of trade will be decisively influenced by the patterns of culture. Businessmen make deals with people they can understand and trust . . .' (p.135).

In 2015 the ethos of self-help and performance investment predominates but is less dog-eat-dog, although workers trapped (because of limited skills or track record or even location) in converging industries will feel all the pressures of *Faster, Faster*. Knowledge creation and complexity management rouse a voracious hunger for highly developed team skills among knowledge workers – finding the right team, working effectively together, recombining and interacting with an outer ring of contractors and suppliers. The 'star' system exists but there is a continuum of capability, with a descending scale of personal economic value, supporting the creation of knowledge, its infrastructure and complexity management. There will certainly be stars among the knowledge creators and those who deliver high-quality complexity management. The best organizations will retain and cultivate complexity managers, but this will be a skill and knowledge base in itself widely applicable and heavily in demand, whether in firms that invest in and have mastered innovation, those that inhabit the cyberworld of info-broking or those engaged in the bloody convergence endgame.

Rough Neighbours

Faster, Faster brings the requirement for organizational change at a speed that means innovation itself becomes commoditized. The world of *Rough Neighbours* experiences change at such dizzying pace that it becomes socially and organizationally unmanageable. Any attempts by organizations to make the needed cost efficiencies and fundamental restructurings to cope with industry convergence create ever-worsening unemployment and commercial underperformance. Governments step in but are unable, either through regulation or other policy intervention, to protect failing industries. This is the grim world described by Huntington, should the West fail to rise to the challenges of the next decade. He points to 'a global breakdown of law and order, failed states and inceasing anarchy in many parts of the world, a global crime wave. . . . The rise of transnational corporations producing economic goods is increasingly matched by the rise of transnational criminal mafias. . . . On a worldwide basis Civilization seems in many respects to be yielding to barbarism, generating the image of an unprecedented phenomenon, a global Dark Ages, possibly descending on humanity' (p.321).

In *Rough Neighbours* political and economic power, such as it is, migrates east, with China as its fulcrum notwithstanding the Asian financial crises of the late 1990s and the ensuing economic and business consolidation. The pre-eminence of Western ideology fades. In the industrialized world governments are forced to chronically high levels of borrowing to pay for exploding welfare demands and consequently push back hard against expanding budgets – privatization of all non-essential enterprises proceeds apace, thereby releasing further competition to fierce and bloodthirsty markets.

The most secure organizational response to the chaos and unpredictability of the markets is to slice deeper into the company, squeezing until the financial and psychological pips squeak. Refocus–redesign–benchmark–converge occurs at speed, with few executive teams having either the time or inclination to look beyond survival to the end of today. Since trading arrangements with those countries which constitute the growing number of rough neighbours are uncertain and unpredictable at best and fraught with selective trade barriers at worst, transnational integration via information technology is mixed. The countries of this world are narrow-eyed in their contemplation of one another; mutual suspicion and defensiveness are the norms.

The fortunate who have employment do reasonably well and there are, of course, stars – but fewer of both of these, since unemployment is common for workers, despite the best efforts of governments to protect jobs. Indeed, enforced job security persuades employers to do less of it. The long-term unemployed have never worked and nor, it must be said, will many of their children. For the capable or those in protected employment, personal performance investment is patchy, dependent on the wealth provided by typically stop–go contract employment, but dominates the lives of many millions of workers who believe it is one of few ways to establish some form of security. Another route to security is through multiple and potent social structures that arise because traditional political, social and economic institutions are seen to have failed. Huntington again:

> People do not live by reason alone. They cannot calculate and act rationally in pursuit of their self-interest until they define their self. . . . In times of rapid social change established identities dissolve, the self must be redefined, and new identities created. For people facing the need to determine Who am I? Where do I belong? religion provides compelling answers, and religious groups provide small social communities to replace those lost through urbanization. (p.97)

In the emerging world of *Rough Neighbours* irrationalism, opposition to science, faith in new ideology – all are viewed as alternative models and paths to personal security. This is so for perhaps a quarter of the population who feel excluded from society, its economic participation and its rewards, but who nonetheless have access to rapid electronic communication. In short, ideologies spread fast.

'Within the company,' argues Sparrow, 'there may be all sorts of curious affiliations stretching throughout and outside the bounds of the firm. Individuals are not necessarily loyal to you, their manager. They're loyal to their affiliation, their ideology, their "tribe" if you will. Different bits of the firm are likely to develop different tribes, centred around a number of powerful individuals who build and defend their empires. Anyone who breaks from the accepted rules of operating is regarded as socially beyond the pale. Getting things done means having to take account of nested pyramids of affiliations scattered throughout the functions of the company. This is one of the difficulties that gives rise to corruption and makes it hard to do business.'

Eventually, after 2015 and protracted instability, a combination of government realism and gradual economic recovery helps the industrialized world move into a form of economic existence much more akin to *Faster, Faster*.

THE WINNING CORPORATION OF 2015

What are the hallmarks of the winning company of 2015? Into what form will today's organizations have to transform themselves merely to compete? To some extent this will depend on the nature and prospects of the world at that time. But in essence, for organizations the variation to be expected from the three scenarios already outlined is one of degree rather than polar extremes. The tenets of *Faster, Faster* operate in all three. They are mitigated by conditions in the *Post-Industrial Revolution*, thus creating the breathing space for niche-building and sustainable innovation, but severely attenuated in *Rough Neighbours*, where convergence and disrupted trading deters investment and innovation. The future, therefore, as best anyone can guess at it, varies around *Faster, Faster*.

Many of the monolithic bureaucracies of today (whether government institutions or vertically integrated multinationals) may still be around, though their structure may well have changed slowly in response to environmental pressures as they struggle to peg themselves against competitors. They are underperforming, however, and are targets for government-sponsored change, privatization, or acquisition and break-up. Some simply fail.

The successful organizations, by contrast, are very different. They are distinguished most obviously by their structure and the differences are felt most keenly by those who operate as workers in the dispersed network from inner core through the web of contract teams that make up what amounts to a virtual organization. However, the essence of these organizations (and what truly makes them different) is the soft stuff: *culturally* they are aeons away from the lumbering monoliths that still cling to survival. Their *values* are distinctive and, crucially, difficult to emulate.

Inner Core and Outer Network

The bounds of an organization are blurred, but also distinct (Figure 1.2). They are blurred because it is hard to pinpoint the end of the network that supports the provision of service or delivery of product. They are distinct because the core of the organization comprises relatively few individuals engaged in only a few executive tasks. There is a leader, sometimes an owner/entrepreneur, whose role is as important as ever a leader's has been. He or she is the person who sets and imposes the context of the business – what is important and what is not, what the organization stands for and where it is headed. As I said in *The New Leaders* (1995), the leader provides purpose over and above the buzz of organizational activity and concentrates attention on what matters. He or she may also be the prime agent of cultural values.

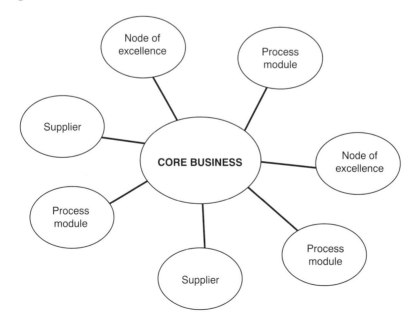

Figure 1.2   Inner core, outer network.

Apart from leadership skills, the personal competencies required at the core divide into five areas:

1. Business strategy
2. IT strategy
3. Product development architecture
4. Complexity strategy
5. Complexity management.

Whether these competencies are defined further by specialist roles is a moot point. Certainly those engaged in product development are specialists, but their chief occupation is at the architectural level: innovation and design around products or services. Specific design assistance is bought in as well from nodes of excellence (e.g. local or dispersed networks providing leading-edge biotechnology, genetic engineering, financial analytics, social and demographic market research, robotics or electronics), but manufacture is outsourced. Business and IT strategy remain part of the core, although an increasingly highly educated elite fulfil these roles, often with higher degrees and substantive first-hand experience in other firms 'out there' in the networks. Everything else is bought in: finance (in large part), as well as IT operations, marketing, sales, human resources, administration, customer servicing, legal services, property and plant management, warehousing and distribution.[1]

These processes are offered as modularized chunks by millions of suppliers worldwide. You contract for the module you require, for the time you require it, at the quality you can afford. The suppliers are specialists, the best of them operating in precisely the same way as the core businesses to whom they supply a service, and many of them globe-straddling in the sense that they are broad and relatively flat (but still retain some hierarchy). They do one thing well, they are sufficiently flexible to provide networked teams all over the world and they can expand and contract according to demand in any local market. So, for example, you might supply excellent customer service for American Airlines at terminals throughout the world, 24 hours a

---

[1] Sound far-fetched now? Despite some early teething problems, IT operations, among a host of other processes, are being outsourced in larger and larger deals. In 1997 DuPont, the Delaware-headquartered global chemicals and energy giant, outsourced its IT operations to CSC and Andersen Consulting in a $4 billion ten-year arrangement.

day, 365 days per year. The terminal staff wear American Airlines uniforms, but some of them, a year later, might be offering precisely the same service on behalf of Lufthansa. As a business you supply customer service to any airline. The brand, owned by the airline, is the only thing that is stable: this is what the customer sees and experiences. Organizations are very careful with their brand. As the organizational world disperses, so is the danger augmented of brand dilution or erosion of the values peculiar to it. In the 1980s this happened to the Pierre Cardin brand as it was stretched from *haute couture* way beyond its capabilities and slapped onto myriad items unconnected with its original special positioning – and paid the price. The danger, in the world of 2015, is as true of multiple brand owners (for example, Coca-Cola's beverages or Banc One's 80 distinct banks) as it is of single core brands (British Airways or Intel).

The new roles are those in complexity strategy and complexity management. There are two reasons for this. First, as noted above, the brand must be protected. It is the most substantial part of the business. Second, and directly linked, the core must retain an unshakeable grip on how the network synthesizes, meshes and delivers. A huge portion of this complexity is invisible, specified and automated by networked computers and rapid feedback and communications. But the bringing together of nodes, both modularized processes and knowledge, combined in ways which provide sometimes marginal, sometimes major, innovative advantages over competitors rests on the creativity, judgement and skill in execution of those delivering complexity strategy and complexity management and, most especially, the defence and maximum utilization of the brand.

The individuals at the core are employed on a variety of contracts, but few are permanent. Most get a base salary plus equity stake and are therefore highly committed to ensuring the success of the enterprise.

In some cases, an increasing number, the organization itself may be temporary. Venture capital is brought to a professional entrepreneur's idea, before pulling together the requisite processes via the web of networks and servicing a tightly defined market need for a year or two, or a month or two. The organization then disbands. This was happening in the late 1990s in Hollywood – as opposed to studios with thousands of employees, there were a rising number of contracted professionals working in temporary teams on a part of the total package. Few members of the organization, such as it is, worked throughout the project.

Treachery and Collaboration

What does it feel like to work in the best organizations of 2015? What is the culture, the ethos?

Leadership, deal making, collaboration, an eye for opportunity, risk taking and willingness to understand and accept the necessary chaos or, more accurately, the sense of being somewhat out of control in this networked world are the pre-eminent social–psychological factors. Just as the roots of economic cooperation are aligned with cultural commonality, to use Huntington's words, so relationship building and trust, which cannot be mediated properly over distance through the wonders of technology, necessitate face-to-face interaction. This is true both within the core and out into the network nodes. 'Eyeball' is still very much a feature of this networked world.

The defining ethos of the successful organization is a mix which, when coalescing in all its constituent parts, itself affords a major defensible capability. Its major cultural features appear in Figure 1.3. As expected, risk-taking and opportunism are important, pursued with eagerness rather than slow caution. Time, of course, has been squeezed. The electronic Web accelerates everything, as do the computers that anchor the Web, many a million times more powerful than their 1990s ancestors. Even traditionally slow practices such as *nemawashii* – Japanese consensus building – despite bearing the same hallmarks of yesteryear (circulation of written proposals vertically and horizontally to all relevant layers of management), have been squashed from a three-month process to a three-minute one. Ongoing improvements to raw processing power and groupware, intranet and internet evolutions have ensured this.

Risk taking and opportunism are intimately tied to an essential optimism, an enthusiasm for new ideas and openness to possibilities. Where this cultural factor, in particular, is missing or constrained by gelatinous internal forces of conformity or hierarchy, so the tendency towards commoditization accelerates. As a consequence, promotion on merit is a value of the new breed of companies. Old prescriptions of age–wisdom and seniority–power still hold back many organizations, especially

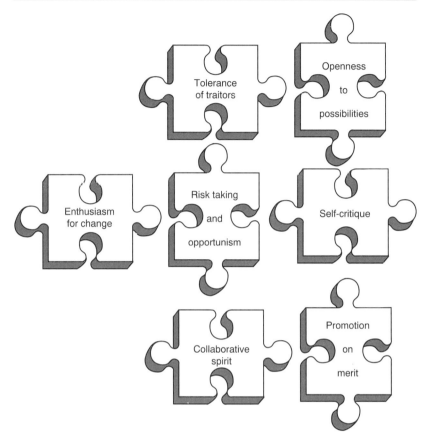

Figure 1.3 The defining cultural ethos of successful organizations.

where national cultural antecedents reinforce this. The obsession with personal performance investment serves also to institutionalize promotion on merit and vice versa.

Collaboration and teamwork are important within the core but especially beyond. Typically this is most strongly felt within focused networks or local centres of excellence where 'eyeball' is more common and trust can be built and sustained. Even so, the nature of commerce means that collaboration can lead to traitors leaving the fold for new and better opportunities. Vindictiveness or severity applied in such cases can simply be destructive to your own organizational advantages. You never know when the old relationship in the new company may assist your business. Moreover, the movement of talented people from one organization to another means that your own organization benefits from time to time as people are attracted to your firm. The net effect of the tolerance of treachery across the best businesses is the transfer of ideas and the creation of new knowledge and opportunities.

No organization in the emerging world of 2015 can survive without, at the very least, an acceptance of change and, at best, an enthusiasm for it. Where it is hardest to build this is where there are generational differences, such as where workers have grown up in a generation used to a fixed way of operating, combined with government policy that endeavours to protect workers' job security. Chris von Branconi, Commercial Director at the German plant engineering group Lurgi makes the comment, 'It's my personal conviction that it's only possible to get change done and achieve a culture of change with new people. It is very exceptional, particularly in Germany, that people who are twenty-five years with the same organization can be convinced that they have to change everything. . . . We're not in the States and the rules for laying off people, in the German environment, are not that you select and lay off the people you believe are not suited to the new organization, but that they are selected for other reasons and you have to work with those remaining.'

Finally, the best organizations of 2015 have a well-developed critical faculty, a capacity to engage in self-critique. This is manifest in the willingness of managers and staff to challenge and be challenged. It is not a critical environment, in the sense of personal attack and office politics. Rather, people have learned to separate the issue from the person. As a result, empire building and turf wars are less of a feature than they might be elsewhere. The firm's attention is directed outwards to winning in the competitive global economy of 2015. As Bill Gates said of Microsoft in an address to the computer science department of the University of Washington in 1993, quoted in Wallace (1997, p.25):

> We are scared all the time. We're always saying: 'Is this the day we've reached our peak?'

2

Big Change – An Unnatural Act

BUT IS IT TRANSFORMATION?

In December 1996, Philip Condit, the new chairman of Boeing, announced 'an historic moment in aviation and aerospace', to wit the $45 billion merger of Boeing and McDonnell-Douglas, two companies that had locked horns in numerous competitive battles over preceding decades. The environmental drivers had been stark and compelling for some time and for at least a year the likelihood of a merger was one of the worst-kept secrets in corporate America. McDonnell-Douglas's civil aircraft business had attenuated to almost nothing, and the rapid post-cold war consolidation of the US and European defence industries in particular and the trend towards the globalization of the defence industry in general had left the firm increasingly exposed. The final straw that pushed McDonnell-Douglas towards the merger (something it had explored with Boeing a year earlier but without positive outcome) was the Pentagon's surprise move in refusing to shortlist the firm for the $150 billion development of the Joint Strike Fighter for the US Air Force and the Royal Air Force. On 1995 sales of $14 billion McDonnell-Douglas was valued in the market at $11 billion, Boeing at nearly $34 billion on sales of $19.5 billion. The merger deal therefore was a lifeline.

For Boeing, with McDonnell-Douglas safely tucked under one wing as a new division of the larger Boeing, the merger offered much-enhanced economies of scale, considerable financial muscle (so essential for new product development in the industry), better coverage and penetration of key markets and, most important of all as we discussed in Chapter 1, an impressive pooling of intellectual resource and technological knowledge. Boeing (and McDonnell-Douglas) have transformed themselves.

So we might say that mergers are a typical and effective route to transformation. They provide dramatic reshaping of an organization which, although a strenuous exercise, can secure much greater leverage, even dominance, in the market. Not so fast! Another case bears examination. Only months after the Boeing–McDonnell-Douglas romance, the stock markets were extending a rapturous welcome to the biggest merger ever of two British companies whose combined market value exceeded $38 billion – this the creation of GMG Brands (later to be called Diageo) between Grand Metropolitan and Guinness. Although the merger had been under secret discussion for three years, industry analysts and competitors such as Seagram and Allied Domecq were taken by surprise.

The environmental conditions, oddly, were akin to those driving the defence and aerospace consolidation. For years the spirits market had been in the doldrums and prospects were not good. Indeed, over the previous five years Grand Metropolitan had underperformed the market by around 40%, Guinness by 50%. Furthermore, executives in the new organization refused to simplify and specialize, instead retaining businesses unrelated to spirits – food, beer and restaurants – and preferring to build an 'agglomeration' as Guinness chairman Tony Greener put it, a giant consumer products group with the express objective of rivalling Procter & Gamble, Philip Morris and Unilever where growth rates far outstripped those in the spirits industry. The new joint chairmen, Tony Greener and George Bull, believed this was a focused business with the core management competence and geographical spread to succeed.

The *Financial Times* was less enthusiastic, pointing to the disturbing similarity of the new Diageo with Pepsico, which also operated across a distractingly wide range of businesses (drinks, fast food, snacks) and had looked to demerge. The conclusion of the *Financial Times* (13 May 1997) was forthright:

> Previous experience suggests that a merger of equals is a prolonged and exhausting process. If that is true within one industry, such as drinks or pharmaceuticals, it is truer across several. Experience also suggests that if the merger is to work, neither company's culture should predominate. Indeed, both have to wither away in the space of a few years, giving place to a third culture which has learnt to forget the 'us and them' mentality. (p.27)

The aspiration of the two companies was laudable. The real concern, however, was that, like many such proposed transformations through merger and acquisition, the new GMG would fail to build and integrate the necessary cultural (social–psychological) elements and would end up destroying value rather than creating it.

This cuts to the heart of big change. As Michael Porter (1990) has argued, 'The behavior required to sustain advantage, then, is in many respects an unnatural act for established firms. . . . Few companies make significant improvements and strategy changes voluntarily; most are forced to. . . . The managements of companies that sustain competitive advantage always run a little scared' (pp.52–3). Our task then is to understand the social–psychological factors that enable firms to 'run scared' and to commit to behaviours that together constitute 'an unnatural act' – for these are the keys that unlock tranformation.

First, however, for those organizations seeking to transform, it would help to understand what transformation is. It should be self-evident that not all change is transformational but, as I remarked at the start of Chapter 1, the word has become somewhat debased, being applied to any change, of whatever form or impact. This proclivity among managers and commentators is understandable – for managers because it adds prestige to what in most cases is the trying, dull but necessary series of adjustments that businesses are called upon to make simply to continue to survive or stand still in today's competitive stakes; for commentators because the humdrum of business change is just that – humdrum – and no one wants to read or hear what is humdrum. So nothing could be more natural than to call all change transformational. Nothing more natural, nor more obfuscating and confusing. The net effect is the fad explosion characteristic of business life since the early 1980s and one which inevitably has the potential to divert, confuse or undermine even the most intelligent and thoughtful of managers. Accordingly, caution is needed: we must try to answer the question, 'What is corporate transformation?' In *The New Leaders* (1995) I tackled this in an outcome-oriented way – in other words, how the organization should behave and what it will feel like after achieving transformation. This expands on Porter's comments and I concluded:

> . . . that the change must be palpable for all employees, that they behave differently and more effectively than before, that the organization is more effective, that it has significantly shifted its competitive position, that it can innovate and adapt on a continuous basis to new opportunities, challenges or threats and that it is able to adapt through

> strategic reinvention by changing the rules, both within and outside
> itself, to create and exploit unanticipated but tangible markets. (p.129)

Another way of looking at this is to examine the scope of change (i.e. how much of the organization and its environment is affected by the change) and the scale of improvement and its impact on the market. Figure 2.1, adapted from *The New Leaders*, demonstrates very clearly that transformation, at the very least, targets the whole company and seeks improvement that reaches, at minimum, the equivalent of best practice. In the optimum, however, transformation includes not only the organizational entity but also fundamental changes to the network (supply chain, alliances and so forth) as well as industry structure itself. Toys 'Я' Us achieved a transformation of the retail industry structure through their huge superstores, with almost every conceivable toy available to customers under one roof and, by squeezing suppliers, at heavily discounted prices – ushering in the phenomenon of the 'category killer'. In this sense, trans-formation attacks both the current and known world *and* the future. It is concerned with the creation of new opportunities, with the ability to junk conventional wisdom and destroy old (often cherished) advantages, to violate established business practice, compete in different ways, shut down competitors' angles of attack and behave in counterintuitive and, indeed, unpredictable ways.

If this is to happen, then big change must too. In the obverse, change of an incremental, narrow, single-process and straight-forward kind is unlikely to transform the organization. This is a statement of the obvious, I concede, but most executives would plump for uncomplicated, narrow, incremental change every time. John Chisholm, the chief executive who led the dramatic transformation of the Defence Evaluation and Research Agency (DERA) makes this point:

> No change is perfect. No process, no organization, no method is cost free. At some level, somewhere the change you introduce is making things worse. You have to be prepared to live with that, to look any one of your people straight in the eye and say, 'I know this is making your job hell, but for these good reasons it's what I'm going to do.' And that's the thing that on the whole stops executives changing things. They don't like taking responsibility for the downside and the complications of change. And the longer you're in an organization, of course, the more awesome that problem becomes for you.

In point of fact, most organizations are strategically, struc-turally and psychologically hardwired to resist modification.

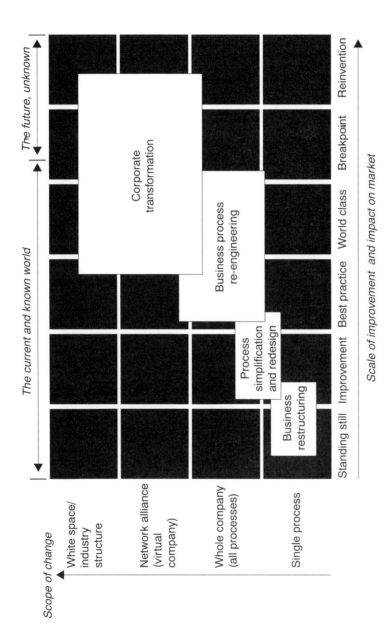

Figure 2.1 The scope and impact of corporate transformation. © Paul Taffinder (1995). *The New Leaders*, Kogan Page. Reprinted by permission.

Resist is too strong a word – it implies an active force against change. Rather the reality of organizational life is that, like organic life, the firm's existence is a product of its history. Its history has shaped it to operate a particular way. History is the patterns of behaviour rooted in a particular environment. Past strategy drives the detailed patterns of behaviour, reinforced by culture, and eventually (though few executives would admit it) culture will come to drive strategy. Change is unacceptable while there appears more to lose than to gain. And here is the crux: there always appears more to lose when, as Michael Porter says, 'a company's past strategy becomes embodied in skills, organizational arrangements, specialized facilities, and a reputation that may be inconsistent with a new one' (1990, p.52). In short, more is invested in the past than the future. This is only to be expected. And this is why big change is the best hope of transforming an organization.

Transformation, we should constantly remind ourselves, must be systemic. It must affect the entire system that is the organization. Thus, substantive change must occur at three levels (individual, group and organization) if it is to succeed. Too often transformation efforts are only concerned with processes, or overemphasize strategic change, or attempt to tackle behaviour (e.g. customer service) without supporting interventions in strategy, capability, and technology.

THE TRANSFORMATION CYCLE

The *sigmoid*, a term chiefly used in anatomy, describes the two crescent shapes that make an 'S', originally from the Greek letter Σ or *sigma*. The sigmoid is a useful shape for two reasons: first, it comprises two parts, one the reverse of the other and, second, when tilted slightly to the right, it becomes a mathematical curve, describing a relationship between two axes – usually time and performance. This has not been lost on either scientists or, more recently, business writers. Jonas and Jonathan Salk (1981) deserve credit for using the idea of the curve to explain longer-term historical shifts and transformations in biological systems, with special emphasis on the difference between the two parts of the curve – the first part representing growth, the second diminishing growth and then decline. Charles Handy, one of the world's foremost business philosophers, has made the same point about organizations. 'The sigmoid or S-shaped curve,' he says, 'describes the way things go in life. They start out with a dip and then, with luck or good management, they grow and move up the curve, but eventually they wane' (1996, pp.23–4). Nicholas Imparato and Oren Harari (1994) tackle the discontinuity issue between one S-curve and the next, arguing that 'the capacity of the organization to "jump the curve" and capitalize on opportunities in a new world becomes the foundation of long-term corporate health' (p.98).

It is therefore helpful to think of an organization's life in two ways. The first is as an extended S-curve (Figure 2.2), with a moderate start, then rapidly improving performance and corporate health over the next period, a sustained time of maturity as growth and performance hits a ceiling, then slowly accelerating decline. This is, if you like, the first part of the sigmoid. If nothing is done to change the organization when it reaches maturity, decline is certain.

Decline can either be arrested or pre-empted, however, by transformational action since this creates discontinuity – *that is, it disconnects the organization from its original path.* Discontinuity is therefore essential. That is why I use the term 'big change'. Quite obviously discontinuity necessitates upheaval, even trauma, but these costs, in financial and human terms, are exacerbated when big change is launched too far down the curve of decline. It may even be too late to save the business. So, the second way of graphically representing the organization's lifecycle is to take account of discontinuities, either forced upon

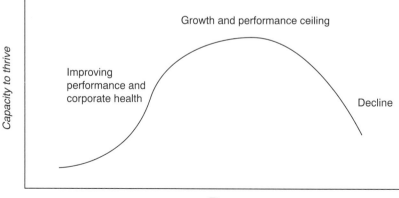

Figure 2.2 The organization's lifecycle: the extended S-curve.

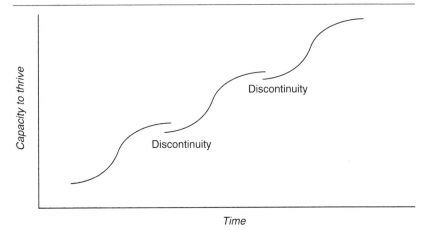

Figure 2.3 Discontinuities and transformation trajectories.

the firm (in IBM's case the popularity of the PC that swept away mainframe hegemony) or initiated by executives (British Airways' second revolution led by Bob Ayling). The S-curve then becomes two or even a series of S-curves or trajectories of big change, each one broken by some kind of discontinuity (Figure 2.3). The extent to which executives leading successful companies are able to scan their strategic environment and launch the new transformation trajectory at the right moment (either in response to current or in anticipation of future dislocations in their business context) thus makes the difference between longer-term corporate success and failure.

If we now drop down into the detail of a single transformation trajectory or S-curve, bringing several degrees of magnification to bear upon it, we discover a number of what I call *transition lines* (Figure 2.4) which make up the trajectory of the curve. These are the main elements of human and organizational effort required to launch and execute big change. The five transition lines are:

1. Awakening
2. Conceiving the future
3. Building the change agenda
4. Delivering big change
5. Mastering change.

Some points to note. First, the five transition lines are *not* linear, sequential phases, one following the other. No trans-

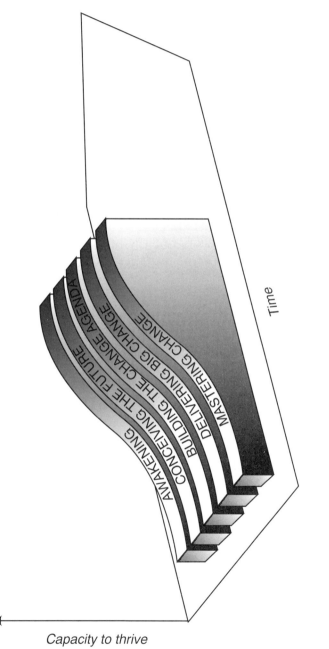

Capacity to thrive

Time

AWAKENING

CONCEIVING THE FUTURE AGENDA

BUILDING THE CHANGE

DELIVERING BIG CHANGE

MASTERING CHANGE

Figure 2.4 The transformation trajectory or S-curve.

formation is accomplished that way. Rather, the transition lines represent different activities in the longer-term change trajectory. Thus, what is real about transformation is its layered multidimensionality and the need for iterative effort. Second, the start points of each transition line are staggered along the trajectory: some actions must begin before others but, again, this is not a sequence, merely a reflection of dependency and relative priority at the outset. Third, the transition lines are the graphic embodiment of clusters of actions which together create the motive force and critical mass for big change to occur. Fourth, the actions and their sequence, however, are highly contextual – they depend on the trigger for change (e.g. crisis or aspiration), the strengths and capabilities of the firm (e.g. financial, human, structural, geographic), its business environment (e.g. high or low growth, expanding, static or consolidating) and its leadership (e.g. cautious or visionary). And finally, fifth, the relative time and effort (i.e. emphasis) expressed by each transition line will vary across the life of the transformation – awakening is clearly more important early on, mastery later.

The actions embodied in each transition line are the subject matter of Chapters 6 to 10. They are also, of course, an articulation of the practical steps that the managers and staff of many of the organizations featured in the research for the book have taken during the course of thinking about, communicating, launching, delivering and mastering big change – in short, they are a routemap for transformation.

WHAT MAKES TRANSFORMATION DIFFERENT?

We should also outline how transformation is distinguished from previous approaches to large-scale change such as business process re-engineering and total quality management. Five characteristics are important here.

First, transformation is *comprehensive* in that it involves the whole organization and requires an *integrated set of solutions*. In the former sense, the change is pervasive, affecting structure, processes, systems, people, business portfolio, collective and individual knowledge and skill, as well as the organization's environment (its markets, stakeholders and regulators). In the latter sense, none of these things can be changed with solutions and interventions that only emphasize one or a handful of change tactics. Single-point responses or solutions that are chiefly incremental in nature will not produce radical shifts in organizational strategy and business performance. (And in this category we must, unfortunately, include most mergers and acquisitions, which are often contemplated and executed for the wrong reasons – typically, to bulk up the organizations involved as a bigger version of the originals and *without any attempt to fundamentally change the way they perform or compete.*) Rather, a multiplicity of disciplines, approaches and interventions, linked and configured, is needed if change of a far-reaching and substantive nature is to be achieved.

Second, transformation may require a *challenge to the fundamental purpose of the organization*. The Rockwell Corporation, suffering under the defence and aerospace consolidation, shifted its sights from defence (some 50% of its revenues in 1985), and therefore disposed of its aerospace and defence businesses – in a deal with Boeing, as it happens, worth $3 billion – and refocused on microchips for faxes and modems. By the early 1990s it supplied 80% of the US fax and modem market. One might argue the same of British Airways which, under new CEO Bob Ayling, began to shift its purpose from passenger transportation to become 'the undisputed leader in world travel'.

Third, transformation may mean *radical performance improvement*. Symcor, the Canadian co-sourcing joint venture between three competing banks, is a clear example of this – the case is analysed in detail in this book. Elsewhere in the financial services industry, telephone banking offers the opportunity for up to 40% reductions in banks' costs. The question is: which banks will be able to bring the right tactics together, fast enough, to seize the opportunity before outsiders steal a march? This happened in the UK car insurance market when Direct Line, to the alarm of its seemingly paralysed competitors, carved out a 25% share of the market within less than ten years of start-up. Direct Line proved that insurance could be sold credibly over a telephone but also that smart mass marketing and customer service had to be combined to execute properly.

Fourth, an off-the-shelf fix will not produce transformation. Importing solutions wholesale from one business to another is to simply take part in the convergence endgame discussed earlier. Thus, mergers and acquisitions can form a part of big change, but alone they rarely trigger or support the breadth or penetrative depth of change that produces genuine value – just as the merger between Swiss pharmaceutical companies Sandoz and Ciba to form Novartis in 1996 was only part of the strategic and tactical changes that the companies needed to tackle to compete effectively worldwide. Transformation requires a combination of strategy and tactics *unique to that business,* tailored to its exact circumstances.

Finally, fifth, the nature of transformation, seen as it really is, without the distortion of fads and fashion, is far-reaching. A necessary condition for and outcome of transformation is *dramatic change in the organization and in the individuals* who make up its collective entity. The transformation of Britain's Defence Evaluation and Research Agency (DERA) was profound both in reshaping the way the organization worked and in entirely changing the day-to-day behaviour of scientists and support staff. This dramatic change was also painful and exciting – sure indicators of the depth of personal growth.

However, big change *is* an unnatural act and the coalescence of these five characteristics – in short, the achievement of transformation – will not occur without tackling the three underlying social–psychological elements in organizations that facilitate human transformation (Figure 2.5). The first is *leadership* (Chapter 3) and by this I mean leadership of substance and not, as is so often the error of firms seeking to transform, simply enhanced management. The second is innovation – not as per invention or product development, but the deeply rooted cultural and individual behavioural determinants embedded in the organizational system and that I have called *systemic innovation* (Chapter 4). The third is conflict and the need, in general, for *conflict escalation* (Chapter 5). We are rather more used to the damping down of conflict. We fear uncontrollable consequences or we are simply socialized to accept conflict as destructive and undesirable. There is, however, a growing body of evidence that the active, controlled stimulation of conflict enhances individual, group and organizational functioning and, as further argued in Chapter 10, is the underlying basis for mastery of the new business logic that transformation aims to attain.

THE LEADERSHIP OF BIG CHANGE

One of the reasons why Microsoft was able to swing in such an abrupt and wholehearted way to embrace the Internet was the

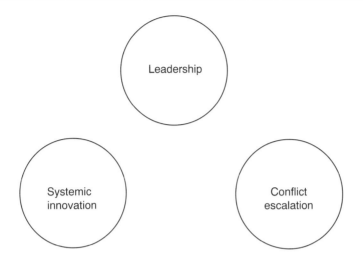

Figure 2.5   The social–psychological elements of transformation.

strength of leadership at the top of the organization. When Bill
Gates sent out to executives his 'Internet Tidal Wave' memo in
May 1995, he was committing the company to taking on something that it had chosen in the past to ignore. He was committing to *transform* the company. Few would have bet on Microsoft
succeeding. The media made comparisons with the overthrow
of IBM's hegemony during the personal computer revolution.
Would the Internet revolution be the undoing of Microsoft?
James Wallace, writing about the subject in *Overdrive* (1997),
noted that by mid-1996, about a year after Gates's memo, more
than 600 programmers had been reassigned to the development
of Microsoft's browsers, the newly created Internet Platform and
Tools Division had exploded to some 2500 staff and Internet
Explorer 3.0, released in August of that year, was regarded as
one of the best in the industry, Microsoft having grabbed a large
chunk of the US browser market (near 30%) by February 1997 –
but not enough to seriously dent Netscape's 70%, as *The
Economist's* sampling of surveys indicates (5 July 1997).
Wallace's verdict on all of this is that 'driven by Bill Gates,
whose burning desire to win and fear of failure compel him not
only to beat his competitors, but to destroy them, Microsoft's
dominance seems secure for a long time to come' (p.294). Or at
least, we might add, for as long as Gates is at the helm.
Powerful, obsessive, singleminded leaders have a habit of failing
to build leadership succession – the fears and suspicions that

make them successful also make them prone to drown, deliberately or no, rising potential leaders in their wake.

Nevertheless, leadership is a critical factor in transformation. If the transformation of a single behavioural system – that is, an individual human being – is complex, so the transformation of large systems – several thousand people – moves towards complexity measured in exponential multiples. Yet organizations achieve transformation. Microsoft is one. Bill Gates maintains that one of the primary reasons for this is that they hire very smart people. Maybe. But NASA have really smart people too and, as we shall see in the discussion of NASA and other organizations in Chapter 5, being smart in an organization under pressure does not prevent uncomfortable and undesirable difficulties. Take another case: British Airways. BA has transformed itself. Ordinary people have been led to achieve extraordinary things. When you spend time with BA employees it is noteworthy how frequently they talk about inspiration, pride and loyalty – the psychological products of strong leadership. In short, leadership matters.

Leadership, however, is poorly understood. Much ink is spilt on the subject every year. In an organizational context the confusion, more often than not, is to do with leadership and management. The two have come to be almost indistinguishable. Indeed, you would be hard-pressed to find any sizeable organization that did not list leadership as one of the requisite behavioural competencies for all management levels, on the one hand, recognizing its tremendous importance, on the other, failing dismally to articulate what it is and how it differs from management. Does it matter that management and leadership have become indistinguishable? Yes. This is not an arid debate. The *management* of an organization is not enough and few individuals warrant the title leader. Warren Bennis (1989) has devoted much effort to articulating the difference between management and leadership and the skills needed to support the two. Management, he contends, is concerned with administration, leadership with innovation. He extends the list:

Manager
- A copy
- Maintains
- Controls
- Asks how and when

Leader
- An original
- Develops
- Inspires trust
- Asks what and why

- Watches the bottom line
- Imitates
- Does things right

- Watches the horizon
- Originates
- Does the right thing

What does all this mean? John Kotter, Professor of Leadership at Harvard Business School, makes the point that 'those who attempt to create major change with simple, linear, analytical processes almost always fail' (1996, p.25). Why do executives chiefly rely on the simple, the linear, the analytical? Because they have been taught to manage and not to lead.

Indeed, the major proportion of effort and funds devoted to management and leadership development (which in larger organizations might amount in cash terms to more than $100 million a year) succeeds in the main in producing better managers, and at best high-performance managers – not leaders. This means that leaders are generally in short supply, change leaders more so.

At core, though, we need to be concerned here with the leadership required to trigger and sustain big change of a kind that produces transformation. Not everyone can do this. Some leaders are suited to particular stages of the organization's life-cycle. Apple Computer's co-founder Steve Jobs has had a wonderful ride. His quirky leadership was exactly right for Apple's start-up, but inappropriate when the company got really big and hit maturity. He was ousted as leader in 1985. In 1996, with the company effectively in decline, he was back (as a part-time advisor to the chairman Gil Amelio), following Apple's acquisition of Jobs' company NeXt Software. In due course there was talk of Jobs persuading former Apple colleagues to return as well to 'help save the company'. He did not need a crystal ball to read Apple's future, nor perhaps Amelio's. On 10 July 1997, Amelio resigned just a week before the company was due to announce third-quarter results – results that confirmed Apple's continuing decline in spite of cost-cutting and other improvements. Amelio could take cold comfort from history: both his predecessors, Mike Spindler and John Sculley, were forced to resign. At the time of writing the question remains whether Steve Jobs is the kind of leader suited not only to the tasks of start-up (entrepreneurial vision, innovation, differentiation) *but also* corporate rescue – tasks in the latter case which are remarkably similar, with the leader as inspirational saviour. In some cases, however, there *are* renaissance leaders, those who have the personality and skills to straddle all the lifecycle stages as an organization moves from emergence, through growth and maturity, and can manage the discontinuity of the S-curve to pre-empt decline. Bill Gates, from all the evidence so far, seems to be one. He has seen the firm through from the start, making it the darling of the stock market in maturity and not only surviving the threat of decline posed by Microsoft's failure to understand and embrace the Internet but transforming the company to remain dominant.

So we must ask, what is the psychology of transformational leadership? There are numerous ways of defining leadership, but I do think that the leadership required to effect trans-formational change is somewhat different and as a result many of the solid, well-researched texts on leadership that abound in bookstores miss the point. They deal with leadership in the stable, mature business, thus leadership that does not have as its overriding *raison d'être* the thoroughgoing transformation of a corporation. To capture the quintessence of leadership in a few sentences is difficult but it strikes me that *the most effective leaders are both a stimulus for and a representation of the organization's collective will.* Leaders, therefore, must trigger the organization's will to change and demonstrate this in deed. The leader is thus both master and servant to organizational members.

At a more detailed behavioural level, the model in Figure 2.6, drawn from some of my earlier research into leadership, high-lights the key elements of transformational leadership: imposing context, risk making and risk taking, conviction, unpredict-ability, and generating critical mass.

Imposing context is to do with interpreting the world for employees, concentrating attention by slicing through the countermanding managerial and organizational noise, convey-ing proportion during short-term success or wretched failure, and saying what matters and what does not.

Risk making, risk taking is perhaps the least developed of skills in large organizations. Yet any business must commit resources in the present to the uncertainty of the future. You cannot run an organization without risk. A leader's thoughts must be focused on opportunity and on understanding (rather than removing) risk. Yes, managers should strive to do it right first time, but leaders should not. Leaders must be prepared to change things, to experiment and to pull the plug on initiatives that, despite

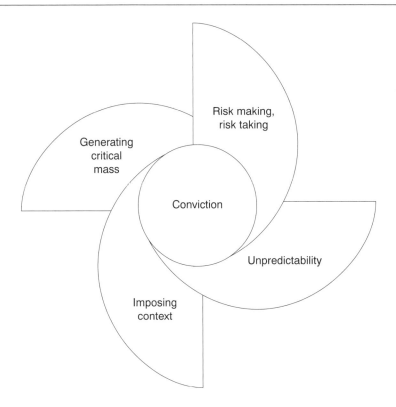

Figure 2.6 The leadership domain. © Paul Taffinder (1995). *The New Leaders*, Kogan Page. Reprinted by permission.

their prestige, heritage, political or personal significance, are failing.

Unpredictability runs counter to everything in organizations which strive for homogeneity, logic, structure, predictability. But the intellectual force behind organizational transformation is entrepreneurial spirit, inventiveness, risk – the unpredictable. In leadership this is about jolting people out of an acceptance of the ordinary by inducing crises and grabbing attention, refusing to sit still, actively disturbing the equilibrium, fixing things when they ain't broke and giving up the past to operate in the future.

Conviction is the emotional driving force of transformation. The *sine qua non* of personal and corporate transformation is that leaders believe fervently in what they are doing. No one will be willing to change if his or her leader lacks conviction about the change. The German philosopher Friedrich Nietzsche made the inspired observation: 'Men believe in the truth of all that is seen to be strongly believed in.' Conviction of this magnitude is the watchword of transformational leaders.

Generating critical mass is the skill of channelling the catalytic collective will created by deep conviction into organizational impetus. Conviction and collective will are immensely powerful but are, on their own, uncontrolled and easily dissipated in large organizations drawing energy to respond to myriad demands, both in favour of change and in defence of the status quo. Leaders get people making decisions, not just talking about it, they gain commitment and compliance, they create urgency and stretch people. They mobilize the forces of change so that cumulatively something greater than the sum total of individual action is reached and sustained.

The leadership of big change will be explored in depth in Chapter 3, drawing out the lessons from business leaders who have experienced both successes and failures.

BUT IS IT SYSTEMIC INNOVATION?

Masayoshi Son, founder and president of Softbank, has a 300-year grand vision for his company. As a provider of digital information infrastructure, Softbank has acquired or invested in over 100 Internet-related specialist businesses. Investors, however, have been jittery about the speed of Softbank's moves and its emphasis on acquisitive growth. Japan's banks shunned the company, fearing its unpredictability and its president's lack of due caution. Instead, Masayoshi Son turned to the capital markets for the multi-billion-dollar investment required to realize his vision. What makes Son unusual, in the Japanese business environment where caution is the norm, is his dedication to speed and revolutionary zeal and his stated unconcern about what others think. Is this innovation?

Bob Ayling, CEO of British Airways, has spoken about the marriage of long-haul air transportation and entertainment. It is self-evident that British Airways has a 'captive' passenger audience at least as large as the major television and media companies. BA carries 32 million people to 170 countries every year. Careful packaging, scheduling and choice of programmes could have appeal across first, business and economy class travellers, but most especially for a younger generation of would-be globe-trotters whose brand loyalty is a great prize.

In-flight entertainment, or IFE in the airline jocks' vernacular, is the way that the industry is already going. Simon-Piers Mahoney, Strategy Development Manager for British Airways, makes the point: 'Virgin is already there, but we're seeking to stay ahead or leapfrog our competitors with the total package, not just movies, games and gambling that we are including in IFE. Hence, the beds in first class and the sleeper seats in Club World. The total IFE package is one strand of an overall strategy of constantly pursuing and meeting what customers want' Is this innovation?

Sears Roebuck, the US department store group, released newly designed pliers in their Craftsman range called Robo Grip in 1996. Sears stores were selling 25 000 Robo Grip pliers a day in the run-up to Christmas and achieved 2.5 million sales eventually, making them, according to Sears, world best-sellers. In a one-month holiday period Sears made a record total of $35 million from the pliers. The design, or rather redesign, was the brainchild of retired engineer William Warheit who called on the assistance of a dentist, Hal Wrigley, in Butler, Pennsylvania. With their different backgrounds they came up with a pair of pliers that could be adjusted with one hand (existing designs need two) by means of a spring-loaded mechanism. Once Sears were convinced and backed the pliers with TV and newspaper advertising, Robo Grip sales soared. Is this innovation?

All these are examples of innovation, but at different levels. As brief as the stories are, important features can be identified: Masayoshi Son's distinctive vision and leadership, the yoking together of contrasting ideas (transportation and entertainment) in constant pursuit of what customers want at British Airways, and the integrated introduction to market of novelty (a clever invention) with marketing and advertising at Sears Roebuck.

It is rather easy to be drawn into complex and detailed debates about how we should define innovation – and related concepts travelling in close company such as creativity and inspiration. I find this leads more usually to obfuscation than illumination. It is enough to say that Michael Porter's (1990) workmanlike description suffices: 'a new way of doing things . . . that is *commercialized*' (p.780). This is broad, but then if we accept the argument in Chapter 1, innovation is the broad response of organizations seeking a defensible capability or barrier to competitors, more and more by harnessing knowledge to new ends.

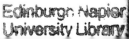

Innovation in this sense therefore is *not* clever design, or distinctive marketing or the re-engineering of key business processes or even breakthrough technologies. In many cases the ideas that seem at the heart of what we observe to be innovation in organizations are not even new. Moreover, innovation that is not integrated into the substance of the organization (i.e. within the total organizational system) will not produce sustainable competitive advantage or longer-term defensible barriers.

But *systemic innovation* will. Organizations that have achieved systemic innovation seem somehow capable of creating *within* themselves the conditions of pressure, necessity or adversity that would normally be *external*. Normally, the weight of history is against the ambitious executive. Quite often industry innovators come from outside the industry, bringing with them none of the encumbrances of conventional wisdom or prejudice.

Pressure and challenge, whether external or internal, create the conditions that drive innovation. Avoiding or minimizing these conditions – the most natural of executive actions – stores up difficulties and organizational fault lines which may in the future tear apart the business. Transformation is very largely dependent on innovation of one sort or another – the markets a firm elects to operate in, the branding it creates, the technology it brings to bear, the products it takes to customers, the speed with which it executes. But all these things can be transitory unless the organization succeeds in creating new clusters of advantages or barriers as fast as or faster than even the most aggressive of competitors. This base level competency requires that the company become capable of sustained transformation – transformation on tap, as it were. But it is a difficult feat. It takes a long time. This in itself requires substantive change at both the strategic and operational levels. At the strategic because the firm must anticipate (or create) and then exploit shifts, dislocations and trends within its industry: complacency about these things, both in the form of assuming them to be unimportant or being caught up in short-term tactical manoeuvring, is to hand an early advantage to competitors. As Bill Gates has said, 'It takes even more guts to bet on the "sea change" when you are the market leader . . .' Change must also be part of the fabric at the operational level because speed of execution, as we saw in Chapter 1, will increasingly differentiate the best from the rest. Execution is also difficult. It is something like a jigsaw puzzle of

1000 pieces: the total picture needs to be built fast, but the picture is changing, therefore you are constantly having to start again.

The CEO of ABB, Goran Lindahl, who took over from Percy Barnevik in January 1997, started the move to emphasize business actions other than the restructuring, cost-cutting and productivity improvements for which Barnevik was most famous. Barnevik formed ABB in 1988 in a merger between Sweden's Asea and Switzerland's Brown Boveri. Although constant improvement and rationalization remain at the core of ABB's culture (as they do at General Electric), Lindahl has talked about ABB's brainpower being directed to higher-margin business, increasing revenues and customer service as well as expansion in developing countries. ABB succeed in this in large part because they *are* able to execute fast: the organization consists of over 200 000 people in 1000 subsidiary firms in more than 140 countries. The philosophy so far stresses being small, interdependent, innovative and highly decentralized.

The ABB case demonstrates an important principle discussed by Michael Porter (1990). 'There is a hierarchy,' he comments, 'of sources of competitive advantage in terms of sustainability. Lower-order advantages, such as low labor costs or cheap raw materials, are relatively easy to imitate. . . . [Even] economies of scale are nullified when new technology or methods make the old ones obsolete, or new product designs have the same effect. Higher-order advantages, such as proprietary process technology, product differentiation based on unique products or services, brand reputation based on cumulative marketing efforts, and customer relationships protected by higher customer costs of switching vendors, are more durable' (pp.49–50).

In short, it is not enough to rely on the lower-order advantages conferred by productivity improvement. Goran Lindahl is building higher-order advantages at ABB. But building higher-order advantages requires big change. Big change, if it is to be successful, requires systemic innovation. And innovation becomes systemic when it has been absorbed and is practised at the individual level by a critical mass of employees.

Rolf Renke, board chairman of ABB Calor Emag Schaltan-lagen, one of ABB Group's German firms, states emphatically, 'Our mindset is a decentralized mindset. We have a very strong profit-centre organization. If I give my profit-centre heads responsibility, then I also have to give them the freedom to act.'

This freedom to act is a cornerstone of systemic innovation. In ABB it is created by structure (small firms, part of a global organization, built around numerous profit centres, all of which is highly decentralized) and matching emphasis on what Renke calls 'finding new ways' (enabling and accepting the generation of new ideas) as well as the more formal product development process which seeks to differentiate ABB products and services.

So, two things are important for systemic innovation: one is the design and structure of work (how the firm is organized) and the other is the ethos of work (the social–psychological factors). Focusing on these two aspects is, however, not sufficient. There is a dynamic relationship with leadership and conflict escalation, but for the purposes of clarity we need to artificially decompose and unbundle, so we will deal with leadership and conflict separately.

It is clear that Bill Gates early on had a very clear concept of how to get· the best innovation and performance from his employees, especially those engaged in software development. The Microsoft 'campus' at Redmond, outside Seattle, is in stark contrast to the original leased offices of the early years (which were standard, unremarkable clones of a thousand office blocks anywhere in the world). In Redmond, Gates created a sylvan landscape within which the first structure resembled an X, maximizing direct light to small private offices but providing employees with areas such as cafeterias where talking and networking would be stimulated. The physical design reflected an underlying belief that small groups working in physical proximity (and, to some extent, in competition with one another) would be innovative and productive. Of course, the infrastructure of electronic communication would assist, but the primary style of working would be eyeball-to-eyeball.

British Airways, as it happens, unveiled a very similar way of thinking when they committed to building their $330 million 'office of the future' at Harmondsworth near London's Heathrow Airport in 1996. From cramped, old-fashioned accommodation at Heathrow's Speedbird House and other widely dispersed office buildings in the vast airport area, the new office complex was an attempt to create what Chris Byron, the BA project director, described as 'a catalyst for change'. The Harmondsworth site is indeed a campus like Microsoft's Redmond. It sits in 240 acres of reclaimed greenbelt land which BA agreed to rebuild into the 'largest public park to be built in the London area this century', according to Byron. BA wanted to use space creatively and flexibly (much like Microsoft), and wanted the building to allow rapid redesign of space as the business unit structure changed in response to market demands. The greatest similarity with Microsoft, however, is in the objective of getting people from different business units to mix, breaking down cherished hierarchies and fostering informality and interaction in the cafés of the central 'street' that links the six buildings or 'houses' as they are known. Moreover, at 'innovation points' you can connect your laptop while having coffee with colleagues. BA faced a tougher challenge than Microsoft because the Microsoft culture that de-emphasizes hierarchy (manifest in individual offices of a standard size, including Bill Gates's, unreserved parking and easy access to senior executives) was designed-in from the outset when the organization was young and small. After all, Microsoft has not been around very long (since 1975) whereas British Airways, in its various historical manifestations, has service and pilot traditions reaching back to the formation of the Royal Flying Corps before World War I. Tackling hierarchy and ways of working at BA is therefore a task of relatively larger magnitude.

What is staggering, though, in both organizations is the unshakeable commitment to eyeball-to-eyeball working at a time when modern telecommunications offer the capability to operate in a highly networked way. In spite of providing the relevant technology – laptops for all, e-mail, intranet applications – BA also wanted people working together in physical proximity. In Microsoft's case the paradox is all the more startling. Randall Stross comments in *The Microsoft Way* (1996) on the peculiar disconnection between the firm's espoused mission to create the wherewithal (via personal computers and Microsoft software) to work in remote ways so that distance of any kind is irrelevant, and the deep conviction (some might say paralysing fixation) of Gates and the executive team that 'telecommuting was not explicitly forbidden, but that most groups had jobs "requiring frequent interactions with others, whether in our hallways, offices, conference rooms, or cafeterias"' (p.21). The company line was that a full-time presence on the campus was best for creativity and productivity – remote, part-time or job-shared working could not be entertained.

Both Microsoft and BA both use the best communications technology, with the core of the Microsoft workforce, the software developers, and in BA the central corporate functions, together on one campus. But where creative spark, networking, and integration are optimized, it is between small groups of workers moving to interact with colleagues no more than a few metres from their workspace.

The physical structures themselves of the buildings in both BA and Microsoft *may* explain something about the innovative capabilities of both companies – more natural light, greater stimulation of interaction, flexibility to reconfigure the space business units occupy and so forth. Of this I have my doubts and research is scant. More likely is the emphasis on small groups and teams, the inevitable competition that arises between groups and, most especially, the tremendously powerful signals and symbolism communicated by the business leaders' tangible commitment to ways of working that are *supposed* to be different and innovative. In other words, everything about the physical and social organization creates the expectation of innovation. It has become systemic. We will return to these considerations in Chapter 4.

BELOW THE SURFACE: CONFLICT AND CONFLICT ESCALATION

Put a question about aggressive competitors to Rolf Renke of ABB and he gives you a strange answer. He briefly acknowledges the strength of competition and increasing market pressures, but then shrugs it off:

> I'm not so worried about competitors. I worry about internal competition. ABB Group is decentralized, therefore we have many similar organizations, maybe not of the same size but many such organizations and therefore much competition from other ABB companies worldwide. They also serve the energy markets. And our business here at Calor Emag is 70% export dependent, so we have to compete with 'duplicated' ABB companies globally if we are to get the export market allocation. Getting market allocation means we have to be one of the front runners in ABB's benchmarking system. You have to be the best in ABB in your market or you will lose export market access. That's the real driving force in the system.

In short, ABB sustains a very real internal competitive market. At the same time, the group tries to make sure that the business units work together and that there is commonality of goals and, especially, values. The key here, however, is that there are many small companies (over 1000), thrown onto their own resourcefulness to fight for survival and win. Conflict is deliberately stimulated.

Most large firms strive to do the opposite, to smooth out, if not obliterate, internal competition. They see it as conflict and conflict is bad. But this is nonsense. As far back as 1969, Walton argued that the absence of stress (because of the damping down and removal of conflict) resulted in conditions in which there was 'no sense of urgency, no necessity to look for alternative ways of behaving, and no incentive for conciliatory overtures' (p.111). Crucially, stimulating conflict when it is absent may boost cognitive flexibility and the ability to deal with complex information. Figure 2.7 expresses the bell-shaped relationship between conflict and performance. Clearly there is an optimal level of conflict, producing a variety of benefits in particular circumstances. By contrast, when conflict is too high, people retreat to more rigid patterns of behaviour, they think less broadly and in fewer 'dimensions', will consider fewer alternatives and tend to see threat where there may be none.

A growing body of research since Walton's original work has expanded his findings, well summarized by Carsten De Dreu (1997) from Amsterdam University. He makes the point that conflict is inherent to all social life and that its avoidance or suppression in organizations can have undesirable consequences

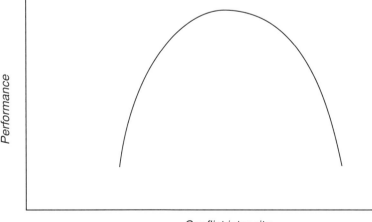

Conflict intensity

Figure 2.7 The relationship between conflict and performance.

such as reduced innovation and a tendency towards groupthink. In fact, explicit competition between groups may enhance cooperation and reduce free-loading. There are equally fascinating and counterintuitive findings about competitive people, who these days generally get a bad press in the faddish pursuit of more cooperative, participative workplaces. (A quick aside: Being cooperative and participative do not in themselves guarantee productive workplaces. It is important that we improve our skills to make these new forms of working effective.) Back to competitive people who, it transpires, are much more creative and flexible with their in-group colleagues when in competition with an out-group – it helps people unite and cooperate, as we know, to have a common enemy. It has also been shown that the active stimulation of inter-group conflict enhances mutual understanding by helping group members define the boundaries of their group and give it an identity – that is, it brings underlying issues out into the open, making them explicit, and sharpens group members' understanding of their goals and interests in relation to the group.

Failure to understand and escalate conflict in appropriate ways has cost one organization several lives and hundreds of millions of dollars. The organization? The US space agency NASA, the National Aeronautics and Space Administration. Despite overwhelming concern for and investment in technical and technological solutions (like many companies), NASA got it wrong, not just once but twice, in dramatic and high-profile style. At 11:38 a.m., 8 January 1986, the space shuttle *Challenger*, travelling at over 3000 kilometres per hour some 16 kilometres above the earth, exploded 72 seconds into its flight, killing its crew of seven. The disaster dealt a devastating blow to the shuttle programme which was already in difficulties from cost overruns. NASA recovered and four years later trumpeted the launch of the $2 billion *Hubble* space telescope – a programme intended to bring the agency back resplendently into the public eye and to demonstrate its resurgent technological pre-eminence. Why? Well, there is no doubting NASA's proud and heartfelt commitment to continuing the exploration of space but nor can one ignore the need to impress the nation sufficiently to secure ongoing Congressional funding. There was a slight problem with *Hubble*, however. It did not work. Its main mirror was faulty and only another costly shuttle mission could solve the problem.

A truly compelling account of the devastating dangers and financial costs of suppressing conflict at NASA is told by Professor Marlene Turner from San Jose State University and Professor Anthony Pratkanis at the University of California, Santa Cruz. In particular they comment (1997, p.53):

> Although there were plenty of warning signs that a potential disaster was on the horizon, they were ignored by the elite team at the United States space agency, NASA. . . . What do these fiascos have in common? In many respects, they share the characteristics of what Irving Janis called 'groupthink' – the extreme concurrence seeking displayed by decision making groups. When groups are susceptible to groupthink, their goals are transformed from the pursuit of effective problem resolution (i.e. identifying possible problems, evaluating different alternatives) to the suppression of conflict at all costs (i.e. launch despite any concerns and contradictory indications).

The symptoms of groupthink as Janis (1972) described them include:

- A sense of invulnerability
- Downplaying or rationalizing threats or difficulties
- Ignoring morally questionable decisions or actions
- Typecasting opponents as stupid or weak
- Pressuring individuals who question the team's actions
- Self-censorship of deviations from joint decisions
- Silence taken as consent
- Selectively excluding contrary information.

Turner and Pratkanis believe that the very history of pride in accomplishments (beating the Soviets to get the first people onto the moon) and the growing self-belief that NASA scientists, engineers, astronauts and managers were an elite created the conditions for disaster. Under inflated expectations from the public and the NASA teams themselves, much energy became devoted, not to making the critical evaluations and analyses necessary for high-quality decisions but to the maintenance of the NASA social identity – an elite organization that could do no wrong. The same could be said of IBM's sudden exposure (and subsequent loss of pre-eminence) in the early 1990s. John Akers' efforts to rescue Big Blue were retarded by the same social dynamics that infected NASA.

What is crucial to understand here is the difference between conflict that arises in terms of issues that are task-related and conflict arising over issues that are social–emotional in nature. Psychologists refer to these respectively as cognitive (i.e. task-related) and affective (social–emotional). Cognitive conflict might occur over strategy, resources, policies, procedures and roles, affective conflict over norms, values and personal or group identity. The key to understanding and using conflict effectively lies in this distinction, since highly desirable out-comes accrue from cognitive conflict, while affective conflict reduces performance and satisfaction and actually promotes rigidity and destructive behaviour patterns such as groupthink. For all practical purposes, then, organizations that perform well are more likely to set organizational and cultural conditions to escalate cognitive conflict and to obviate affective conflict. It is no surprise, therefore, that those organizations with deeply rooted, powerful cultural norms and values (Boeing, British Airways, Microsoft, Levi Strauss, Nordstrom and the like) are resilient and better able to handle change. There is stability and widespread concordance of affect – in one very important way people are socially–emotionally at one with each other right across the organization. They agree on and support the common values, norms and aspirations of the firm. These values and norms may well be written down as part of some mission or value statement, but as likely as not there will be differences between the actual and the espoused. What is important for transformation is that the actual values and norms are held by sufficient numbers of employees that they form a critical mass, not that they are written down. Furthermore, while people may firmly agree on the cultural values that bind them together (even though they may not be able to articulate them), at the same time there may well be fierce cognitive conflict – over strategy, budgets, markets, resourcing, policy and so on. ABB embodies this apparent paradox. More on the practicalities of using conflict for transformation in Chapter 5.

THE CULTURE OF LEARNED HELPLESSNESS

Probably one of the greatest hurdles a company faces when it attempts to transform is a pervasive sense of learned help-lessness. Many organizations that need to change have become locked in the spiral described in Chapter 1, with market pressures ratcheting up, competitiveness ratcheting down and a cost-cutting culture driving out those employees who might think and behave differently. It is hard under circumstances of decline to do anything other than downsize. The business has become locked into a fixed way of doing things. The executives' strategic and investment legacy forces them to stick with what they have. The range of things they try becomes narrower and accordingly they rarely have an impact. They are not effective in their own work environment and nor are most employees. Soon, fewer employees try to effect change. The fewer employees who attempt to make a difference, the less likely employees generally will feel that they can affect anything in their working environment and the less likely it is that effective, action-oriented new joiners will stay (or even join in the first place). So the spiral continues.

The concept of learned helplessness is due to Seligman (1975) who developed the theory in clinical psychology settings to account for depression. In any setting people may acquire a sense of helplessness when confronted for a period of time with uncontrollable aversive stimulation – i.e. exposure to stressful events over which people have no control. This helplessness later tends deleteriously to hamper their performance in other stressful situations that they *could* in fact control. However, they appear to lose the ability and motivation to learn to respond in an effective way to the new stressful circumstances.

When such helplessness permeates an organization because of the spiral of decline and reaches a level of critical mass, the culture itself may become dominantly one of learned helplessness. In British Airways before the first transformation was initiated, this was the case. But it need not be precipitated by an obvious decline. All too often, small start-up hot-growth companies charge ahead faster than any of their bigger rivals because of a combination of drive, ingenuity and entrepreneurial flair in the individuals that they attract. But growth itself means that they inevitably recruit (for good logical reasons) more and more conventional people with bureaucratic tendencies. The new employees, dedicated to process, structure, hierarchy, command and control may steadily reach a critical mass that outweighs the original entrepreneurial energy. They come to dominate the company and the culture. A belief system can then quickly spread that it is not possible to do things as quickly or effectively as before, or to take the same everyday risks. Hot-growth becomes no-growth. The culture becomes one of helplessness. The behaviour and cognition of employees in a state of learned helplessness are characterized by:

- Passivity in the face of pressure and demands
- Failure to initiate action that might resolve the current difficulties
- Beliefs that one cannot take action to resolve problems ('there's nothing we can do; it's out of our hands')
- Disinclination to be encouraged by occasional successes in the mistaken but unshakeable belief that the success did not occur because of their own actions but was merely by chance or circumstance ('it won't happen again: it had nothing to do with us . . . we were just lucky')
- Low expectations of effectiveness, even when successful ('I can't see things coming right; why should they?')

Transformation cannot proceed unless this change in culture is signalled early on and then driven into the organization. As John Chisholm, CEO of DERA, says of the early days of that organization's tranformation:

> Indeed, the main point was to get a culture of change. That's fundamental. I had to get the organization to overcome its helplessness and get it into people that anyone, anywhere can make things happen. There had to be a culture that every problem, every issue is resolvable. And it's up to you to do it.

3
The Leadership of Big Change

RAISING THE DEAD

In the late 1980s Sears Roebuck, the giant US retailer, was doing a wonderful imitation of IBM: it was doing its best to be moribund. Both organizations had been known for innovation and awesome service but were now suffering disastrous criticism and a customer exodus because of arrogance, rigid inefficiencies and corporate fatigue. Both made huge losses, chairman Ed Brennan of Sears contemplating from the 110-floor Sears Tower a mammoth $3.9 billion splash of red in 1992. Massive, energy-sapping reorganizations had failed to deliver desperately needed change. Wal-Mart, upstart discount-chain, overtook the venerable Sears as America's leading retailer. Then Arthur Martinez arrived to take on the job of Sears Merchandise Group CEO, cutting 50 000 jobs, closing 113 of the poorly performing stores and (shock, horror) pulling the famous Sears catalogue. A number of the 'non-core' diversifications, particularly into insurance and real estate, were sold off, as was the other famous Sears icon, the Sears Tower in Chicago. Apart from cutting costs and getting *out* of markets, Martinez also forced the full-line stores business (representing nearly 60% of total revenues) to define a prime target market (mothers of middle America) instead of attempting to be all things to all comers and pulled the supporting infrastructure in behind this. In addition and by contrast, after getting the top job in 1995 Martinez hitched Sears' future growth to a totally different engine – in what he described as his 'off-the-mall growth strategy', smaller specialty outlets away from the big shopping malls and traditional Sears stores, the Home Stores dealing in 'heavy-duty' hardware, garden supplies, tools and electronics equipment, the Auto Stores selling and installing tyres, batteries and related goods (as opposed to the 'softer side of Sears' as the company's marketing drive described its range of women's apparel). Martinez's transformation was a marvel: by 1996 Sears had delivered $1.27 billion earnings on $38 billion sales and for investors was way outperforming both Wal-Mart and the tightly run consumer brands companies like Coca-Cola, Walt Disney and Kodak.

IBM, similarly, bounced back from near-death – under the leadership of Lou Gerstner – where John Akers, the previous CEO, had presided over a $5 billion loss (when securities analysts in early 1992 were projecting a $4 billion profit!). Akers had not been idle. He tried very hard to turn Big Blue round, cutting, for example, an unprecedented $1 billion out of the research and development budget, slicing thousands of jobs and reorganizing and decentralizing on a heroic scale but was undone finally and symbolically by having to announce IBM's first dividend *cut* ever. On 27 January 1993 Akers resigned.

Big organizations have it within them to bounce back from adversity. Seasoned investors know this. At its worst, during 1993, the value of IBM shares sank some $75 billion. By early 1997, however, the rebound under Lou Gerstner had recovered all of that and more, surging to a record high. Revenues of $76 billion, profits of $5.4 billion made it the top-ranking computer firm in the world. Indeed, as *Business Week* (26 May 1997) reported, several canny investors did very well out of IBM, buying shares when the company had sunk to its worst haemorrhaging in 1993 and the stock price had collapsed. The very fact that such organizations are so large and globe-straddling, with gigantic revenues pouring in from all over the world and such enormous share of market, means they have sufficient cash flow to generate mountainous balance sheets, enabling them to claw their way through the bad times until the right leader can make a difference at a substantive level within the business – like Lou Gerstner or Arthur Martinez. In short, all is not lost for the corporate dinosaurs of today. The right leader can make a significant difference to their fortunes. The corporate dead can be raised.

But what makes the right leader? In Chapter 2 we started to open up the concept of transformational leadership and looked at the leadership domain: imposing context, risk making and risk taking, unpredictability, conviction, and generating critical mass. Leaders who are capable in each of these elements of the domain can transform organizations. Leaders like Gerstner and Martinez create a strong emotional attachment from employees and inspire people to do more than they otherwise might. They are able to raise executives' and employees' ambition, to establish a shared ownership of purpose or mission and to motivate people to go beyond self-interest for the organization's greater good. This is not because of some mysterious charisma, but because of the way they behave, the things they do. The most effective leaders are both a stimulus for and a representation of the organization's collective will. Leaders, therefore, must trigger the organization's will to change and demonstrate this in deed. The leader is thus both master and servant to organizational members. Let us look at the evidence under each of the leadership domain headings.

Imposing Context

Martinez was quick off the mark when he took over Sears' Merchandise Group. The finances had to be put right. Survival was at stake. He closed stores, trimmed the workforce and, importantly, gave the organization a focus it had long lacked. It seemed to have escaped Sears' executives who their customers were. Once it was a high-growth company that was able to sustain high growth by redefining its market in line with population changes in the USA – in the 1900s targeting farmers through mail-order, then in the 1920s switching to retail outlets aimed at both farming and urban blue-collar buyers, in the 1950s becoming *the* maker for the American middle-class family. In the 1980s Sears seemed badly confused and Arthur Martinez in the early 1990s redefined what its business should be and began to impose a new context for the business, speaking to the organization and, through Sears' advertising, to the market about the 'softer side of Sears' and, quite literally, 'We're not who you think we are'. He was clearly focusing the company on its middle-income customer and, in doing so, placing growing emphasis on extracting maximum value from its brands such as Craftsman, DieHard, Weatherbeater, Kenmore and, of course, Sears itself.

In April 1995 British Airways began to brief leading design consultants to come up with a new identity for what, until then, had been 'the World's Favourite Airline'. Here, like Sears, the brand had been recognized as a huge asset that could be used in new ways. (Remember, in Chapter 1, we said that in the dispersed organization of 2015 the brand would be the most substantial part of the organization and the prime force for organizational coherence: in Sears and BA there is the early recognition of this.) Bob Ayling and his team intended to take BA through a second big change at least as fundamental and far-reaching as the original had been during the 1980s. The new context for BA was to be its internationalization – through to the core. This meant matching service to an increasingly international customer base (60% of BA's business originates outside Britain). Ayling started to tackle a number of strategic and tactical challenges built around the announcement of the new mission of BA: to be the undisputed leader in world travel. Nothing about airlines in this. The context was much broader, moving, as the new mission statement explained, 'into other world travel-related areas', but the core theme was powerfully reinforced by the new image capital: that BA regarded the whole world as its customer. Out went the earlier successful but sober (and uniform) design with its echo of the Union Jack on aircraft tails and in came images from around the world, each one distinct – a Celtic knot, Chinese calligraphy, paintings from the new South Africa, a North American 'whale rider' and so on. The new context was also underpinned by a commitment to adjust staffing so that customers would be able to receive service from staff who spoke their own language – an adjustment that meant replacing 5000 BA employees with more highly skilled staff, including cabin crew speaking languages other than English.

Imposing context can be as much about management style and culture as about strategy and marketing. Clive Dolan, managing director of Siemens Plessey Electronic Systems which, until its recent sale to British Aerospace, accounted for virtually all of German firm Siemens' defence business profits, faced the need to transform his company following the defence industry consolidation affecting Boeing, McDonnell-Douglas and others worldwide during the 1990s. As hard as it was to get started on the 'hard' business issues of the organizational turnaround when he got the job in 1993, Dolan also came up against what I call the 'underground' stuff – the way the executive team had learned to operate, the hidden agendas and hierarchical, aggressive management style. He says:

We were making losses – this was endemic and I had to put it right. But also the way the management team worked was like internecine war. We just had battles all the time. At the same time, as MD, I was expected to be on top of all the detail – technical, business, strategic . . . The change programme started in earnest when I wanted to change the way we worked as a team. I was being expected to behave in the old way. I didn't.

In leading big change, imposing context means making it absolutely clear what is important in the organization, what its markets and strategy are, where it has come from and where it is going, and demonstrating what the culture and values of the executive team should be and thus, by extension, what is expected of employees. Nothing will change unless the top team changes. This is as much about signalling change as about operating differently. In the case of Sears, Martinez actually got rid of most of the senior executives, replacing them with non-retail specialists. Typically the business media read this (correctly) as a tactic to bring in new thinking, but missed the importance of the symbolic statement of change that this connotes, both inside and outside the company – Sears *is* changing. Likewise, Lou Gerstner at IBM brought in more than 60 new executives in the second year of Big Blue's big change, his aim to 'quicken the process of transformation'.

Risk Making, Risk Taking

In an interview with *Fortune* (28 April 1997) Arthur Martinez explained what he thinks about big change:

A turnaround is a financial recovery. A transformation is much more. It's all about changing the structure and the approach of the business, and re-educating our people to feel comfortable outside a command-and-control environment. It involves getting them used to risk taking and innovation. (p.110)

Martinez killed off the famous Sears catalogue, that many called the soul of Sears and which had been around since the turn of the century. The traditional Sears mainstay of big stores, he promised, would also go the same way, being replaced by a completely new retail model, one based like Disney on the power of consumer brands delivered through outlets that may not even bear the Sears name. He knew that risks were called for and still would be and that they have to be demonstrated in deed or employees would not follow his lead. So, for example, he promoted and supported executives who had languished under the previous leadership because of their off-the-wall ideas and proclivity to take risks.

This can be hard on the executives who grew up under the old way of doing things. Clive Dolan acknowledges this: 'I was acutely aware that I was taking big risks and that this was hard for the management team. Some took to it easily, most were very uncomfortable for a time. When you're changing the whole organization, people tend to lose faith, people panic and go back to what they know.' However, the necessity to take risks, to ask questions about what needs to change and then commit to changing them is overriding. In truth, if you're not making mistakes, you're not doing anything. Looking back on over two years of transformation effort at Siemens Plessey, Clive Dolan muses:

> At its heart, launching change like this means having to take the risk of letting go of the reins at some point. And that means that you are unleashing a complex, writhing organization into the unknown. You know that at any one time all the parts of it aren't working perfectly, but that's the only way you learn what does work and what doesn't . . .

Unpredictability

One of the difficulties leaders face in firms that must change is the apathy, cynicism or learned helplessness of employees: 'It's been done before. It'll never work. It can't be done.' People get into a rut, the culture gets into a rut – or to use Clive Dolan's words, 'skepticism becomes a way of life'. Transformational leaders are able to jolt people's scepticism, to get them out of a rut, to challenge the status quo and to move outside the pattern. Such leaders grab people's attention in organizations where it has become the norm to view things from only one particular (limited) perspective, where the company way is the only way and, quite simply, everything is logical, rational, uniform – utterly predictable – but is killing the business. Arthur Martinez has committed Sears, in effect, to give up the past and operate in the future by questioning the fundamental basis of American retailing in general and Sears' history and traditions of retailing in particular. In transforming the company, Martinez would have no sacred cows. Command and control was out. The old culture and way of doing things was a drag on change.

Clive Dolan makes a similar point: 'It's very easy to become seduced into a particular way of working because that's the way the organization and its culture constrains you, and that's what had happened to us . . .' Dolan tried twice to kick-start the transformation of Siemens Plessey and, like Sears before Martinez, this was on top of numerous changes to organization structure. 'We had become obsessed with organization!' Dolan laments. 'We had made constant changes to organization structure, but the disturbing fact was that the sum total of all our efforts was producing diminishing margins and a growing frustration among the workforce.' One of the ways that helped make the change happen down at the grassroots was Dolan's clear commitment to doing things that were completely different from what was expected by the old, ingrained, still all-powerful culture. A key leadership message delivered and reinforced by Dolan helped sufficient numbers of people to believe that they could change things. He said to employees, 'I invite you to challenge authority. If you do, I will support you.' Dolan goes on to add, 'This was symbolic, but symbolism is more than just theatre. Process alone misses the point. The symbolic helps people to see that they too can change.'

Inviting employees to challenge authority has the effect of legitimizing the escalation of cognitive conflict and thus of clarifying issues and solving problems. Ultimately this conflict begins to break down the ossified bureaucracy and inward-looking, in-bred culture.

Conviction

Perhaps the most distinctive mark of transformational leaders is their utter conviction. It's not that they never change their minds – witness Bill Gates' about-turn on the Internet, or Arthur Martinez's surprising redirection of Sears towards small, free-standing specialty outlets selling hardware. But once they commit, they put their conviction on the line. They make it utterly clear what they believe in and especially so when trans-formation is called for. Clive Dolan:

> It simply isn't possible to make a transformation in the way people do things unless you are bold in your assertions and stretch the horizons

... but above all are totally resolved to change your company. .... It's
my conviction that transformation needs to be driven from the top. If
your people don't feel that you believe it, it won't happen.

Pierre Gravelle, now president and CEO of the Canadian co-
sourcing venture Symcor, led the dramatic transformation at
Revenue Canada, including Customs and Excise, when he was
deputy minister in the early 1990s. This was an aggressive
programme of modernization and process re-engineering in a
government bureaucracy whose culture and ways of working
had always emphasized rules, policing and enforcement but
whose objectives were to become not only efficient but also
client-centred and fair-dealing, thus facilitating voluntary compliance rather than enforcing it. The gap between reality and
vision was vast, seemingly unbridgeable. 'We managed to
deliver the goods,' says Gravelle, 'because of a single-minded
determination about the change. You must be personally
impatient for one hell of a long time ... You can see I get
very excited about this, because we were building for the
future.'

Generating Critical Mass

Conviction is the thing that mobilizes employees, gets them to
commit to a new context or new vision, but such catalytic
energy is readily dissipated if leaders fail to channel it by
building the right operational and management infrastructure,
getting people to make decisions and not just talk about it, and
then rousing the workforce to operate at pace, with a sense of
urgency – most times in complete rejection of the way
management and workforce currently operate. Typically, the
organization's structures and measurement systems drive
inappropriate (old) behaviour. Says Clive Dolan:

When you ask managers, who are already finding that they haven't got
enough people for business as usual, to provide substantial numbers of
people to run a change programme, then you find out how open-
minded, flexible and resilient they really are! And of course the problem
is that those same managers have a vested interest in maintaining the
current organization and status quo. They've grown strong because of it.
But you have to get them to realize that their jobs really consist of
making change happen as a norm ... You have to put new measures on
them to change their behaviour and when they don't meet those
measures you have to be prepared to push them hard.

Pierre Gravelle's experience of big change at Revenue Canada yields an important lesson about critical mass as well – if a level of critical mass is not achieved, you are in danger of building a house of cards. He relates a story of the early days of change at Revenue Canada when senior managers were going through some gut-wrenching reality-facing:

> At my first 3-day intensive session on the future of the organization with 200 bright, dynamic managers – but of the 'old school' – one of my high-fliers in the group came up with a graphic. And he says to everyone: 'You know, we've embarked on a journey, up a very steep hill. We're all in this bus, waiting for it to get moving but we're just passengers; at the moment there's only one guy pushing the bus and that's Pierre. But the way it's got to be, if we're to succeed, is that Pierre will be up here steering and we'll all be pushing.' That's just to illustrate that over time, once there is employee buy-in and manager buy-in, this has a multiplier effect. In any event, you should never do these things by yourself because the moment you leave, the whole thing falls apart – it isn't lasting.

The Leadership Domain

Are you a transformational leader or simply a high-performance manager? Are there sufficient numbers of people in your organization to lead big change? Although the best way to answer these questions is through more comprehensive psychological assessment, the questionnaire below will give you a rough and ready indicator. Fill it out yourself or, better still, get peers and other colleagues to assess you.

Directions: First read all of the twenty behavioural statements in the questionnaire, then choose only *ten* that strongly characterize the day-to-day behaviour of the person you are rating and tick them. Scoring instructions and a leadership profile are given at the end of this chapter.

1. Ensures that major tasks/projects are on track   [ ]
2. Lifts people's sights to show them what they can achieve   [ ]
3. Insists on hitting deadlines   [ ]

Figure 3.1 Big Change Tours Inc.

4. Makes it clear where the business is
   heading   [ ]
5. Monitors people's performance
   carefully   [ ]
6. Encourages people to do things
   differently, to take risks   [ ]

7. Focuses on running the business
   efficiently [ ]
8. Constantly demands new ideas and
   perspectives [ ]
9. Avoids exposing the business to
   uncertainty and risks [ ]
10. Imparts a sense of adventure and
    excitement [ ]
11. Makes the best of how the
    organization presently operates [ ]
12. Experiments, turns things upside-
    down, challenges people [ ]
13. Ensures that mistakes are not made [ ]
14. Articulates strong convictions and
    ideals [ ]
15. Manages his or her reputation [ ]
16. Creates a sense of pride and trust in
    working with him or her [ ]
17. Emphasizes standards and procedures [ ]
18. Generates energy and urgency in
    others to get things done [ ]
19. Insists that people operate within clear
    limits of authority [ ]
20. Sustains pressure so that people
    achieve more than expected [ ]

Note: A more comprehensive assessment is
available from the author.

BIG CHANGE *IS* THE BUSINESS

It is hard to transform an organization. Sears' Arthur Martinez
would agree with Pierre Gravelle, president of Symcor, that
financial recovery or delayering the organization – hard as those
things may be – are simply 'playing at the margins', to use
Gravelle's taut phrase. Transformation is not a project. It cannot
be separate from what the business is and does. Looking back
on eight years of big change effort at Revenue Canada and his
success in transforming the organization, Gravelle is sanguine
but realistic about such change. 'Managing fundamental, long-
term change within any large public institution, including

changing the corporate culture,' he concluded in an address to
senior US government officials in Washington, DC, in late 1995,
'is a significant and protracted endeavour, lasting longer than
the much quoted seven-year span.'

No one knows this better than Clive Dolan. When the former
Plessey Company became part of Siemens Plessey Electronic
Systems in 1989, the organization underwent more or less
continuous change in response to the demands of customers all
over the world. Customers still wanted state-of-the-art battle-
field radar and communications technology but, increasingly,
were demanding software-intensive systems and wanted them
delivered faster and at reduced cost. Executives tried in a
number of ways to shift the organization and were encouraged
by some notable successes, but it was soon clear that these were
piecemeal and were not tackling the whole organizational
system. In fact, as Dolan admits, the things that went right did
so rather more through good luck than judgement. Focus and
coordination across the company was lacking. After accepting
the top job in October 1993, Clive Dolan learned the hard way
about transformation. Despite his active encouragement and
sponsorship of standalone change programmes designed and
driven by individual functions, the inconsistency and general
inability of Siemens Plessey to improve performance was
becoming a source of deep frustration. Dolan takes up the story:

> The bottom-up change route simply wasn't going to produce a dividend.
> . . . It simply wasn't enough. I determined that we needed to do
> something more dramatic and wide-reaching . . . but people were
> saying, 'What price corporate transformation when I've got a business to
> run?' In simple truth there isn't a choice. What they were actually saying
> was, 'I've got a business to run into the ground!' Here's where the
> strength of your conviction is really tested, because you have to have the
> courage to say to them, 'Your business *is* the change programme.'

It was only at this juncture, when senior managers began to
understand that change was not a part-time activity for them
that any hope of achieving a critical mass of change effort was
realized. Change became what the business did every day,
driven from the top but legitimized by every executive and
senior manager in word and in action. To make sure this happened, Dolan was relentless in reinforcing the same message,
not only by saying what mattered but also by demonstrating it.
For example, time and again he came across managers who

complained that they couldn't do the change programme *and* their day job. Dolan's response was unequivocal. 'Right,' he would say. 'Then do the change programme.'

To launch big change successfully and to prevent it becoming unglued at some future date, then, requires a number of leadership actions. We have already in this chapter explored some of the personal psychological dimensions of transformational leaders but we must also set out the key leadership actions that executives need to take during the course of initiating and sustaining big change. Action List 1 gives the headlines.

Action List 1   Leading Big Change

1. Choose the right team for the change.
2. Unite the team and permit no backsliding.
3. In crisis-driven transformation, big change starts by diktat, not by consensus.
4. Communicate the essence of the change time and time again.
5. Never abandon your change agents.

THE RIGHT TEAM

The Defence Evaluation and Research Agency (DERA) has roots in Britain's national armaments industry stretching back before World War I. Formed as the Defence Research Industry in 1991, the organization brought together the non-nuclear Research Establishments of the Ministry of Defence. DERA employed 12 000 staff and was widely known around the world for numerous key inventions and contributions to the innovation that has made Britain the second largest defence equipment exporter after the USA. But DERA was in crisis. It was on a slippery downhill slope. Subject to all the maladies of a slow, bureaucratic government body, DERA was unequal to the task of responding to rapidly changing military needs. The less responsive they were, the less support they received from government. The less support they received, the less funding (then $1.3 billion) was directed their way and, of course, the less they were then able to respond. The cycle of decline was clear and potentially deadly. John Chisholm was offered the chief executive role at that time, but before accepting the job he gave the ministers a list of six preconditions. Matters, however, were not to be that simple, as Chisholm confirms:

> As usual, in composing such a list, I started with the least demanding at the top and worked down to what I expected would be more difficult. That was the last I heard for five weeks. I assumed that a more accommodating candidate had been found. Then the Home Secretary rang and I heard that my list had been agreed. What had caused the delay? Had there been a difficulty? It turned out to be the very first item, one I had considered the least contentious – that I must be able to choose my own team. Coming from the private sector I was seeing for the first time one of the myriad secondary controls under which so many public sector organizations must labour. It just never occurred to me that an executive set the challenging task of transforming a large organization should not have the perfect liberty to choose those lieutenants that he would want with him in the coming battle.

Chisholm was obliged to take a course of action over which other chief executives, such as Arthur Martinez, have much greater freedom. Indeed, Martinez replaced most of the senior team when he arrived at Sears. Chisholm, with a critical eye, looked within DERA. Many of the executives had passed their sell-by date but he managed to select the few key individuals who not only were possessed of the right technical and business skills to take on the job but were themselves frustrated by their perceived lack of freedom to get on with things – in short, they were highly motivated to lead change. Within a matter of weeks he had formed the team he needed. The gravest difficulty was the financial staff he had inherited. They had been steeped too long in the traditional government bureaucrat brew of rules and rulebooks and proved culturally and technically incapable of providing effective financial accounting services. Chisholm recruited a finance director from outside to undertake a complete renewal of the department. As all this was happening, Chisholm began the reorganization of DERA but, as he is keen to emphasize, 'the details of the structure were nowhere near as important as the choice of the individuals within it'.

Similar action was taken by Desmond Smith in the first year of his appointment as managing director of the $4.5 billion South African financial services group Sanlam. With years of indifferent performance behind the company, including some big losses, and with the growing threat of international competition that followed the profound changes in the political landscape of the country, Sanlam needed to change fast. In the first twelve to eighteen months Smith replaced about half the general management. It was clear to him that a number of executives just did not see things the way he did and would not have been able to make the change. They were balking at everything. He gives an example:

> We identified information technology as critical to being a world class player, but the current team weren't up to it. I took out the top eight guys in our IT division, scouted around outside the company but couldn't find anyone suitable and decided to appoint a marketing general manager running one of the regions. He had an IT background but had been a marketer for the last twelve years. I wanted a manager who understood business and business needs and who could shake up the IT division, get them focused instead of playing with themselves in their little ivory towers.

So the lesson for leaders is not so much about getting rid of an old senior team as about selecting the right team to take on change. Hugh Teasdale, director of Downstream Businesses at EVC, the $1.2 billion European Vinyls Corporation, is unequivocal on this score. 'From my experience with ITT in Europe, the Middle East and Africa and here with EVC,' he says, 'if you're starting out to change the organization, never compromise on appointments. Unless you've got the right person in the right job, properly compensated and motivated, you've lost 85% of the battle – and the converse is true, especially at the general management level.' Teasdale goes on to make a related point that organizations facing the need to transform inevitably face, especially if the organization has a long-serving culture. This concerns the tendency, particularly at senior levels, to view the job and its incumbent as one and the same. 'Never let the organization,' Teasdale continues, 'be designed to accommodate people in particular roles. That leads to compromises and you will always suffer because of it.'

Ad Scheepbouwer, managing director of PTT Post, one of the first postal services in the world to be privatized and to compete internationally, sums up nicely, 'What you find in starting change like this is that there are a lot of people who can tell you what the problems are, but only a few who can give you solutions and those are the people you need.' However, once you have got the right team, their value in facilitating the transformation is incalculable. Vernon Sankey, CEO of Reckitt & Colman, the $3.8 billion household and pharmaceutical products company who sell famous brands such as Lysol, Dettol and Disprin in 120 countries, maintains that transformation is impossible without the right team – 'right' in terms of the people in it and the way they work together. 'A leader,' he says, 'becomes closely identified with the transformation, as if he or she is the person that makes the difference, but that's inaccurate. In my experience the leader not only inspires but gains inspiration from the team.'

UNITE THE TEAM AND PERMIT NO BACKSLIDING

In addition to the 'Think Weeks' that Bill Gates takes to go off alone and ponder Microsoft strategy and competitor actions, the team also have 'retreats' where they consider the future and spend time together, and the top management group meets once a month to make decisions on the business. Gates, perhaps more so than many other CEOs, steers the Microsoft ship himself but, nonetheless, the coming together of the top team and Gates' regular review meetings with numerous product development teams is an essential part of the ongoing process of creating a unified and common understanding among managers. At the time of playing catch-up on the Internet, this relationship and communication infrastructure allowed Gates and the top team to be close enough to the action in Microsoft to push the right buttons to transform the company.

At the start of any big change, getting the right team together, as we discussed in the previous section, can happen fast and work well, but it can sometimes only be half the challenge. The other half is uniting the team around the need to change the company or sustain the change. Moreover, although the chief executive's deep conviction is enough to start change, it is never enough to sustain it. There has to be a unified executive team who come to hold to the same conviction. At Siemens Plessey it had become perfectly obvious to Clive Dolan that despite the best efforts of the management team members individually, they simply were not spending enough time together. On the surface what was lacking was the need to come to terms with Dolan's vision of the company's future and then work out what would get them there, but under the surface some equally important dynamics needed to take place. 'So despite the time pressures and difficulties,' Dolan says, 'we took three days away from the business to simply get our thoughts straight. During these three days we developed from the vision a framework of how we were going to make the change within the company happen. We bared our separate agendas to each other. We got to know each other considerably better and collectively determined that we would commit to using the new framework as a means of bringing about change.'

Upon all this was dependent the future success of the change programme. During that first three-day session Clive Dolan and his team jointly committed to spend 40% of their time (two days per executive every week) on change instead of the usual running of the business. To bring the implementation of change right to the top of the executive team's agenda and imbed this in the way they conducted themselves, they scheduled a second monthly meeting, in addition to the regular executive meeting. This second meeting focused exclusively on change implementation and within weeks Dolan and his team were using this monthly event not just as a way of ensuring that collective sponsorship remained strong and cohesive but to force the pace of change. 'Everyone in that team,' Dolan affirms, 'had to be unified. We allowed no backsliding. I said to them: "We are involved in a change programme; we will change. People in this team have had their chance now to change and if they can't or won't, they will have to go."'

The Right Way

There are times when a leader must move out ahead of the flock, go off in a new direction, confident that he is leading his people the right way.

Nelson Mandela (1994, p.514)

START BY DIKTAT NOT BY CONSENSUS

If you are looking for management fads, you could do worse than alighting on the notion of 'consensus'. There seems, these days, an almost overwhelming pressure to stretch consensus as far as it will go in organizations. It is said that consensus will get people 'bought-in' and 'on-side' and that consensus will ensure they are less likely to 'resist change'. And yet although consensus *is* important, it is a matter of timing. Rushing to build consensus too early, particularly at senior levels, can be fatal. Why? Because people expect their leaders to lead and not to ask for their agreement and commitment at an early stage. This is especially the case when people feel under pressure, circumstances are unfavourable, the future is uncertain and they are suspicious of a new leader – all, of course, conditions typical of many incipient organizational transformations and most typical of those that are crisis-driven. Ian Preston, the former CEO of $3.8 billion ScottishPower, one of the leading privatized British utilities, once said to me: 'If you're in the throes of a major change programme like we are, there's only room for consultation and not consensus. Consensus is for the stable environment . . . but who's stable these days?' Duncan Whyte, a one-time Arthur Andersen partner, joined ScottishPower in 1988 as finance director in the prelude to privatization and worked with Ian Preston to lead the huge change to the company. Whyte is now responsible for developing aspects of the group's business (energy supply, electrical retailing, telecommunications and contracting services) which together will establish the basis for ScottishPower to compete successfully in developed markets increasingly demanding multi-utility service offerings. Thinking through each of the substantive programmes of change that he and his colleagues have led in the company since 1988, Whyte states without hesitation:

> You have got to drive forward initially regardless of your people, almost without taking them with you – by diktat. Now I'm sure that is contrary to what people like to hear, but it starts with diktat. Of course, this is a timing thing. Pretty soon you need the programmes to get people involved, but you don't start from consensus; you start from a clear statement by the executive team of where you want to go . . .

Decisive steps that set the tone for change are called for during the early stages of transformation – especially in organizations that are transforming from crisis. They are as important in signalling the fact that change is happening as they are in reinforcing or building a new leader's credibility. When Lou Gerstner stepped into John Akers' shoes at IBM in 1993 he did what he had done more than a decade before when set the challenge of transforming American Express: he set about managing largely by diktat, particularly in the early days. American Express and IBM were, in their own ways, remarkably similar – both at one time rich and arrogant with byzantine management hierarchies and both fallen on hard times with inward-looking, unimaginative cultures that were struggling to find answers. Gerstner at once began to push through changes around him, many times by-passing the regular chain of command, thereby implicitly flattening the old hierarchies and shaking people up. Paul Carroll, in his analysis of the collapse of IBM (1993, p.353) paints this picture of Gerstner in the days and weeks after his appointment:

> He effectively abolished the Management Committee, saying that he didn't believe in rule by committee. Gerstner also tried to forbid anyone from making a formal presentation to him using foils. For a while, executives didn't know what to do. They could barely speak without their foils. But Gerstner insisted that if someone had something to say, they should just say it. Gerstner, in general, dispensed with the formality of IBM meetings. . . . He asked quick, tough, almost rude questions. Then he wound things up in perhaps fifteen minutes – while the more formal Akers might have let the same meeting go on for an hour and a half. . . . Gerstner began walking around, sticking his head into people's offices to ask how they were progressing . . . Gerstner began using e-mail to communicate with people and didn't bother relaying questions down through the hierarchy . . .

COMMUNICATE THE ESSENCE TIME AND TIME AGAIN

John Kotter, of Harvard Business School, posits the following startling equation in his book *Leading Change* (1996). Assume that the total amount of communication received by an employee in three months is 2 300 000 words or numbers. A typical change vision (consisting of one 30-minute speech, one hour-long meeting, one 600-word article and one 2000-word memo) might be communicated in some 13 400 words or numbers over three months. Do the calculation: $13\,400/2\,300\,000 = 0.0058$. In other words, the change vision for the three months in which executives are communicating it captures around half a per cent of an employee's total exposure to the blast of organizational noise. Now, although this equation neglects to factor in the quality of the change vision message, the inspiration with which it is delivered by executives and the motivation of employees to change, it is also true that most employees have heard this all before. So the half per cent soundbite, even doubled, trebled or quadrupled, is straining credulity.

In my wanderings I struggle to recall a single executive who has led big change who does not comment on how, initially, they badly underestimated the need to communicate. From his experience with 42 000 employees at Revenue Canada and Customs and Excise, Pierre Gravelle makes a point which captures the tactic that otherwise might be missed. 'Sustaining a service quality focus requires daily reaffirmation and reinforcement – internally for all managers and employees; externally for clients and stakeholders.' The first point about daily reaffirmation might be considered motherhood (although most organizations still fail in this), but the second acknowledges the systemic nature of organizations: the organization is the people and processes that make it up, but it functions within a further net of systems – customers, suppliers, stakeholders. The message of organizational change will transmit fastest and most powerfully when managers, employees, customers and other stakeholders hear the same insistent message from every quarter and not just from the executive team.

Just kicking this off can be gruelling. Clive Dolan of Siemens Plessey: 'I personally spoke to all 3000 employees on their own sites in groups over a period of about 30 days. . . . [But] people had seen it all before and whilst I was encouraged by the enthusiasm shown by some, I was in little doubt that there was a thick core of cynicism running through the organization which had been tempered and honed by years of dissatisfaction.' Apart from the personal executive commitment and effort, the organizational energy required can be enormous. In British Airways' first transformation during the 1980s two training programmes central to the effort were launched: Putting People First (PPF) for the entire workforce and Managing People First aimed at the managerial population. Colin Marshall was present at four out of every ten of the PPF seminars – an amazing time commitment for any chief executive.

As daunting a challenge as all of the above is, it is still only the beginning and it is all one-way: top down. Many organizations, unused to the level and scope of communication messages and media demanded in transformation, go only this far. And it is not far enough. 'Not only,' says Pierre Gravelle, 'did I need to give the same messages all the time but we had to deliver this through all forums and mechanisms. We had to get employees to shift from being passive listeners to active participants.'

Sanlam CEO Desmond Smith agrees. At the start of the change programme in 1995 they consulted with staff, customers, and brokers to identify the detail of the changes they needed to make – ultimately the 'fifteen migration ideals' that would demonstrate how Sanlam had transformed if they were successful in changing. In particular they surveyed 7500 of the 14 700 employees on a one-to-one basis, or in groups or through questionnaires, asking as one of the key questions, 'Where do you think you can help us to bring about the change?' Some of the responses were surprising. 'They said they wanted to work in an environment,' Smith remembers, 'which was far more performance-driven and output-oriented and an environment where initiative would be recognized and rewarded. How they thought they could help us with the change, they were saying, was in improving productivity and client service.' Smith and his team were beginning to get employees both to understand and to actively contribute to the change. In addition, Smith's team discovered that staff's preferred route of communication was via their immediate superior and so began to gear ongoing communication during change implementation to this delivery mechanism.

In the communication stakes it is, as the examples above show, possible to underestimate the willingness and enthusiam of employees for change. This is undoubtedly the case in organizations that have simply been managed badly – where freedom of action has been constrained for a long time, or initiative drowned, or executives have failed to offer employees a compelling, inspiring vision of what they could, with effort, attain. There is, perhaps, no worse a lapse of leadership than to dam up, knowingly or unknowingly, the collective motive energy of an organization. But the assumption is easily made that employees will resist everything or that they are not equal to the task, especially when executives are appointed from outside, as Ad Scheepbouwer from the Netherlands' PTT Post will vouch:

> You tend to underestimate the value of the people already in-house when you come in from outside, from the private sector. You think,'All these people are civil servants. They probably don't know what to do.' But it struck me later that there were a lot of very good people around who were willing to make the change, who were saying,'We should do it. Let's do it. Let's improve quality, let's improve productivity, let's improve profit, let's develop new services – because in the past we were

never allowed to do such things.' So there were lots of reasons why
people had been held back. They really had an enormous drive to prove
that they were as good as, or better than, all these other people coming
in from outside.

The counterbalance to this, as we said before, is that some
executives and employees will never make the change and will
always be a drag on your best transformation efforts. At PTT
Post the whole of the top management team was replaced by
individuals from IBM, Unilever, Alcatel and other firms at the
outset in 1988 and some 40% of managers below this have now
similarly come in from the outside, most tellingly in sales and
finance. The communication of change is clearly boosted by the
tangible fact of change in the make-up of the workforce and the
new energy and ideas new recruits bring.

NEVER ABANDON YOUR CHANGE AGENTS

In the deliberate mess triggered by tearing up old processes and
ways of working, the individuals who pull the organization
forward to build the new context or vision and communicate
this to their peers, customers and suppliers are the prime agents
of transformation. They frequently face criticism and resistance,
bewilderment and scepticism and in the early stages are unlikely
to be surrounded by a critical mass of enthusiastic supporters of
change – not because people are unwilling, but merely because
the heart and the mind are engaged at different rates. It is
straightforward to understand the intellectual argument for
change. It is much more difficult to commit at an emotional
level, to abandon the emotional attachment (pride, pleasure, the
feelings of being effective in your job and making a difference)
to how things are and have been. As Clive Dolan discovered at
Siemens Plessey, 'managers have a vested interest in maintaining the current organization and status quo. They've grown
strong because of it'.

The psychological concept of self-efficacy or perceived personal effectiveness, first developed by Albert Bandura (1977) is a
critical part of behavioural and therefore organizational change.
Personal change is mediated through the cognitive and emotional experiences of mastery arising from successful performance. But the strength of people's convictions in their own
effectiveness in a particular set of conditions determines whether

they will even attempt to cope with multiple changes in the organizational environment. Elevating people's perceived self-efficacy (and therefore their expectations of success) means that their efforts will be more active and more sustained. But these expectations of self-efficacy are built up from different experiences, primarily by performance accomplishments – that is, people's success or failure in particular environments. Repeated success working in a particular way, with a given set of processes and a prevailing culture (especially if the occasional failure is experienced but overcome along the way) will lead to strong self-efficacy expectations in that environment: this is how I can be successful again. Transformation sets about destroying that environment. So while the expectations and patterns of behaviour become strongly established, it should be no surprise that employees freeze in the old way of working when directed to operate in another. They have no other way to behave.

How do you rebuild employees' self-efficacy expectations? Since behaviour is established in the first instance through performance accomplishments, this is also the best way to change it, but it requires intervention by someone, at the personal level, to kick-start and sustain the learning process. Who? The change agents. The champions of transformation who are already committed to the change and can intervene to help people to behave differently, by modelling the new behaviour, by themselves tackling the difficulties of new processes or culture, and by instruction and coaching. Increasing self-efficacy breaks down the culture of learned helplessness so endemic in large corporations.

So change agents, who are few and far between at the start of transformation, are the facilitators of behavioural change throughout the organization. Usually, early on, they receive substantial support from executives who realize their worth and at a time when the enthusiasm for big change is running high – at least among executives. The danger is later on when the pace slows, when it is natural to assume, because of the massive effort applied over a year or more, that change has been embedded in the organization. At this juncture, it is easy 'to take your foot off the accelerator', as ScottishPower's Duncan Whyte confesses, and through oversight or by declaring victory too soon to 'put people in positions where you leave them abandoned'. In ScottishPower, they have learned this lesson and invest heavily in training, education and support.

At Molson Breweries, which holds the dominant share of the market in Canada, this lesson was learned later than it might have been. Following a merger in 1989 with Carling O'Keefe Breweries (part of the Foster's Brewing Group) in anticipation of a more competitive beer market in Canada, Molson embarked on a big change programme whose early phase was aimed at massive rationalization and cost reduction. In the process, of course, like many organizations worldwide, Molson slimmed down its middle-management workforce but, with the best of intentions, as Michael Smith, Vice President, Organization Effectiveness, concedes, 'we spent a great deal of money and time on those we fired, making sure we treated them sensitively and with full support. Meantime, for those managers who remained and who were helping to lead the brunt of the change and for whom the change was most profound, we did nothing to help them make the change.' Now, Michael Smith has launched targeted leadership development for this group and acknowledges, 'We should have got it running earlier so that the change message was cascaded better and earlier . . .'

Leaders must be alert to these dangers and continue to offer support and reward – both tangible and symbolic – to those who continue to make change happen, especially when the organization is well down the path of transformation.

Transformational Leader or Just High-performance Manager?

To check your profile as a transformational leader or high-performance manager from the Leadership Domain Questionnaire on page 71, follow the instructions below.

(a) Give yourself one point for each of the ten tick-marks.

(b) Questionnaire items – odd numbers (1, 3, 5 and so on): if you score seven or more on the odd-numbered items, put your dreams on hold of transforming your company. You are much more comfortable as a manager and follower, or the leader of a stable, successful business that does not need to transform (how long can that last?). Your preference is for controlling performance, monitoring progress, hitting shorter-term objectives and deadlines and making sure the organization operates efficiently and in an orderly manner.

(c) Questionnaire items – even numbers (2, 4, 6 and so on): if you score seven or more on the even-numbered items, you have a preference for transforming the organization rather than maintaining it and probably have a history of getting into trouble with colleagues because you always want to change things, offer new ideas even when business is running smoothly, raise people's ambitions to greater heights and demand a lot of intellectual and emotional energy from them. Working closely with high-performance managers to follow your lead, you have the potential to make transformation happen.

(d) Mix of both odd- and even-numbered items: you are confused! You like tinkering around the fringes of change, but prefer the fallback stability of keeping things under control, avoiding too much exposure to risk and uncertainty. You would probably be willing to accept and support transformation, but at heart would prefer someone else to lead it.

4

Systemic Innovation

PERSUADING THEM TO SMILE TOO

'The thing that was sacrosanct in the 1980s,' Strategy Development Manager S-P Mahoney observes about British Airways, 'was to make sure that we delivered a customer service change. This was a huge driver for us because we knew it had been horrendously poor. In terms of where BA has come from, getting that foundation right has been critical but the manner of our success means we may have some difficulties in the future.' British Airways has achieved a remarkable transformation. From losses of around $400 million in the financial years 1980 to 1982, being a drain on the public purse and its acronym BA jeered at as 'Bloody Awful', the company has been successfully privatized, has shown consistently improved profits and share price and in business circles has acquired a different epithet, 'Bloody Awesome!' Of course, the transformation was painful, involving in 1981 massive staff cuts (from 53 600 to 47 750) that reached a low of 36 000 in 1983. Pay was frozen. The business footing was changed 180 degrees so that operational management delivered to the specifications of marketing people who, in turn, took their steer from customers – a novel concept for an airline at that time.

The story so far has been widely told and I do not wish to repeat it here. More instructive are the lessons to be learned about the type of organization that BA has become through the process of big change and the new challenges the company faces. Bob Ayling launched a second transformation soon after his appointment, just ten years after BA was privatized. This had four main strands, predicated on some simple strategic facts. Sixty per cent of BA's business originated outside Britain: it was, therefore, not the country's flag-carrying airline; it was an international operator whose headquarters is based near

London. In its European operations it was easily undercut by smaller, aggressive new entrants – EasyJet, something of a virtual airline, Air UK and Debonair – who together with the national airlines in the crowded European market were squeezing BA profits. The airline's global ambitions, too, were threatened if a suitable partner for the massive transatlantic market were not found. This was especially the case given the progress of other airlines in jointly forging global route networks to tie up large market segments.

The four strands of Bob Ayling's new transformation were an attempt to deal with the global market – both its threats and opportunities. First, much time was devoted to the pursuit of a mega-alliance with American Airlines which would capture for the two airlines clear transatlantic dominance – a marriage denounced by competitors as a stranglehold on the highly profitable transatlantic business and, at the time of writing, mired in unresolved antitrust difficulties. Second, Bob Ayling reassured shareholders and analysts by announcing his Business Efficiency Plan to take out over $1.5 billion in cumulative operating costs over three years – the net effect of this being job losses, pay cuts in some jobs, a squeeze on perquisites and employment conditions and, of course, outsourcing of targeted services. With staff making up 30% of total costs, they were an obvious target. In Mahoney's words, 'Every department has to justify its existence. If its work can be done better and cheaper outside, then there is obvious pressure on us to consider outsourcing.' Third, at the same time as the company was taking out low-skilled jobs through redundancy and early retirement, Ayling committed to taking on 5000 new, higher-skilled employees and, among cabin crew, there would be a higher proportion who spoke at least one of the languages of BA's worldwide customers. Last, Ayling started to put in place the new branding and image making that would support the new mission for BA to be the undisputed leader in world travel – hence the internationalization of the brand (fifty new culturally diverse artistic designs expressing the new identity, from aircraft tailfins to ticket wallets and airport lounges), the aim of achieving an 'open and cosmopolitan' style of service, and the 'global, yet caring' tag. In all of this Ayling faced a severe test from thousands of cabin crew unwilling to accept new terms and conditions and ground staff who were resisting the sell-off of BA's catering unit. The *Financial Times* reached this conclusion:

. . . Mr Ayling has clearly failed to convince many of his cabin crew of the need for change. They have more direct contact with passengers than any other staff: if they are dissatisfied, customers can sense that immediately. Mr Ayling's task is enormous. It will not be enough to persuade his cabin crew not to strike. He has to persuade them to smile too. (26 June 1997, p.9)

So this is a company that has struggled, not once but twice, with transformation. In the latter instance BA's concentration of effort has been to sustain its ambition as industry leader and, despite the real difficulties that BA has fought to overcome over the best part of two decades (difficulties that all transforming companies must face), it has been remarkably successful. In many ways British Airways owes this success to crucial elements of innovation which, though not always there, are now deeply embedded within the culture, as we shall see in the course of this chapter. In addition, and perhaps most important, we shall also examine some of the hidden fault-lines, *themselves a product of forging this innovative organization and culture,* that run through the business today and that must be addressed if Bob Ayling's new revolution is to be realized.

Inspiration

Indeed, what evidence is there that those sublime intellectual events known as 'inspiration' involve any conscious thought? Most often our best ideas are served up to us out of our unconscious while we are thinking or doing something perfectly irrelevant. Inspiration probably depends on some sort of repetitive and time-consuming pattern-matching program which runs imperceptibly below the level of consciousness searching for plausible matches.

J.L. and C.J. Gould, The insect mind: physics or metaphysics? In Griffin (ed.), *Animal Mind – Human Mind* (1982, p.292)

ECONOMICS OR PSYCHOLOGY?

One of the difficulties inherent in the application of innovation, particularly what I call systemic innovation, to organizations is that for a long time it has been considered the preserve of economics rather than psychology. Business process re-engineering (BPR), in shifting effort away from vertical, hierarchical operating across functional boundaries towards 'flat' teamwork in 'strings' of activities defined as business processes, has, to paraphrase Adrian Alsop (1996), the wherewithal to promote creative potential and innovative teams because of the focus on team autonomy and high levels of communication and interaction that go hand in hand with flatter, cross-functional team structures. However, one of the outcomes of BPR has so far been to assign pre-eminence to the reduction of headcount costs and thus to increase the demands on workers. A psychological view would have shown that the implicit or explicit expansion of job demands on individuals in general leads people to focus on extrinsic work rewards (pay, promotion) rather than the intrinsic rewards (excitement, satisfaction, fun) so important for encouraging and sustaining innovation. BPR, as typically executed, therefore, can be damaging to corporate health. In addition, as argued in Chapter 1, an overriding focus on cost reduction and utilization of assets drives out those who do not fit the growing cost-reduction culture and reinforces intolerance of different or challenging (creative) points of view.

Of course, productivity improvements via cost-cutting or BPR and determined efforts to install innovation are not either/or solutions. The real strategic challenge is to create the organizational conditions to enable a firm to improve productivity and to innovate – even if the two philosophies, as we have seen above, are by their natures somewhat incompatible. John Chisholm of DERA elaborates on the difficulties of doing these two things:

> What makes the task particularly challenging is that we have to serve customers in an orderly way and deliver products. We have to be able to commit, with complete assurance, to achieving results. All of this requires firm *process*, but we also have to do it without snuffing out the spark of innovation, which is inherently iconoclastic – it's something that breaks rules.

At heart, though, innovation is concerned with harnessing knowledge to new ends. Listening to this statement, many executives think at once of product and service development and of specialist groups of workers working in wacky environments to come up with new 'things'. Certainly new product introduction (NPI) has an important place here, but harnessing knowledge to new ends should run the gamut from clever strategic analysis and thinking (e.g. Microsoft technology guru Nathan Myhrvold's ongoing analysis of the future, closely mapped onto corporate strategy) through intelligent decision making and action by frontline staff at the customer interface (Nordstrom's commitment to 'satisfying the unreasonable customer' or British Airways' empowerment of all staff to 'put people first', especially where it counts – with the customer). Another good example here is DERA, whose existence depends on producing innovation at the leading edge of defence technology. John Chisholm puts it this way:

> A lot of the innovative value of the organization comes not from the brilliant bit of science in one part, but from the linkages of quite different sorts of science brought together to create understanding or break-through at a linkage intersection. For that to work you have got to have a coherent organization that pulls together.

Siemens Plessey's Clive Dolan, by contrast, is less upbeat about progress towards embedded innovation throughout his company. He recognizes how hard it can be to get the message across, get it understood and then start to change things. 'I don't think we've been that successful on that front,' he concedes and adds a key point, 'People still think in terms of product, not in ways of working.'

His comments resonate with Vernon Sankey, CEO of Reckitt & Colman, the $3.8 billion household and pharmaceutical products company who sell famous brands such as Lysol, Dettol and Disprin to more than 1 billion consumers every year. With a history reaching back to 1814 and operations in 120 countries, Reckitt & Colman were a devolved and decentralized business that had grown successfully throughout the twentieth century right across the globe largely because of the autonomy given local entrepreneurs to exploit the brands. 'The problem,' Sankey contends, 'was we were so decentralized that a tremendous level of knowledge was created all around the world, but was never really shared.' Sankey recognized this when he became CEO in 1991, at a time when the firm's share price reflected the market's view that something needed to be done. Moreover, as Sankey admits, 'Our performance had been sustained by acquisition alone.' Sankey launched a global transformation of the organization as a 'real step change to move forward' and one that would, for the first time, properly capitalize on Reckitt & Colman's worldwide strengths and resources. What Sankey wanted to do was gain leverage from the dynamics of pooling world-class ideas and expertise between global teams (transferring skills and expertise where they could be most effective, if necessary), in addition to integrating product innovation and development activities globally to speed the launch of new products or using buying power on a world scale.

So, knowledge pooling and sharing across the organizational network and at many levels – not just in product development – is a key commercial advantage. It provides the tools for harnessing knowledge to new ends, but for successful transformation the aspiration must be to embed this, to make it systemic. The main actions needed to do this are given in Action List 2 and are expanded in the rest of the chapter.

Action List 2   Building Systemic Innovation

1. Create the expectation of innovative practice: nothing is more powerful than self-fulfilling beliefs.
2. Trigger internal conditions of pressure to do constructive damage to the status quo.
3. Build the ethos for innovation: small teams, eyeball-to-eyeball and creative climate.
4. Change the people-mix to get idea diversity, both in top management and via general recruitment.
5. Ensure the execution of new ideas: innovation without execution is wasted effort and will stall transformation.

CREATING SELF-FULFILLING INNOVATION

In 1948 Robert Merton brought to the attention of the world the notion of the self-fulfilling prophecy, a psychological phenomenon widely practised but seldom consciously or systematically. The idea is a simple one: what you believe to be the case about someone or a group of people may create a reality that in itself confirms the belief. This has been tellingly demonstrated in learning and development, most notably in experiments in schools where psychologists administered IQ tests to children and then shared the results with their teachers. However, the psychologists also told the teachers that certain of the children in each class could be expected to show substantial IQ increases over the duration of the year. Of course, the psychologists had merely identified these 'special' children at random as part of the experiment and themselves had no indication of the children's potential. The startling result was that the children who had been 'identified' as *expected* to make IQ gains did indeed make the gains. Why? For no other reason than that the expectation had been powerfully set. Therefore the teachers treated the targeted children differently, paying them more attention, giving more feedback to them and thus creating *elevated expectations* in those children themselves. Numerous psychological investigations have confirmed these findings over the decades and, in particular, have shown that positive changes in people's performance, achievement and self-esteem are driven far more effectively by commending them on their current effectiveness, creativity or performance (i.e. making it clear that you believe they are already effective in a particular area) than by trying to persuade, exhort or threaten them to do better.

The implications for organizational life are profound. If you expect employees to be difficult, to show not the slightest creative spark or to underperform and then treat them accordingly, then that is precisely what you will get. By contrast, if your clearly communicated expectation is that employees are highly motivated, creative, responsible and proud of their customer service, then employees are likely to respond appropriately. Naturally, the expectation must be powerful – that is, it must not be undermined by CEO or top team actions which communicate the opposite. In short, the challenge is to create an utterly convincing set of beliefs.

This brings us back to the culture of learned helplessness described in previous chapters. In such cultures, employees believe that they can have no impact on events around them – they are helpless. But when such a belief system is challenged by leaders who, rather than exhorting people to change, demonstrate convincing expectation that employees can make a difference, that they can innovate, then positive changes in behaviour are likely to result. Such behavioural changes are most substantive and most sustained when employees (through a leader's expectations) come to attribute the positive behaviour to their own values, self-efficacy, and abilities and not to short-term *outside* forces that have induced them to change.

Well-known business leaders such as Gates at Microsoft, Branson at Virgin, Martinez at Sears, Marshall at British Airways and Welch at GE have implicitly created expectations of innovative behaviour, both in their senior management cadre and in the organization at large. Moreover, we have already seen how at Microsoft and British Airways the signs and symbols (i.e. expectations) of innovative practice are reinforced in the headquarters environment – innovative architecture, the 'campus' environment, reconfigurable office space, cafeterias and meeting places, physical mixing of departments and teams, and high availability of communications technology. Moreover, the expectation of innovative practice in transforming companies soon moves to the market, with customers and shareholders, who then act (both consciously and unconsciously) to sustain pressure for new ways of doing things – customers expect high standards; analysts expect growth and impressive stock performance.

In triggering such expectation in the first instance, however, executives are usually up against the avalanche of old culture, processes and systems that are finely tuned to reinforce the 'traditional' way of doing things, even to protect the sense of learned helplessness, and especially to stamp out changes to the status quo. Any expectation of innovation, therefore, will be regarded with alarm in many quarters. Pierre Gravelle began to create the expectation early on during his transformation of Revenue Canada:

> I said to myself that I must exchange ideas on change with CEOs in other organizations so that I myself was getting new ideas that could be applied in the Revenue Administration. Also, in the early stages at the three-day sessions with my top groups of managers, I invited CEOs and other executives along to speak about their experience of change and to talk to my managers.

Sears' Arthur Martinez did the same thing, in one instance getting Disney's CEO Michael Eisner along to speak at an annual executive convention. It is no secret that Martinez admires the transformation of Disney and their innovative use of brands to build growth.

But in both these examples, the usefulness of the content derived by an audience of managers listening to chief executives of other companies is pretty close to zero. We have all experienced presentations of that sort. But it does not matter. Of far greater value is the symbolic message. In the Sears case, Martinez was establishing a completely new benchmark company – not a retailer but a consumer-brands organization that has successfully altered its fortunes. And in both the Martinez and Gravelle cases, expectation was being powerfully constructed, an expectation that ran something like: 'Here are others that have radically changed. They can do it. We can do it. This organization will change. You all have the ability and motivation to help me change it.'

CONSTRUCTIVE DAMAGE TO THE STATUS QUO: TRIGGERING INTERNAL CONDITIONS OF PRESSURE

The implication of John Chisholm's earlier comment that innovation is inherently iconoclastic is too often missed by executives. The tearing down of the old, the breaking of rules, the overturning of convention and accepted wisdom, these are not the actions of normal people in typical organizations. And yet the equally unnatural act of transformation requires their energetic pursuit. It is not enough to strive just for the new; executives must inflict, as Symcor's Pierre Gravelle colourfully puts it, 'constructive damage to the status quo'.

What Gravelle means by this is that new ways of doing business rarely emerge only from positive intent. This permits old ways of operating to retain their force. Constructive damage means, at times, doing away with existing policies, processes, programme delivery and the like to pressure employees, then faced with the imminent prospect of many of the old ways of working being despatched to oblivion, to find or create alternate, innovative solutions – i.e. solutions that are not simply reiterations of old ways of operating. This is not to abandon strategic or tactical control and pressure employees to invent, willy-nilly, a thousand different ways of performing their work when one will do. The broad parameters of newly defined process and system architecture need to be articulated first, so that innovative ways of working are designed within a coherent whole (lessons picked up later in this chapter under 'Ensuring the Execution of New Ideas'). But the thrust of constructive damage is to force new behaviour at the individual level.

For example, on arrival at IBM in 1993, Lou Gerstner made it clear he did not hold with the notion of managing by committee and therefore dismantled the old IBM management committee structure, in effect forcing single-point accountability onto executives, to accept and stand by their decisions and actions. To the alarm of many (and evident relief of some), Gerstner himself started to bypass the often byzantine formal management processes that had long dominated Big Blue's culture. The effect, in due course, was a galvanizing jolt to the corporation. Managers read the writing and began to follow suit. The vacuum created in sweeping aside traditional formalities was quickly filled by new, faster and more innovative structures and procedures. Ways of working began to change.

Static organizations that, like IBM in the early 1990s, find it near-impossible to change also tend to choose as benchmarks those that are in the same industry, often the same country, and tragically the same performance band. Rarely do you witness executives identifying *process* benchmarks outside the industry or country or some way above the nearest performance band. Even industries, it seems, huddle together like sheep. The chief financial officer of a large insurer once proudly related to me that he was radically widening his team's horizons by seeking out best practice, not merely among those few organizations regarded as close competitors but in other insurers in other countries. I pointed out that the big insurers, wherever they were in the world, were doubtless doing the same thing. Had it occurred to him that they would all be copying each other? Would it not be better to break the mould entirely and seek benchmarks in a whole variety of industries? It was obvious (and startling) that such ideas were utterly alien to him. What hope, then, for systemic innovation in such a business? By contrast, Duncan Whyte describes what they did at Scottish-Power:

> At first we hired consultants to do comparative studies of how we performed against the American utilities and we found that we were above average, but not in the top 25%. So we set targets for things like efficiency, safety, customer service and so on. Benchmarking then became a way of driving the business. What started out as targets turned into a way of life. Soon we extended the benchmarking, not just the utilities but comparing ourselves to Federal Express, British Airways and others . . . It was all driven by the desire to be the best in world terms and to be recognized as such.

The British Airways culture is active in support of constructive damage. How? 'The culture,' declares S-P Mahoney, 'in some ways rewards people for fighting the system and breaking the rules. Although many people here prefer to play by the rules, you have to push the boundaries in order to really benefit personally in your career.'

At the formal level, BA's move to the Harmondsworth offices was a means by which managers and employees could, in my terms, do deliberate damage to the old ways of working. Traditionally, employees kept vast, uncoordinated libraries of paper documentation, often (as is the case with millions of workers worldwide) just on the off-chance that a particular memo, or letter or piece of information was needed at some future date. Moreover, keeping paper was symbolic of the underlying old culture of 'information is power' – something that BA executives wanted to destroy. They wanted information to flow freely, to be more accessible and to enhance speed and quality of decision making. While this was the aspiration, the reality was that there were no common standards for filing or classification and the paper explosion continued unabated with diminishing returns in the value and dissemination of information or knowledge. BA launched 'Operation Paper Mountain' to reduce the huge volumes of paper kept by individuals in thousands of offices all round Heathrow. Three objectives were touted for the move to Harmondsworth: *Minimizing Paper*, *Streamlined Communications*, and *Effective Teams*. The first two were aimed at shifting the organization quickly to adoption of fast, reliable electronic communications and data storage while clearing as much paper as possible.

Chris Byron, the Harmondsworth Project Director, says, 'The training that accompanied the physical adjustment also emphasized key cultural messages at the same time – for example, how technology can support the business processes.' And the third objective, *Effective Teams*, was ostensibly aimed at grasping the missed opportunities for wider interaction, sharing information and ideas and being involved beyond the traditional bounds of department or workgroup. But it was also intended to sweep to one side the old hierarchical structure which was getting in the way of the need for ever faster communication and decision making: no one, including senior executives, had exclusive use any longer of an office, including Bob Ayling, the chief executive. Instead, announced Chris Byron just before the move, the top team would work from 'team space, allowing them to be much more visible, accessible and involved in the workplace'. This was a deliberate signal to the organization from the very top that hierarchy, in and of itself, was no longer tenable. 'We are still very hierarchical,' admits Byron, but adds, 'The new building provides the facilities for anyone to do their job and not to play to their status.'

BUILDING THE ETHOS FOR INNOVATION

St Luke is the patron saint of craftsmen, artists and doctors. If you are seeking to build the right ethos for innovation, look no further than St Luke's, a British advertising agency based in London, whose mission is not the sort of boringly wordcrafted, let-us-offend-no-one statement typical of most organizations. 'To open minds,' is St Luke's purpose, 'by creating fascination in ourselves and in our clients.' The company is small, employing around 80 people with revenues a shade under $110 million, but its creativity is a cut above the rest – and, of course, in the advertising world creativity is everything. Responsible for powerful, attention-grabbing ad campaigns for companies like United Distillers, Boots, The Body Shop, Ikea and Eurostar, St Luke's formed in 1995 when two of the directors, Andy Law and David Abraham, put together an 'earn-out' from US *wunderkind* ad-agency Chiat/Day, which had just been sold to media and advertising goliath Omnicom in the USA, following acquisition-driven debt repayment problems. After meeting with the new owners, Andy Law had decided that being swallowed by Omnicom was not something he personally would permit. He told colleagues back in the London office that he was leaving and that they should make up their own minds. Everyone in the UK office of Chiat/Day decided to join him.

The earn-out involved Law and Abraham paying Omnicom $1 to buy the London office of the old Chiat/Day and a seven-year payback deal based on a percentage of the profits – worth about $2 million. The agency broke away and their clients came with them. There were 35 staff in the newly independent St Luke's and they needed to decide what to do with themselves. 'We locked ourselves away,' remembers Chairman Andy Law, 'in a room with no windows for three days and imagined we were on a desert island. Then, without preconceptions, we tried to answer the question, "What would the perfect company be like?" We developed a pretty good idea and from that we formed a cooperative.' *Every* employee has shares in the company, distributed equally and without concern for rank, salary, or tenure.

The philosophy of St Luke's is radically different from other agencies. In place of the norms of most ad agencies – layers of staff, autocratic style, strict hierarchy, dog-eat-dog scrambling in the promotion stakes, big egos and big offices – St Luke's has created a virtually flat structure ('apprentices' and 'practitioners' in St Luke's parlance) with few formal organizational arrangements, participative decision making (they set their own salaries!), upward and downward performance reviews, no secretaries 'owned' by directors and, like British Airways, no offices, merely client rooms (that clients can use in collaboration with St Luke's staff) where campaigns are initiated and run. All facilities (even personal computers) are shared so that a true collaborative ethos prevails. Andy Law elaborates:

> At the start we looked at what gets in the way of creativity so that we could design a way of working that releases creativity. So in our own very simplistic way we wanted to transform each individual's own potential. We decided that creativity is not enhanced by all the usual things you find in advertising agencies – habit-forming, bureaucracy, fear, hierarchy. We knew we must let people's values, aspirations and imagination flow freely.

Growth was an ambition and so the design of the organization evolved to accommodate and stimulate this. Everything revolves around 'creative cells' (at present four) which get away from the 'one big blob' problem that could have hobbled growth. 'We moved the organization and the culture into bite-sized chunks which are more manageable,' says Law. Each cell operates as a group of owner–entrepreneurs, stimulating involvement, interest and intimacy with clients. Once a cell reaches a size of 35 people, it must offer ten of its members to form a new cell. New cells, however, grow more by members' understanding the skills and aspirations of the people in them than by market or industry needs. The chairman's role is to provide the vision for the company and the support to structure the formation of new creative cells.

There are undoubted difficulties created by the minimalist approach to hierarchy and structure. 'This is not Utopia,' Law freely admits. 'Although we don't really have office politics because there is no hierarchy and people are completely involved, the way we work creates complex interpersonal relationships.' Everyday disputes in a team concerning a campaign or some other business agenda can boil over into personal territory and the high level of uncertainty created by the lack of structure, job roles and rules of working can be stressful. Moreover, it remains to be seen whether the 'creative cell' structure, dividing and multiplying *ad infinitum* and the cooperative management style can succeed as the agency gains size. Nevertheless, the ethos of St Luke's is distinctive and effective and there are lessons about both innovation and transformation to be learned from its structure and its ethos.

Ethos might, in organizational psychology, more properly be described as climate. Climate is the conglomerate of attitudes, feelings and behaviours which characterizes life in the organization as opposed to the values, norms and belief systems that we term culture. Culture is hard to influence. Climate is more amenable to intervention and management and can exert a powerful influence on organizational processes such as problem solving, decision making, communications, coordination and control as well as learning, creativity and motivation (Ekvall, 1996). Goran Ekvall, from the University of Lund in Stockholm, has identified a number of dimensions of organizational climate which have been shown, through a series of 15- to 20-year longitudinal studies in various countries such as the USA, Britain, Sweden, Germany, and Spain, to have a significant bearing on innovation in organizations. These are:

1. *Challenge*: emotional involvement of employees in the organization's goals and operations.
2. *Freedom*: independence of behaviour exercised by people to share information, start initiatives or take decisions.
3. *Idea support*: the way ideas are treated – i.e. encouraged, supported or countered.
4. *Trust/openness*: the emotional safety that comes because there is no fear of reprisal, ridicule or the exploitation of ideas without due acknowledgement.
5. *Dynamism/liveliness*: the extent to which there is psychological turbulence – surprises, new things happening, a feeling that work is buzzing or fast-moving, rather than 'the usual'.

6. *Playfulness/humour*: spontaneity and ease as opposed to a gloomy and serious atmosphere where joking and laughter is viewed as inappropriate.
7. *Debates*: the degree to which many voices are heard, discussion is accepted and people clash over ideas rather than simple obedience to rules and ways of working.
8. *Conflicts*: inappropriate personal and emotional clashes in which the atmosphere is clearly one of 'warfare' and ideas are shot down because people dislike each other.
9. *Risk taking*: tolerance of uncertainty, the seizing of opportunities and active experimentation as opposed to staying on the 'safe side' or procrastination.
10. *Idea time*: the amount of time employees can and do use for developing ideas, rather than an unrelenting squeeze on time because of routines and other pressures.

During the course of his work with numerous organizations, particularly those that could be distinguished as either innovative or stagnated, Ekvall concluded that the dimensions most specially connected with creativity and innovation were Idea Support, Debates, Risk Taking and Idea Time, but that four of the dimensions seemed to make the crucial difference between a workgroup climate that promotes radical innovation and one that supports only incremental improvements. These were: Risk Taking, Dynamism, Freedom, and Debates. An important point to remember, too, is that these dimensions can, to a very large extent, be influenced by individual managers.

At St Luke's, Microsoft, British Airways and other successful organizations employees clearly show behaviour typical of many of the Ekvall dimensions, although the appropriateness of one dimension of behaviour or another varies between industries. These behaviours are evident at BA in the everyday language of managers, who talk about 'being brave' (risk taking) and 'freedom to get on with things' (freedom), in the company's commitment to interactive team-based working (trust/openness), in the sense of many managers all over the BA world struggling with difficult questions (challenge) and in the intensity of debate over fundamental strategic and tactical issues. Other elements of culture and climate, however, can work against innovation. Because of the still hierarchical nature of the company, it is common practice for senior BA managers to 'bump' meetings when something of greater (relative) importance arises. This causes no little disruption to managers and staff at lower levels who are left to reschedule meetings and accommodate their bosses. It can also lead to resentment and personal conflict, emotions that undermine innovation.

Some fascinating findings on the behavioural practices and wider management actions that distinguish highly innovative and less innovative companies are included in the survey report at the end of this chapter.

CHANGING THE PEOPLE MIX

A sure-fire way of turning off the pipeline that feeds your team and organization alternate perspectives and innovative potential is to keep the same people around the whole time. In many companies there is still little cross-functional movement, even in the course of an individual's career – both at staff and management levels. Organizations in stasis tend to have static employee populations: people only move up functional lines; team composition remains the same or, at best, people of a very similar background and training join the team; recruitment trends become fixed on clones of existing employees and managers. During recruitment the words 'I know how to pick people' are frequently heard spilling from the lips of supervisors and managers, usually meaning 'I never fail to pick someone like me!' Even when more sophisticated human resources systems are implemented to create job moves and encourage resource sharing, managers kick and scream in protest at letting members of their team move elsewhere. These proclivities are understandable. We naturally, and unconsciously, gravitate to groups that we perceive to be more like us. Given the choice we prefer to recruit individuals who share our thinking and ways of operating. It is easier to form teams where there is minimal disagreement and we abhor conflict, if we can possibly avoid it.

All these actions, formal and informal, conscious and unconscious, limit the potential for innovation. For transformation to happen, changes in the top team composition are essential. Whatever their strengths, members of the executive team are likely to think and act in very similar ways, especially if they have worked in the organization a long time and are unconscious keepers of the old orthodoxies. This was the fatal disease at Sears Roebuck before Arthur Martinez arrived. He changed people alright, but more importantly hired big-hitters with backgrounds and viewpoints from *outside* the retail sector. New people from different industries bring new ideas – a key requirement for Martinez whose own career is dominated by retailing. He, in particular, needed a team with wider exposure. The same is true of IBM's big change: in 1994, during the first 12 months of the transformation, Lou Gerstner and his team hired more than 60 new executives (to bring new perspectives and as Gerstner put it, 'quicken the process of transformation').

Gerstner himself was an industry outsider. Although market analysts tend to worry about the industry knowledge of incoming chief executives, more often than not it affords no advantage – and may even be downright limiting – to spring from the same industry. Lou Gerstner knew next to nothing about making and selling computers when he stepped into John Akers' shoes at Big Blue. He had joined McKinsey & Co. as a consultant, following an engineering degree from Dartmouth and a Harvard MBA, and some years later was given a consultancy engagement to assist the new CEO of American Express, James Robinson III, irreverently called Jimmy Three-sticks by Amex wags. Gerstner was tempted away from McKinsey to join Amex and in 1985 was made up to president. Having helped turn round Amex's performance he then went to RJR Nabisco until discussions opened with IBM. As a result of being a computer industry outsider, what passed for computer industry wisdom cut no ice with him and would not pass unquestioned. In 1996, for instance, he told *Fortune* (29 April, p.59):

> I start every day with customers, but this is an industry that starts every day with technology. It is driven by its technological accomplishments, which are enormous. But what's happening in the marketplace is being driven by customers. The Internet's been around for 25 years. What made it suddenly emerge? Well, the real issue is that customers are changing the way they're thinking about information technology.

And when CEOs come not only from the same industry, but the same organization? They themselves must change. Vernon Sankey is a Reckitt & Colman man through and through, having spent decades with the company. When he kicked off the global transformation of the company following his appointment in 1991, he realized not only that all his executive colleagues were imbued with the old culture but that he himself would have to change if he was to stand any chance of succeeding in Reckitt & Colman's transformation. With coaching and the use of psychometric feedback on management and leadership style he worked hard to begin to understand better how he currently operated and how he needed to change. He says:

> Changing yourself, changing your behaviour is very difficult. Before this I tended to dominate discussions, I listened poorly, didn't want to spend time on the issues behind the issue; I was in a tearing hurry and wasn't taking anyone with me . . .

Equally he acknowledged that some of the skills they needed both in the top team and elsewhere in the company around the world were simply not in place. 'Some people had to go,' he continues, 'including some in the L&F acquisition in the US – they wouldn't make it. We needed new recruits and differences of viewpoints were essential, still are. Just in my team now, fifty percent of them are new and the kinds of skills each person brings are quite different. Forty percent of people in the executive teams in the businesses round the world are new.'

Differences of background and viewpoint should be encouraged at senior level and their example cascaded, but they are unlikely to happen unless the people mix is changed. The same is true at other levels in the organization. Despite the enormous difficulty of laying people off and adjusting the mix in Germany, ABB's Rolf Renke has been reducing year by year the average age of department, division and function leaders by recruiting younger, well-educated employees. Moreover, these managers are actively encouraged to make changes in their career. 'Also,' Renke points out, 'we hire every year a lot of people from different high schools or universities in Germany and we target the guys who are mostly loaded with a lot of new information and ideas from their research.'

ENSURING THE EXECUTION OF NEW IDEAS

Innovation as simply 'new ideas' misses the point. If we go back to the Michael Porter definition of innovation as a new way of doing things which is commercialized, it is clear that the *execution* of new ideas, new knowledge or new ways of working is paramount. For the organization to gain commercial leverage, it follows that execution of new ideas must happen at a level of critical mass. There is only really one way of doing this and that is through empowerment. Much talked about, much misunderstood, empowerment as it should operate is well articulated by John Chisholm at DERA.

At DERA, Chisholm was very clear about the change strategy that he would employ to transform the old public sector bureaucracy into one of the world's foremost defence science and technology organizations. He focused on two parts in the change strategy: processes and empowerment. Process we shall deal with in a later chapter. On empowerment, Chisholm remarks, 'Giving individuals personal goals and targets and holding them responsible for their achievement is absolutely basic to making any large organization run effectively.' But what he found, to his surprise, was that empowerment was countercultural. He explains why, in public sector organizations all over the world, this is usually the case:

> The ethos of the public sector is to smear responsibility across a number of functional commands, thus ensuring any decision is taken on a departmental basis. This is not without merit when political decisions are to be made – it ensures they are given a thorough scrutiny before being made public. The trouble comes from the natural tendency for the practices at the top of an organization to permeate through it. The processes for formulation of policy are disastrously inefficient when applied to the implementation of policy.

In creating the new DERA, Chisholm and his team began to set up a devolved management structure. Goals, and the targets within those goals, were then cascaded down the structure. Crucially, the departments that previously had wielded power – finance, personnel, contracts – were turned into service functions whose existence depended on the quality and relevance of services provided. This was not, of course, all smooth sailing. In empowering managers and staff, Chisholm was also throwing responsibility onto people in the operational areas to define the detail of how all of this would work, to apply themselves to discovering new ways of doing things, to take some risks – in short, to innovate. And this was aimed at everyone – critical mass again – not just a few elite groups of 'innovators'. What started to happen was frustrating but a valuable lesson:

> We found that some of the old culture kept bubbling up. People began to design bureaucracy back into the organization! This was the instinct

of the old culture. What we continually have to do is try to back away from the instinct to bureaucratize, towards one which is less inclined to mandate highly prescriptive procedures and ways of working and more inclined to build the quality of the individual, empower the individual and allow the individual to innovate within a framework.

British Airways, as a service organization that depends on the personal interaction between each employee and each of 32 million customers (as well as the value chain behind this) put enormous effort into getting the people change right. Two training programmes central to the effort were launched: Putting People First (PPF) for the entire workforce and Managing People First aimed at the managerial population. As mentioned in Chapter 3, CEO Colin Marshall was present at four out of every ten of the PPF seminars, demonstrating a very high level of commitment to change. But what the BA executive team wanted to build *was* commitment – commitment to act, to do things differently, to innovate. This could only happen through active role modelling by the leadership of treating people with respect. As BA's S-P Mahoney puts it:

> We've taken 50 000 people and we've instilled an ethos of empowerment into everybody, and that includes people who load bags into containers or handle freight or drive forklift trucks. It's also in the revenue accounting area or in telephone sales. Whatever anybody is doing in the company, they have been empowered.

But empowered to do what? Under Sir Colin Marshall, BA's culture was fashioned into one which enables all employees to make decisions about how to *improve* face-to-face customer service, the interaction with suppliers, business processes and anything else on which the organization depends for its success. 'The product is the people,' Mahoney says. This means that employees use their brains. They make decisions on specific actions. They try things. They are individually responsive to other individuals, whether colleagues, customers, or suppliers – anywhere in the value chain. Multiplied up from the individual to the business as a whole, this generates enormous motive power, especially where BA employees come up against the unexpected or the non-standard. It is here, in the shifting seas of the service industries where customers are endlessly demanding, that they win over their competitors. British Airways employees come up with and act on good ideas. They are expected to and they do.

Yet these initiatives, though they loom large in the life of British Airways, are subsidiary to the really fundamental core of what will make BA successful in the future. S-P Mahoney again:

> We've empowered everyone. People therefore feel good about themselves and about being enabled to make decisions. Also, we manage people in the cargo sheds or the terminals – in other words, behind the scenes – with exactly the same style of empowerment. Put this together with our structure and it means that we have a problem: we can't get the basic processes right. This is true of baggage handling, punctuality, on-board hand baggage policy and so on. Being empowered to make decisions on what size bag passengers can take on board sounds like a petty issue, but in the scale of things it's pretty important. If you travel to Zurich on a busy Monday morning and one of the aircrew makes a decision that you aren't allowed to take a particular piece of hand baggage on board, chances are a week later on a flight that's just as busy, one of the aircrew will decide that you can take it on board! Passengers therefore are left wondering what's going on.

Getting consistency into the execution of processes is very important. It directly affects the customer service experience. For example, if freight or baggage handling is subject to individual (and therefore quite random) acts of empowered decision making (which may not be aligned with a colleague's), even if the actions are well intentioned, then freight and baggage may arrive late or not at all or, as is hoped, may be exactly on time and delivered to the right place. In short, customers experience annoying swings in quality and consistency. This was the feedback that BA was getting in its major reviews of service and operations.

British Airways needs to create a two-stream organization now: tight, high specification of requirements coupled with team empowerment for particular processes and loose, highly individualistic empowerment to other areas of the business (strategy, marketing, sales) including, in most cases, frontline customer contact.

Indeed, many of the behind-the-scenes processes are factory processes, much like those in a manufacturing firm. The system of empowerment in manufacturing processes is quite different from that of a customer contact area. First, the process is paramount. The individual interaction with colleagues or customers is not. Second, the team and not the individual are empowered to make changes. And the changes must happen in a very structured way. Any one individual can identify a problem and suggest an improvement, but the team as a whole is responsible for adjusting the process, so that everyone then works to the *new* process.

The two-stream model does not, therefore, proscribe empowerment among the individuals running the process. Continuous improvement would then be impossible. It is just that the nature of the empowerment is different. The difficulty that BA faces is, as Mahoney, says, 'that we're not good at process. We don't think that way. We don't operate that way.'

An alternative, and the object of much attention in BA, is to outsource everything, in precisely the manner described in Chapter 1. BA would then become a virtual airline. This raises obvious concerns, however. 'A lot depends,' Mahoney worries, 'on whether you can get the service providers to deliver the brand consistently.' Reckitt & Colman's Vernon Sankey ponders the same dilemma: 'Do we need manufacturing plants all over the world? What do we really do as a business? We sell great brands. It's clearly too soon yet, but I can in the future envisage that we might outsource plants, and a lot besides.' Innovation, after all, is about asking and answering such questions.

A Survey of Current Best Practice in Innovation

By Dr Trevor Davis, lead-author of the Coopers & Lybrand Management Consulting Innovation Survey

In 1997 Coopers & Lybrand and Henley Management College conducted a survey of best practice in innovation among *The Times* top 1000. In the course of the work, respondents were measured on their performance in generating revenue from new products and services. This provided a means to understand the practices of the top 20% in comparison to the others. The data highlighted a key difference between the high performers and the remainder: for the highest performers innovation is a fundamental organizational capability and new product introduction (NPI) is merely one aspect of this capability. So the narrow view of innovation as NPI no longer holds true in the best-performing companies. Furthermore, in shaping innovation in an organization there seem to be four key areas of focus that distinguish the top performers:

1. Innovation management style
2. Idea management
3. Climate control
4. Leadership.

Innovation Management Style

The overall innovation management practices of the top 20% can be characterized as either *managed* innovation or *open* innovation. Managed innovation is a systematic, planned approach to innovation that places emphasis on a high frequency of adaptive changes, with a more cautious approach to breakthrough changes. Innovation is one core competence among many, rising and falling in importance as needs require. The defining ethos of this approach to innovation could be expressed in a question and answer:

> 'Where do new ideas come from?'
> 'Generally the board and senior management.'

Open innovation, the second style of innovation management, is a more flexible, less structured style that encourages a portfolio management approach to all forms of novelty. Innovation is a dominant core competence, more like a basic value in actual application in the sense that there exists a clear template for innovative behaviour. Here the question and answer would be:

> 'Where do new ideas come from?'
> 'Top-down and bottom-up. It's a two-way process.'

Both of these styles work well in generating shareholder value but it is likely that the open style is increasingly able to outperform the managed.

Idea Management

Perhaps the most striking feature of the highest-performing organizations is the extent to which they have constructed explicit and tacit processes for the management of ideas. Figure 4.1 shows the major components of a scalable idea management process synthesized from the survey respondents.

In this context scalable means visible and accessible to all levels of the organization. For example, this process model is applied to innovation award schemes as much as to the conduct of specific problem-solving sessions. This is quite different from a frame of reference that separates core processes from problem-solving processes, using different models for each.

A key antecedent condition for the process model to operate effectively is the appropriate climate – i.e. the context which encourages and supports individual and group creativity. This context has been described by Ekvall (1996) and is included in the section preceding this survey

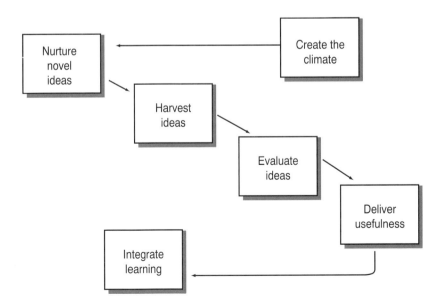

Figure 4.1 Process model for idea management.

report. With this in mind it is important to ensure that managers have the skills and willingness to support this climate building.

One of the difficulties most organizations face is the natural tendency to squash, at an early stage, novel ideas – 'won't work, doesn't make sense, will cost too much, won't convince people, it's awful' and so forth. Nurturing novel ideas enables ideas to be developed and augmented and the top 20% achieve this by a balance of divergent and convergent activities in idea generation. Especially important is the need to ensure that criteria which act as hurdles to idea development (e.g. cost and other practicalities in application) are deployed much later in the process than occurs in less innovative organizations.

The survey data suggest that the top performers place emphasis on systematic collection of ideas, not just suggestions. This is manifest in the near-fanaticism with which they collate and record ideas. Nothing is lost. And, not surprisingly, the highest performers tend to have the greatest expertise in the application of groupware and intranet communication: idea sharing, transmission and collection is therefore quicker and more widespread.

Evaluation in the top 20% is deferred longer than in the poorer performers. This prevents ideas being killed when they are most vulnerable. Practical mechanisms to achieve this are the use of reward systems that positively promote novelty and the allocation of risk capital to enable extended development of ideas without the financial constraints typical in many organizations.

In order to deliver usefulness, the top performers deploy their traditional approach of innovation as a business process for the development of new products and services. On this aspect there is little difference in the survey between the top 5% and the remainder of the top 20% performers. Most organizations have re-engineered their new product introduction process in ways that are so similar that the process has become homogenized across industries and sectors. Fretting about improving this process further is probably unnecessary: the likely gains will be incremental and tiny. Much better to concentrate on the first three elements of the total idea management process and to devote some time and effort to integrating learning and knowledge generated from the innovation process. In short, the best organizations strive to get better.

Climate Control

As with idea management there are marked differences between the more and the less innovative organizations in the manner in which they address organizational and work unit climate. Several of the dimensions of creative climate originally identified by Goran Ekvall (1996) were tested in the survey and there is a sharp demarcation between the top 5%, the top 20% and the remainder. In the top 20% many of the elements are in place, but in the top 5% there appears to be a more effective balance across the organization. In addition, the top 5% view climate as dynamic (manipulable to suit a given set of trading conditions) and therefore actively control the climate in their firms. The climate indicators drawn from the work of Ekvall that were examined in the survey were:

Challenge and involvement
Freedom
Trust and openness
Idea time
Idea support
Debates
Risk taking

The top 20% of survey respondents confirmed that employees were energized and motivated by involving them in setting challenging targets for the introduction of change (*challenge and involvement*). People were more likely to be allowed to define much of how their work is performed, to take the initiative to seek out information and share it (*freedom*). The highest performers encouraged the expression of honest opinions and were unlikely to retaliate if an opinion ran counter to received wisdom (*trust and openness*). A number of organizations reported that employees were allocated time to explore possibilities and potential. The poorer performers, by contrast, were more inclined to bow to time pressure and accept the obvious options (*idea time*).

The highest performers avoided the premature evaluation of new ideas by institutionalizing the use of well-established creativity tools – suspending judgement, maximizing idea flow, looking for possibilities in all contributions in order to avoid early criticism, squashing of ideas and so on (*idea support*). Likewise, the more innovative organizations were more likely to endorse the use of effective meetings and other group processes to engage people in debate, thereby valuing a range of diverse viewpoints and experiences and unlocking new possibilities. In the lowest performers debate was characterized as 'an excuse for not making decisions' (*debates*). Finally, the highest performers tended to measure their business performance in ways that allowed employees to work effectively with ambiguity and uncertainty, in particular empowering people to try things even when outcomes were unpredictable or unknown. The balanced scorecard approach of Kaplan and Norton (1993) played a role here and although the most innovative had the strongest focus on financial success, this was counterpoised by willingness to allow longer payback periods for innovations (*risk taking*).

Leadership

Leadership has a central role to play in innovation. Climate is broadly affected by the leadership style of key managers. It is their behaviour that will cause climate changes. The survey reconfirms this view. All respondents recognized that leadership is required to bring about change and that, as novelty increases, the demands on the skill of leaders increases too.

However, the leadership role was perceived to be different and operated differently in the top 20% than in the remaining organizations. In the highest performers leadership was seen as less hierarchical and more facilitative and situational – the 'leaders' were senior figures concerned with organizational goal-setting but also those people, at whatever level, who could influence climate directly. In the lower 80%, ideas were seen to cascade primarily from the top of the organization and the leaders were the 'top'. For these organizations, middle management was the prime conduit for disseminating messages on change and direction but not for influencing climate directly.

Becoming More Innovative

Perhaps the greatest challenge to organizational innovation is spreading the behavioural changes needed for enhanced leadership and climate beyond the boardroom and senior management. The most innovative organizations in the survey appeared to share a common approach: this was to identify those employees who were the most influential early adopters or champions as role models and advocates for the changes needed. In this way the bulk of the organization could be quickly 'infected' with the new operating style. Just as with product or service innovations entering the market, this approach carries the same risk: rejection by the majority if the benefits of the change are not persuasive to them. To minimize this risk, the most successful place the emphasis on quickly communicating the necessary change via those managers and supervisors who are closest to the front line.

Six Steps to Innovation Heaven

Analysis of the survey data pointed to six steps that were important in creating and sustaining innovation. These were:

1. Explicitly tackle climate and culture – the need for the climate dimension of 'freedom' (in the sense of employees defining their own work and seeking out and sharing information) was mentioned more frequently than any other.
2. Invest in management and leadership development across a broad front.
3. Ensure that additional 'idea time' is one of the planned outcomes from process change.
4. Modify recruitment and promotion criteria to favour managers and supervisors who are more able to adapt and to manage climate.
5. Involve customers directly in the nurturing of novel ideas.
6. Modify organizational structures to give greater organizational freedom and control to a wider population of managers and supervisors.

Finally, one of the distinctive features of the top 5% was their wider use of information technologies in the idea management process. This was aimed at fulfilling two objectives: first, capturing deeper and more intimate knowledge of the marketplace and, second, facilitating organizational feedback and learning.

5
Conflict Escalation

HUBBLE, HUBBLE, TOIL AND TROUBLE

The National Aeronautics and Space Administration (NASA) suffered two high-profile disasters within years of each other. First was the tragedy of *Challenger*'s explosive end only a minute after blast-off, taking the lives of seven crewmembers. Second was the failure of the *Hubble* space telescope, four years after *Challenger*. Both stories are briefly related in Chapter 2. There have been other embarrassments, notably the loss of an important weather satellite and the $1 billion loss of the *Mars Observer*. The vast funding, for which NASA missions were famous or infamous (the two *Viking* trips to Mars during the 1970s set American taxpayers back $3 billion in 1997 dollars) and the principle of superredundancy (duplication and replication as fail-safe back-up), in addition to the enormous weight of intellectual and technological know-how brought to bear in these great enterprises were, incredibly, inadequate to the task of safeguarding NASA from catastrophic failure. On the contrary, it is likely that such conditions, together with the spur of public scrutiny in the form of increased Congressional oversight, were in general *responsible* for breeding a social–psychological milieu, under the surface of NASA's elite professionalism, which over time actually diverted attention away from critical analysis of alternatives and de-emphasized the importance which might otherwise be accorded contradictory indicators.

Simple technological solutions to problems were missed. Straightforward quality assurance tests were not put in place. In the case of *Hubble* alone, for example, NASA investigators later confirmed that an optical instrument, ironically called the null corrector, had been assembled incorrectly. The Perkin-Elmer Corporation and Hughes Danbury Optical Systems agreed in

1993 to pay the US government $25 million in an out-of-court settlement, but it was also concluded that lax NASA supervision and deadline pressures contributed. *Hubble*'s mirror flaw had apparently been spotted on previous occasions but had been dismissed. The pressure to live up to its reputation encouraged instead the avoidance of controversy in everyday work and the protection of NASA teams' preferred shared identity as exceptional workers in an exceptional organization. So far had this defensive, uncritical milieu developed that, at the Senate hearings examining the *Hubble* bungling, one of the NASA officials responded in all earnestness, 'We know what we're doing. We're clever' (Chaisson, 1994, p.191).

On 10 February 1992 President George Bush asked for the resignation of Admiral Richard Truly who had run NASA since 1989. In his place there came an outsider. From TRW where he had been vice president and general manager of the Space and Technology Group, Daniel Goldin became NASA's ninth Administrator in 1992 and set about moving with the times. Early on he set the tone by continually ramming home the same message of 'faster, better, cheaper'. As *Flight International* reported in 1995, the bureacracy and the bulk were gradually sliced away, reducing the 215 000 workforce by 55 000 and NASA's budget by $15 billion over five years, the more to approximate the original 1950s vision of a small, fast, flexible engineering organization focused on space exploration. In place of the big-budget blockbuster missions like *Viking*, *Voyager* and *Pioneer*, the new NASA would build and launch smaller, cheaper, faster missions. There would be no more cargoes bursting at the seam with fancy scientific gadgetry, multi-replicated back-up systems and over-ambitious plans – all of those things had contributed to intense pressure to succeed and thus escalated affective conflict, thereby promoting mechanisms to protect the image of NASA employees. In contrast, the successful *Pathfinder* mission that landed on Mars and analysed soil and rock samples in July 1997, for example, cost under $200 million and Goldin planned to reduce the average cost of future unmanned spacecraft. The new budget-conscious emphasis and the new ways of working that Goldin imported from TRW started to alter the way NASA scientists thought of themselves and operated day to day. A more self-critical, less image-obsessed ethos had been injected.

Robert Capers, in an article for *Academy of Management* in 1994, for example, reported that Goldin created a new Office of

Continual Improvement to educate NASA teams on total quality. This was followed by quality councils in each of NASA's field centres. More crucially, Goldin introduced the notion of independent evaluation of those projects running behind schedule or over budget. The review procedure was painful and direct, raising the level of conflict dramatically but pinpointing required action and stimulating proactive problem solving. In addition, he started to recruit more women and people from minority groups, thereby shifting the traditional make-up of NASA personnel and creating some of the conditions for alternative ways of viewing the world.

Goldin's instinct was to debureaucratize an organization that had become overweight with inappropriate paperwork and administration and whose original culture of change, experimentation and exploration had been suffocated by the remorseless rise of a culture of 'official procedure' – it is notable that in the 1950s professional administrators at NASA could almost be counted on one hand but by the late 1980s almost a fifth of the workforce were administrators. Goldin started to push accountability down the NASA layers, encouraging all employees to offer suggestions for improvement and change and to take limited risks in pursuit of better approaches to working. None of this was easy. In common with many organizations, much of the resistance in NASA came from middle managers, feeling that their status and power had been threatened. A critical measure of Goldin's progress in transforming NASA, however, was that the workplace 'temperature' *had* risen. Internal perturbations that fire up cognitive conflict and shift employee thinking and action away from building and maintaining a widespread social identity or posture are, as we shall see, indicators of early success.

CONFLICT INTENSITY: STASIS, PARALYSIS AND TRANSFORMATION

Futile, destructive, unsatisfactory – these are epithets applied to conflict in virtually all management books. It is hard to find a good word spoken of the concept. Certainly, in theories of change management the strong inference is that conflict must be identified, managed and reduced. Left alone, it will fester. Problem-solving tactics are typically brought to bear to *de-escalate*, to bring conflicts to a speedy resolution. Many organizations offer training in conflict management as a standard feature of supervisory and management training curricula. Positive morale and improved organizational performance are usually touted as the benefits of effective conflict management. All of this is somewhat at odds, though, with the truth.

First, what do we mean by conflict? For our purposes here, conflict is active, often contentious dispute, debate or disagreement, typically triggered or accompanied by the presentation of contrary or opposing information. Second, what are its real effects? Escalated to optimal intensity, conflict produces many social–psychological and organizational benefits either never exploited in the passive view of conflict as 'unacceptable' or even suppressed by normal conflict management approaches. Some of these benefits, catalogued by Evert Van de Vliert at the University of Groningen in The Netherlands (1997), include:

- Motivation and energy to deal with underlying problems
- Making underlying issues explicit
- Sharpening people's understanding of real goals and interests
- Enhancement of mutual understanding between different groups
- Stimulation of a sense of urgency
- Discouragement to engage in avoidance behaviour
- Prevention of premature (and therefore dangerous) resolution of problems.

Having read this list, now think of your own experience of organizational change. Most, if not all, of these benefits will be relevant, no matter what size and scale of change you have experienced. Generally, however, the idea of conflict escalation is counterintuitive, not least because in the short term it is aversive: it creates increased stress, might lead to obstruction and delays, involves additional effort and could be awkward or embarrassing for a time. In short, there are obvious costs. Moreover, people are typically short term in outlook, particularly in organizations. Feeling the pain *now* is not a condition in which anyone is likely, on the assumption of deferred performance and psychological benefits, to invite an escalation of the pain.

The situation is magnified when the ambition is corporate transformation. Conflict de-escalation will more likely be emphasized in the mistaken belief that the rapid resolution of obstructions, difficulties and disagreements will allow the firm to get on with the job of transforming. The real effect, however, will be to constrain decision quality, reduce creativity, breed disaffection or even withdrawal among many employees, defer deep-rooted conflict until later and suppress controversial information that might subsequently have a devastating impact on the business. There is some of this tendency, usually to a greater than lesser degree, in all organizations. Especially succcessful organizations. Consider two such icons of corporate worship – Daimler Benz and Microsoft. In the case of Daimler Benz, executives had set their sights on making inroads to the mid-size and small-car market, considered to be the way of the future but one which the makers of high-quality Mercedes Benz luxury cars had largely ignored. The future of the A-class 'Baby Benz' over which its engineers had laboured (and journalists had initially enthused) came under question in 1997 when test-drivers from Swedish magazine *Teknikens Värld* managed to tip the car onto its side during a routine slalom avoidance manoeuvre called the Elk test (replicating avoiding sudden hazards like elks on Swedish roads). The media fallout from this seemed to take Daimler Benz by surprise, but after some initial defensiveness (blaming the tyres that were fitted, claiming the Elk test was an extreme manoeuvre unlikely to be performed by normal drivers), they rapidly set out to fix both the car design and the damage to the image of the Mercedes Benz. All well and good, but there were deeper social–psychological difficulties. As far as conflict suppression is concerned, there were clear indicators of the presence in Daimler Benz of the conditions that lead to social identity maintenance. Here was a highly successful organization, revered for its engineering excellence and safety innovations. But it was also under pressure to get the car out quickly, following several years of cost-cutting and efficiency improvements, and, in particular, to turn a profit on building a small car that customers would expect to have the same unqualified advantages of safety and high standards as its bigger, more expensive stablemates. Under these conditions of threat and pressure, it appears that managers deep in the bowels of the organization began to engage in behaviour not unlike that of NASA scientists, engineers and administrators: they put up a front of concurrence, pretending that everything was alright when unpalatable evidence of the A-class's design was apparent. Indeed, senior managers subsequently began to look closely at why communication channels had failed to feed such unpalatable evidence up to a level where corrective action could be initiated.

The potential existed, similarly, at Microsoft for many of the conditions that contribute to conflict suppression and that hamstrung NASA: the powerful, dominant leader, the elite groups of employees, the overwhelming expectations of securities analysts and shareholders that Microsoft stock inevitably goes *up*, the public image, reputation and history of having things their own way with Windows and DOS. Things nearly did go badly wrong when executives and employees were staring so hard into the future that they could not see the future around them in the form of the Internet's potential. One of the reasons they could not see its potential was because the Internet was regarded by Microsoft executives as a real threat to the company's security. It was thought that being hooked-up via thousands of employees' PCs would enable outsiders to breach security or introduce a virus. Few PCs on the Redmond campus had more than an e-mail connection to the Net. Microsoft had indeed succeeded in protecting itself from the Internet – and all its opportunities. Fortunately for the company, it did have mechanisms in place for conflict escalation. One of the best routes for this is through employee suggestions, critique and challenge and it is true that for a long time Bill Gates has actively sought ideas, critique and comment from employees, direct to him either in person or by e-mail. With the Internet effectively blocked to employees, however, Microsoft had also shut down employees as a source of challenge. Their very ignorance on the subject was a strategic black hole. (This at a time in the evolution of organizations when, we must remember, having the infrastructure to access the richness and complexity of knowledge is fast becoming both a defensible barrier and a competitive advantage.)

What saved Microsoft has probably more to do with Bill Gates himself. He was worried about the Internet (and it is easy to forget that this was before the media explosion had propelled the Internet into the limelight) and he was pushing colleagues to look more closely. Thus, as a result of the Microsoft culture he had helped create of active search for external challenges, the Internet threat (and opportunity) was under review for some time by Microsoft executives Russ Siegelman and Nathan

Myhrvold before the company's 1995 strategic about-turn. Sluggish it might have been, uninformed and indecisive it was not. Part of the Microsoft ethos therefore, despite the apparent arrogance and singleminded win-at-all-costs mentality of its leader, is concerned with collection of data (both supportive *and* controversial), intense debate and democratic expression of contentious views.

In many organizations there is certainly the appearance of such behaviour. People in groups can be especially adept at conflict avoidance but give the impression of necessary contentious debate and smooth team functioning, usually by concentrating debate on peripheral issues – debate that is 'full of sound and fury, signifying nothing', as Shakespeare neatly put it. Turner and Pratkanis (1997) have demonstrated in their psychological research that cover-up behaviour of this type is most often observed where groups perceive they are under threat (i.e. seen to be inadequate or not delivering), yet fear the consequences of appearing so. They therefore take action to present a falsely positive image, clamping down hard on disagreements, debate and contrary information that might split the group's cohesion around the positive image. The threat therefore pushes team members towards a concentration on efforts to deal with the *threat* – efforts (maintaining the group's image) that have nothing to do with actual work demands – thus reducing the time and effort devoted to the real tasks at hand and ultimately impairing decision making and performance. In short, protecting the shared identity of the group becomes more important than the goals of making the best possible decisions and taking the most appropriate action. Case in point: NASA during the 1980s.

These conditions in organizations are make-or-break as far as transformation efforts are concerned. If nothing else, transformation efforts are constantly challenged by the need to integrate seemingly opposing – conflicting – interests, simply because the scale of change is so great and all-inclusive. Suppress cognitive conflict or allow the intensification of affective conflict (i.e. that which is social–emotional and to do with personal or group identity) and transformation efforts will either founder or fail. Overstimulate cognitive conflict and similar consequences will befall executives.

The stasis–transformation–paralysis (STP) curve in Figure 5.1 highlights the chief performance impact at progressively higher

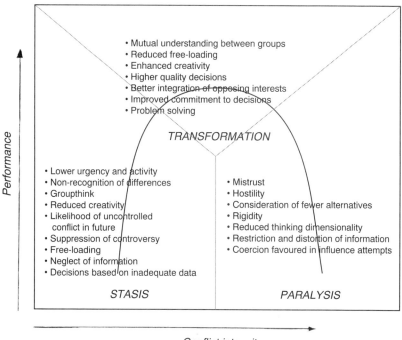

Figure 5.1 The stasis–transformation–paralysis (STP) curve.

intensities of cognitive conflict. At low intensities, the organization is, in effect, in a kind of stasis. There is lower activity and
urgency, avoidance of responsibility – even free-loading – as
well as neglect of relevant information, reduced creativity,
failure to diagnose problems and recognize differences or
demarcation issues and a strong proclivity for making decisions
without adequate information.

At very high intensities of conflict, the organization might be
described as paralysed: mistrust and hostility are probable
outcomes, together with rigidity in behaviour patterns and
concomitant reductions in both thinking dimensionality (i.e.
perspectives on an issue at hand) and consideration of
alternatives. There is also likely to be restriction and unwitting
distortion of information, with coercion being favoured in any
influence attempts.

At optimal intensities of conflict, transformation is facilitated.
Free-loading is reduced because the conflict prompts the identi-
fication of weaknesses and shortcomings in colleagues with

success being seen to derive from personal competence. (Case in point: Daniel Goldin's introduction at NASA of independent project reviews.) Higher-quality decisions are made because relevant data is brought into the open for active problem solving and less energy and time devoted to group identity protection. The factors behind opposing interests emerge more clearly and conflict stimulates individuals to define where they stand, producing as a consequence mutual understanding between groups. This helps groups ultimately to move towards integration in line with superordinate goals (such as vision, mission, strategy) and generates greater commitment to decisions.

TRUST AND CONFLICT

As discussed in Chapter 2, the key to using conflict effectively is understanding the difference between cognitive and affective conflict. Affective conflict is concerned with the self, particularly as this relates to personal or group identity and is characterized by emphases on norms and values. Generally people instinctively understand this difference – they can tell whether conflict is to do with task (situation and action) and emphasizes intellect and analysis, or concerns ongoing relationships with other employees and with the organization and brings into play emotions such as anger, jealousy and mistrust or pride, loyalty and a sense of unity.

British Airways has powerful values and norms. Ask BA employees about these matters and they will tell you, like Chris Byron, Project Director for the office move to Harmondsworth, 'It's not just a job. It's almost a way of life. . . . Every person that works for British Airways is very proud of British Airways and externally we will defend it. We are tremendously loyal, amazingly loyal. That's not loyalty to any one individual; it's loyalty to British Airways.' Part of it is to do with the livery and the world-class advertising and PR. Staff turnover is generally low and people would love to work for the company. Every day at BA's Meadowbank recruitment office there are thousands of unsolicited applications.

Even though the company has powerful values, staff do not go around with the new mission in mind, nor are they able to articulate on demand a set of formal values. But the values are there nonetheless: safety, security, proactive and spontaneous goodwill to the customer, excelling in a crisis – some written down as explicit value commitments, some not. These values are the core of the company. Yet, at the same time, there is conflict. This was actively encouraged early on during the transformation in the Putting People First seminars and other types of motivational workshops. These events were not just one-way inputs of training, as Chris Byron relates:

> We tried to encourage staff to make decisions and do what they could in their own job. But on the training programmes there was intense debate about how far you could go, what the actual constraints were and how you could participate. We needed to be clear about the constraints within which you can make decisions. But there's always this issue of where the line is drawn, you know: how much can I actually do?

The same was true with the management seminars. Over a number of years while he was CEO (he is now chairman), Sir Colin Marshall spent a couple of hours on each of more than 100 seminars with some twenty-five managers in the room, encouraging critical debate and challenge to the way things worked. Initially managers were startled and suspicious. They were used to the old hierarchical culture, more like the airforce than an airline. He was aiming to build debate and critique into the business at large by giving tangible legitimacy to such behaviour in the form of his own presence and behaviour at the seminars. He was raising the level of conflict.

This continues to be felt. Chris Byron noticed this very clearly in the project team gearing up for the headquarters move to Harmondsworth. 'Although we argue and there are different levels of tensions, the one thing we've got in common is that every single person really wants us to succeed. Everyone is determined this is going to work, even if it means we're all working weekends. It's very important to us.' So, tension and argument around the complexity of the task but deeply felt emotions of pride, loyalty and unity around the objectives. Cognitive conflict at optimal levels; affective conflict held in check by deep-rooted values and norms. There is stability and widespread concordance on common values, norms and aspirations. These things bind people together and create trust. Trust is at the heart of what enables ongoing, sometimes fierce, conflict over the task-related challenges of running the business.

CREATING AND EXPLOITING CONSTRUCTIVE CONFLICT

In the course of our deliberations on conflict we have dived into an area of considerable sensitivity. Conflict escalation is, at best, undervalued, at worst actively displaced in favour of peace-making initiatives. Conflict management interventions, to give them their due, at least get some of the way there in that they sometimes bring conflict out into the open. But usually this is to provide catharsis for the parties involved and the primary objective remains one of smoothing the waters. Conflict is mostly viewed as undesirable and unproductive. What a small but growing band of scholars and practitioners is arguing for, however, is escalative intervention so that the benefits outlined earlier in this chapter might accrue to organizations and the people in them.

Moreover, since I have repeatedly described transformation as an unnatural act for companies and we have witnessed some of the profound challenges and difficulties that assault those who try, it must by now be obvious that conflict cannot be avoided or dismissed, nor the necessity to understand and more effectively intervene in situations of conflict be neglected. Further, it is clear that competitive advantages will accrue to organizations that do more than merely 'manage' conflict – in the scale of big change we would expect that ultimately conflict induction and intensi-fication would speed transformation and contribute to greater success. After all, some executives in organizations that have transformed instinctively take actions which escalate conflict. That they do so instinctively (either without conscious or stated intent) is laudable, but more could be done if executives explicitly understood conflict and engaged in its deliberate induction and escalation.

The balance of this chapter is devoted to extracting the lessons on conflict both from applied research and a number of organizations and then elaborating a few important actions for exploiting its usefulness. I declare immediately, however, that the psychology of conflict escalation in organizations is new (though much of the pure research dates back to Robbins in 1974), it is counterintuitive (and therefore people are suspicious of it) and it carries risks (if handled inappropriately). Still, the risk of transformational failure is high anyway, from both a personal and organizational point of view. So, if you are looking for safety and a risk-free route to transformation, then read no further. If not, take a look at the key actions for conflict induction and escalation which appear in Action List 3.

Action List 3   Escalating Conflict

1. Seek out 'difference' and embed challenge and self-critique: organizations with these values breed insight and therefore tend to anticipate and respond to problems and opportunities faster and more effectively than competitors.
2. De-escalate conflict over values: surface common norms, values and goals and ensure that people 'act together'.
3. Build internal market pressure: create market forces inside the organization to identify underperformers both at the departmental, team and individual level and to improve productivity and efficiencies.
4. Tool-up managers for conflict escalation: because conflict escalation is counterintuitive, managers need to overcome in-built reservations and learn when and how to use it.

THE MERIT OF INSIGHT THROUGH CHALLENGE, DIFFERENCE AND SELF-CRITIQUE

One of the norms in Reckitt & Colman, as you might expect in a British company that has been around since 1814, is that people are very polite to each other. Such norms are, of course, desirable but they can conceal hidden demons. 'The company,' says CEO Vernon Sankey, 'is almost too polite. In the past it's been so nice that the real issues haven't come out because people were so polite to each other. They're much more subtle. Therefore saying "no" in a rough or difficult way isn't part of the norms, but that doesn't mean to say that people aren't thinking about it. And they can undermine in different ways.'

Sankey was concerned that these norms and the behaviour of people below the surface of polite interaction would get in the way of aligning the top team around a unifying theme embodied in the new vision, the strategy and the transformation imperative. As he concedes, there was the ever-present danger, accentuated in Reckitt & Colman during the global transformation effort, of 'talking about and agreeing on one set of actions and then behaving the opposite way.' As a consequence he kicked off some work to define leadership behaviours. One of these was *Challenging the Status Quo*. This was an explicit way of stating the desirability of challenge, debate, intellectual argument – conflict escalation. Crucially, the articulation of leadership behaviours was supported and reinforced by measurement, sharing of feedback in the top team and a link through to remuneration.

A similar tack was taken by John Roberts, Chief Executive of the Post Office in Britain who has insisted that either the chairman or himself, plus a member of the executive team, attend each of the strategy and leadership training events for different levels of senior managers. Their presence is to provide input and to raise debate. He relates this anecdote:

> As part of the preparation for one of the courses, I had just received a list of about thirty issues that the course participants wanted to raise with me, like, 'Why are we doing this?' or 'Why is X drifting?' And all of that is fine because we've tried to encourage a culture here where you are challenged. But it struck me this time that there can be a tendency to read challenge as, 'Why aren't *you up there* doing more to solve this?' So one of the lines I now take is to drive home the message, 'Hold on a minute! It's not just us up here. It's all of us in this room who have to be doing something. What is each of us doing to help?'

The same explicit encouragement was made by Pierre Gravelle during Revenue Canada's transformation. He was clear that employees, long used to a civil service milieu of hierarchy, rule following and enforcement of compliance from taxpayers, would have to be fully engaged in building the new service-oriented culture and in influencing how change was developed and delivered. Consequently, he was active in encouraging employees to challenge conventional ways of doing business and getting them involved in working within teams to improve service delivery. But Gravelle went further. 'We also had to enlist,' he says, 'the support and ideas of our chief interlocutors *out there*. These were the Canadian Bar Association, the Canadian Centre of Chartered Accountants, the various tax practitioner groups, accountants, industry associations and so on. We organized ourselves by setting up business advisory committees and the like so that we could tap input and support from these various streams, getting them to challenge us and building support among them over three or four years.'

When Gravelle was appointed president and CEO of Symcor (a case analysed in more detail in Chapter 7), he began to assemble a management team for the new organization, drawing on executives mainly from each of the three competitor banks involved in the joint venture. Of course, each of the executives came with views, opinions, ways of working and cultural values rooted and nurtured in their previous employers. The potential for conflict was high but Gravelle knew that this in itself was valuable:

> Our different cultural baggage is at conflict every day and this is very healthy. It helps us to bring to the table different experience and perspectives. While it may be difficult at first, it enriches the decision-making process and maybe the solution as well. It's based on insight as opposed to simply a quick fix – doing things that we've done in the past.

So here is the crux: conflict prevents tempting, easy, short-term solutions and ultimately – in the course of confrontation, active expression of difference and intellectual analysis and debate – it brings *insight*. This is applicable to the top team or any team in the organization. It is a concept that British Airways seem to have grasped, at least in the sense of expanding their horizons to encompass a global view of their customers, made tangible in the new corporate imagery that reflects what Bob Ayling describes as 'our focus on international routes and our intention to build global alliances'. More critical, though, is the question of what it truly means to be a global company and, as BA's S-P Mahoney argues, that will be determined by the airline's willingness and ability to absorb into its ranks people from many other cultures around the world:

> I think that enabling us to be influenced by other cultures of the world will be a significant competitive advantage, provided we can be brave enough to do it. The implications of trying to do it are huge. . . . To change the fabric of the company means that we would have to have a sizeable distribution within our customer contact and management population that is actually made up of these cultures. That would allow who we are and the decisions we make to be motivated and driven by the way that these cultures work.

ACTING TOGETHER: DE-ESCALATING CONFLICTS OVER VALUES

St Luke's, the British advertising agency created in a breakaway from the old Chiat/Day, described in Chapter 4, takes values and ethics *very* seriously. The agency was born out of frustration with what the advertising industry had become and an aspiration not only to create the perfect company but also, in chairman Andy Law's words, 'to transform the way the advertising industry works.' No small ambition. Within the company there is no room for the values and norms of ego, greed, habit (doing the same things the same way without thought), power, fear and seniority that are the everyday driving forces in the advertising world and many other types of organization besides. Honest, ethical advertising is the company's purpose. Employees talk about the company's 'Total Role in Society' – how it interacts with all its stakeholders, whether shareholders, employees, clients, competitors, the environment, or consumer groups. The talk is not idle: the company's common ownership (*all* employees own *equal* shares) is the bedrock upon which such values can genuinely live. Employees are involved in virtually all decisions – salaries too. The company is owned by a trust and a five-member council governs it; one of the trustees must be an outside lawyer, the others are representatives from the directors and employees, with employees electing their representatives. Collaboration and cooperation are real, rather than buzzwords – employees, including directors, 'own' neither desks, personal computers nor any other physical resource.

This does not mean that St Luke's is a calm paradise without conflict. Intense debate is common, but it is almost exclusively channelled into day-to-day creative ad issues and business requirements. Affective conflict occurs but is minimized by the structural and cultural arrangements of St Luke's. The values of ethics, honesty, collaboration and change are constantly reinforced and ensure that people act together in concert.

Despite its growth (more than doubling revenue in two years to around $110 million), it is easy to dismiss St Luke's as an off-the-wall, quirky outfit at the periphery. The advertising world certainly did – until the company started to grab business other agencies wanted, attaining a pitch conversion rate of 80%, well up on competitors, and narrowly missing being voted *Campaign*'s Agency of the Year in 1996 after only its first year of operation (it was runner-up to Abbott Mead Vickers BBDO). More than this, however, St Luke's is a model of how knowledge-based organizations of the future may well operate.

St Luke's has some 80 employees and revenues of $110 million. At the other end of the scale is ABB, with 200 000 staff and revenues of $36 billion. The differences between them, however, are not so dramatic. In 1988, after the formation of Asea Brown Boveri Group, one of the early actions of the then CEO Percy Barnevik (now non-executive chairman) was to communicate a set of policies and values that would help to bind the diverse population of employees around the world in a way that enabled them to act together in pursuit of the new organization's objectives. ABB's mission and values were documented and communicated with zeal by Barnevik himself and his managers. There was much made of 'pulling in the same direction' and retaining a 'single sense of purpose', reinforced by consistent use of the ABB brand name and logo to sustain cohesion and gain leverage from unity. This is difficult when you have more than 1000 companies in 140 countries, taking worldwide revenues of $36 billion. It is especially difficult when you have also created an internal competitive market where individual ABB companies are openly competing for export market allocation, as discussed later in this chapter, and there is the danger of multiple ABB offerings to confused customers.

The pursuit of unity and cohesion in so large and diverse a group is possible for two reasons. First, there is a genuine commitment to it. As Rolf Renke of ABB Calor Emag makes clear, 'The main point is to find win–win cooperation with our foreign colleagues.' The same commitment is made real by the fact that ABB document and communicate a set of values and ways of working, including their operational and functional policies, signed by the CEO and given voice by him in countless presentations and personal interactions. Second, there is a strong expectation that local managers themselves be responsible for spreading and reinforcing the values. This is facilitated by the distinctive profit centre structure (around 5000 profit centres) and the flattened hierarchy. This makes for small teams in fairly small companies (2300 employees at Calor Emag in 12 profit centres) and the emphasis on team leadership and individual accountability to make the values live.

The values are not especially distinctive when compared to other corporations. They are: corporate unity, business ethics,

customer focus, employee focus, quality, environmental protection, and action orientation. Like St Luke's, however, ABB puts
substantive effort into sustaining and communicating the values
– that is, making sure that a critical mass of the 200 000
employees worldwide are socially–emotionally at one: they
agree on and support the common values, norms and aspirations of the company.

ABB has had years to build these values and continues to do
so. In the course of transformation, however, with all the fluidity
and chaos that is the inevitable accompaniment, these things
take time to build. Producing glossy sheets of paper with
aspirational values can have little impact, as Chris von Branconi,
commercial director at Lurgi, a subsidiary of Metallgesellschaft,
discovered.

Metallgesellschaft, in 1994 Germany's 14th largest industrial
group with 258 subsidiaries, was hauled from the brink of
collapse in a billion-dollar capital injection and cash aid package.
For some time Metall had grown phenomenally with charis-
matic Austrian Heinz Schimmelbusch at the helm, expanding
from its base in metals and mining into a huge conglomerate.
But in late 1993 Schimmelbusch, the chief financial officer and
four board members were fired. Staggering losses had been
incurred in trades on oil futures in the USA just when global
petroleum prices were falling. Declared at around $200 million,
the losses were abruptly disclosed as nearer $1 billion and were
thought to be much higher. Following the rescue and with its
market capitalization halved, Metall was forced into the agony
of massive restructuring and downsizing. For subsidiaries such
as Lurgi the programme of change meant interventions 'where
every project had a major, direct impact on the balance sheet' in
Chris von Branconi's words. However, Metall later launched
a 'vision programme' to focus effort on clients, technology,
quality, the environment, profitability, markets and culture. Says
von Branconi:

> The culture element was very much the priority but it soon had little
> credibility at Metallgesellschaft and certainly lost out completely here at
> Lurgi . . . When you've had a very rough ride, you need to be able to get
> out of trouble at a certain point in time and get to a more normal
> situation. That's when you need the chance for culture to regenerate. If
> there's no natural basis again from which a new culture of confidence
> can grow, then it will become very difficult in the long run to achieve
> this.

Building new cultural values therefore is dependent on three criteria. First, the timing is important. When a company is in trouble and has to go through the gut-wrenching actions so common at the start of transformation – laying people off, chopping out layers of hierarchy, fixing the finances, changing processes and people's jobs and making huge demands on their time and energy – attempts to build new values will fail if they follow close on the heels of actions that inevitably trigger negative emotions (shame, fear, anger, frustration).

Second, it is important to objectively assess the old values and define the new – but not to announce them, yet. Some of the old values may well prove to be a brake on transformation efforts, so it is as well to understand what they are. Value assessment requires you to discover precisely what it is that the organizational environment, right across the firm and at different levels, expects and rewards. Given different circumstances, what are the patterns of behaviour that managers and employees will exhibit? Will they be more inclined to do this, or that? New values, on the other hand, spring from leadership vision, from creating and beginning to impose a new context for the organization, but they are worthless without a third and final step.

In the third step, values must be built on the reality of organizational success, not on its promise. Because everything is in turmoil early in transformation, employees find it hard to see genuine success in what is happening around them. Everything is hard work. There is little to celebrate. They silently ask questions about how sustainable the transformation is. This usually means that values either emerge naturally from what the organization becomes or are successfully grafted onto organizational life only following massive changes to what DERA's John Chisholm calls 'the underlying reality' – the processes of the organization, the way the organization works. He also makes the point that inspirational pieces by the CEO, culture change workshops and training that try to push new values are worse than wasted, unless this underlying reality has changed. 'One of the first things I did on arrival,' Chisholm states, 'was to stop the new management training programmes. I could see that they were rapidly leading to disillusionment. Managers were spending a week hearing about the brave new world but then returning to the bleak unchanged reality.' Ultimately, however, victories do come and that is the foundation for expressing and spreading new values throughout the organization. Pierre Gravelle of Symcor agrees:

> There is no magic solution. You have to articulate a minimum set of values: what do we stand for, how are we different from competitors? So you make an affirmation of some very basic principles, but when a company is very much in transformation, the cultural values will grow and expand over time. You need to have some fluidity so that employees and managers will have the opportunity to ultimately shape and mould the culture. The mission statement and values statement are never real until they have been lived. Lived, but also changed, modified, thrown out of the window a couple of times!

Ad Scheepbouwer of PTT Post puts it like this: 'If you talk about culture, the important element is that people feel they're on the side of a winner. That applies as much to junior employees as it does to senior management, because everyone wants to be proud of something they know is flourishing.'

To summarize then:

1. *Do not attempt to build a new corporate value set during or imme-diately following financial turnaround (downsizing, large-scale lay-offs, disposals)*: the flood of negative emotion (affective conflict) will be too high and will defeat you.
2. *Assess the old values and define the new*: the old are expressed in the reality of what employees are expected to do and for which they are rewarded; the new spring from vision and future context but remain only words until tested, modified and embodied in the reality of organizational successes.
3. *Build new values on the reality of organizational success, not its promise*: when the underlying reality has changed and people witness its success, that is the time to link new values to the emotional experience of winning.

BUILDING INTERNAL MARKET PRESSURE

To achieve the transformation of the $4.5 billion South African firm Sanlam from a bureaucratic, inward-looking local insurance provider to a world-class, international financial services group, managing director Desmond Smith worked with his colleagues to identify fifteen migration ideals. One of these was to move the company from a bureaucracy to autonomous business service units that contract for and buy services from each other. For a company that had traditionally been run on slow, largely inefficient functional lines, this was a dramatic change, but Smith knew that the idea of internal markets would bring huge and continuing improvements in productivity and efficiencies, to the extent that every business unit was 'running its own bottom line'.

The basic form of the internal market was to create three types of business sectors:

1. *A marketing sector*: This would be responsible for distributing and selling the various products and services generated by the product sectors.
2. *Product sectors*: These would include, for example, unit trusts, individual assurance, group benefits, health, and asset management. Each of these sectors would take full responsibility for its products and services – market research, design, development, promotion and administration.
3. *Service sectors*: These would provide support to the rest of the company and would include human resources, corporate communications, actuarial, financial and legal services, corporate facilities and business systems.

In setting this up, governance rules were compiled to determine the mutual relationships of services with other sectors. The rules took the form of a set of guidelines on which services are rendered and the extent to which product and marketing sectors are compelled to use those services. 'So you will now find,' Smith says, 'that our Individual Life people will contract with our Asset Management company for the management of their assets, and with HR for things like payroll administration. Then they agree certain benchmarks and the structure of the fees – which are performance related. Some pretty hard bargaining goes on. . . . So every business unit now has its own direct expenses and value-for-money services contracted from the other business units.'

Within the vast conglomerate that is ABB, the complex organizational arrangements (strongly decentralized business units, tiny numbers of headquarters staff, fast and efficient reporting and control system) also produce the same heated internal competition that Sanlam now feels, but this time on a global scale. Germany's ABB Calor Emag lives with the challenging ABB principle of 'think global, act local' every day. This is true both in operations and customer delivery, with especial emphasis on ABB's own stringent benchmark standards. Calor Emag must hit these benchmarks to retain its export allocation (the German subsidiary is 70% export dependent) and to secure ongoing development work on product refinements or new products – work which might otherwise be shifted by beady-eyed business area managers to another better-performing subsidiary in another country.

In addition, managers in ABB companies are expected to be 'givers' rather than 'receivers' – that is, to recruit and develop good people but be willing to release them for other key roles, especially global management positions at the forefront of the group's expansion. The new CEO Goran Lindahl has targeted Latin America and other emerging economies. What is more, Lindahl is continuing along Barnevik's theme of sustaining ongoing cost cutting by demanding productivity improvements of 6–10% a year, applied not only to engineering and production but also to administration or sales. Soon after taking over as CEO he also set the ambitious goal of raising the global order intake from $36 billion (1996) to $50 billion by 2001. ABB Calor Emag's Rolf Renke expresses the continual sense of pressure that managers and employees in ABB feel:

> The decentralization of the ABB Group is a very good idea. It's the key to a lot of the success we've had in the past because all these smaller companies are flexible and have close customer relationships. Also, each of the organizations depends on its own success. There is no big brother behind to help us out. We have to make sure of our own profit and do everything we can to survive, because ABB would kill us immediately if we didn't make profits.

The pressure that Rolf Renke and his 200 000 colleagues worldwide feel produces a constant stream of analysis, debate, testing, exploration and informed decision making – the hallmarks of conflict escalated to a moderate, constructive level. But, as we saw in the previous section, to prevent conflict running out of control and producing destructive personalized battles there is a strong drive to 'pull in the same direction' around a cohesive set of values. Much is made of fairness, openness, and trust, with the clear expectation that what counts in the first instance is the manner and example set by senior managers.

Now, the creation of internal markets to escalate conflict among business units, as in Sanlam's case, or even between subsidiaries, as in ABB, need not be as far as it goes. Many organizations are searching for ways to reduce rigidity and sluggishness in the very nature of job design. Process re-engineering has pulled the spotlight onto this area and team-based approaches are usually the result. Even in teams people can be hemmed in not only by rules and controls but also by the definition of what their job is. Job descriptions thus become comfortable defensive earthworks behind which employees become accustomed to shelter from the fluid demands of the business and the varying needs of customers.

DERA's John Chisholm recognized that, in addition to all the other change that was needed to transform the organization into the world's foremost defence science and technology enterprise, they would have to tackle the way they looked at a person's employment. Having already set about smashing the old organization structure with its bureaucratic functional departments such as finance, personnel and contracts, to replace it with an internal market for service function suppliers, Chisholm brought the same thinking to bear on the design of employees' jobs. It had long been the case that the organization was defined by *posts* – pretty well static job descriptions linked systematically in a hierarchy of fixed grades. The implied emphasis therefore was on doing the things prescribed by the *post* and not doing the things required by the customer. There were horrendous implications for management too, giving rise to a control and enforcement culture that hobbled decision making. It takes no great imagination to see the intolerable rigidity forced on the whole organizational entity. 'We now think of everything we do in terms of *projects*,' declares Chisholm. 'Everyone's job is only defined in terms of those projects in which he or she is currently engaged.' The effect was startling for employees and managers and a dramatic turnaround in the way DERA worked for its customers, as Chisholm relates:

> A mark of the new system working is how difficult it has become to produce a traditional telephone book. This used to be the bible of where everyone in the organization sat. And very useful it was too. Everyone had their own tally code which uniquely described their post in the hierarchy. A quick glance at the book and you knew precisely to whom you were talking. No more! The project management system busts the rigidities of the old hierarchical system. Buoyant areas attract new staff,

declining areas organically shed them without the need for obtrusive senior management interference.

The gearing of all work in DERA to the new project management system also provided the basis for a new pay and grading scheme. This set out a more continuous path along which individuals could develop and advance without putting arbitrary roadblocks in the way in the form of the fixed grade hurdles. The best employees regularly collided with these hurdles under the old dispensation, damaging motivation and holding back skill enhancement. Most important for DERA, though, was how the project management system affected the performance of individuals through the new pay and grading scheme. 'The new scheme,' says Chisholm, 'relies on the working of the internal and external markets for staff to demonstrate the worth of individuals and then reward those personal characteristics – such as teamwork and professional skills – which are most important to DERA.'

TOOLING-UP MANAGERS FOR CONFLICT ESCALATION

What has preceded has been a discussion of some of the macro-escalative interventions that might be applied in a systemic and organization-wide manner. In this section we deal with some general conflict guidelines as well as escalative and de-escalative interventions amenable to individual action.

At the outset we should point out, however, that most organizations do not run on the basis of trust and openness. Rather, these are laudable aspirations. Even in the smallest of firms the reality is one of cognitive and affective conflict – disputes over strategies, resources and tactics; setbacks through frustration, jealousies and anger. Trust and openness are, anyway, misunderstood, misrepresented or miscommunicated in most cases. These values have come to mean peace making, the smoothing of turbulence and polite interpersonal interaction. Yet, as we have discovered in this chapter, such tactics can have a detrimental impact on organizational effectiveness and retard transformation efforts. It would be helpful therefore if a greater number of managers (and external advisors) were skilled in the purposeful induction and escalation of conflict.

Conflict escalation starts with leadership. Some leaders, especially those who are better suited to the tasks of transformation, demonstrate unpredictability (described in the Leadership Domain model in Chapter 3) and unpredictability is itself a form of conflict escalation – in any employee and at any level. In leaders, however, unpredictability is heavily leveraged by the real and symbolic power invested in them. Unpredictability is noticeable either in the consequences of such leaders' actions or in the actions themselves. Sears' Arthur Martinez, for example, questioned the unquestionable. The company's traditional notion of retailing through the famous Sears catalogue was thrown out. The assumption that retailing growth comes through more big stores was thrown out too. Building a retail model around brands, *à la* Disney, was in. Delivery of the brands through small outlets (that do not bear the Sears name) was in too. IBM's Lou Gerstner shocked executives by tearing up the long-established rules of how IBM executives behave. His often explosive style got attention and blew people out of deep ruts. Siemens Plessey's Clive Dolan was expected to behave as his predecessors had behaved. He did things differently.

But leaders could do more. And so could their managers. This section is an attempt to offer some guidelines for doing so.[1] I list four general guidelines and four specific interventions:

Guidelines
1. Learn to fight fairly.
2. Establish conflict protocol as normative behaviour.
3. Differentiate before you integrate.
4. Target 'comfortable' business units for conflict escalation.

Interventions
1. Build minority dissent within a majority position.
2. Implosion: accentuate likely risks and threats.
3. Perspective multiplication: build up multiple perspectives, especially where there is the danger of groupthink.
4. Victory or defeat: Raise the stakes to either/or alternatives.

---

[1] In elaborating the guidelines I must acknowledge the excellent scholarly work catalogued by Evert Van de Vliert (1997).

Guideline 1: Learn to Fight Fairly

In the course of organizational life, disputes and disagreements inevitably arise. The usual response of those involved is to take entrenched positions and for the conflict to become personalized and emotional, sometimes leading to disaffection or complete withdrawal from interaction. Few people in organizations, if any, will have escaped the experience of those meetings in which team discussions deteriorate into harsh disagreement and then mutual hostility, after which no business can be transacted. Recognizing that conflicts do occur and that, most of the time, it is better to avoid affective conflict, managers should learn to fight fairly, with dual overriding objectives: to progress the task-related business at hand and to sustain the relationship between those in dispute. To achieve this managers need to be able to explicitly communicate and implement rules for fair fights and either rise above the ensuing fray or bring in an outsider (from another department) to administer the rules. The rules, however, should *not* be aimed at de-escalating task-related conflict – a tempting proclivity whose consequences are undesirable.

What should the rules be? There are four main rules, but others might be relevant in the culture and context of different organizations. The rules are:

1. *No knock-out blows*: the objective is not to overcome or defeat those with opposing views.
2. *Reciprocity*: all the parties involved (disputing teams or individuals) must be regarded as equals and therefore be allowed to fire back. This is essential (but difficult to accomplish) when those in conflict are at different hierarchical (i.e. authority) levels.
3. *Honesty*: generalizations, bluffing and underhandedness will rapidly produce affective conflict and should be proscribed. Reliance on evidence and facts should be promoted.
4. *No ultimatums*: their effect is to polarize the parties involved and to halt task-related progress.

Guideline 2: Establish Conflict Protocol as Normative Behaviour

Armed with rules for fighting fairly in specific circumstances, an ambitious leader's next step would be to establish the same protocol more widely, embedding norms such as tolerance of diverse viewpoints, examination of opposing recommendations without reservation and an overriding framework of cooperation, even during frank and intense debate. Having the norm of overriding cooperation in place makes it plain to team members that it is in everyone's interests to collaborate, share and speak openly. Case in point: ABB's ongoing efforts to build and sustain a culture in which all 200 000 employees 'act together'. A crucial point here is to make a crystal-clear distinction between political manoeuvring and personal attacks (which lead to disaffection) and open, honest disagreement (which leads to task-related progress and higher-quality decisions).

These norms should be cultivated first in one-off events (strategy away-days), then built into the regularity of management life (executive committee meetings and so on) before adjusting the assessment, appraisal and reward systems of the organization to reinforce them. This sequence establishes the norms and legitimizes them through senior management action, then builds them into the reward structure of the rest of the organization.

Guideline 3: Differentiate Before You Integrate

The natural tendency of people is to move towards agreement if it is within sight or, if it is not and positions have become hostile, to adopt belligerent them-and-us postures that protect identity ('*they're* always wrong; *we* get our facts right; *they're* just being difficult'). People at work will tend under conditions of low-level tension or conflict to move fairly rapidly towards integration – i.e. early agreement – except, of course, that what passes for agreement often turns out to be misunderstanding or a poor decision. Why? Because rapid and premature closure excludes material facts, data and perspectives. In other words, integration is happening at too shallow a level – the level of polite agreement, if you like, that Reckitt & Colman's Vernon Sankey describes, agreement that masks genuine differences or misunderstandings.

The rule, therefore, is to get the sequence right. Express differences first, then proceed to integration and unified decision making. In other words, for it to be really effective conflict must be escalated and then mitigated. The real danger lies in unknowingly striving for integration ('Right, let's get this agreed and out the door!') before dissent or alternative perspectives have been aired. Naturally, the temptation to do this is strong, especially when a commitment to transformation releases a mainspring of time pressure. Inevitably, this postpones conflict to a less opportune moment (e.g. when those actions triggered by the rush to integration and decision making start to go wrong) or drives them underground to resurface in political manoeuvring, resistance or sabotage. A second danger lies in failing to move to integration, thereby prolonging the intensity of conflict for too long. The STP curve shows that this ends in individual or organizational paralysis.

Guideline 4: Target 'Comfortable' Business Units

Before Goran Lindahl was appointed CEO of ABB, one of his roles as a member of Percy Barnevik's executive team was to identify areas of the conglomerate where management had become complacent or too comfortable and go in to shake things up. In a sense this follows the counterintuitive aphorism: fix things when they ain't broke. In its largest possible manifestation, the action of merging with another organization or acquiring companies is the deliberate escalation of conflict. The Ciba and Sandoz 'merger of equals' to form Novartis in 1996 was chairman Alex Krauer's way of overcoming the 'complacency of success', as we shall see in Chapter 6.

Within an organization, tactics for shaking things up in this manner include:

- Moving managers or changing the composition of the business unit's top team
- Introducing urgency by elevating objectives or standards
- Creating competition between teams or business units
- Identifying contentious operational issues and ways of working before inviting the team to address them
- Bringing in consultants to uncover and highlight improvement actions.

Intervention 1: Build Minority Dissent Within a Majority
Position

Again, leaders often provide a spur to building minority dissent.
Some cases in point: Clive Dolan's invitation to Siemens Plessey
employees to challenge authority; Vernon Sankey's explicit
encouragement to challenge the *status quo* as an everyday part of
leadership behaviour in Reckitt & Colman. In a sense those who
elect to stand outside the consensus (despite the fact that we are
inclined to regard consensus as a good thing) are helping to
escalate conflict.

Nonconformity, disagreement and opposition are all escalative actions. They can, of course, be destructive. All conflict can.
What is important is that such actions occur or are encouraged
to occur at appropriate moments (for example, in the course of
moving towards a critical strategic decision) and are not prolonged to the detriment of organizational performance and
progress. One can visualize minority dissent as a gate or even
series of gates through which a piece of analysis or a decision
must pass (Figure 5.2). The likely decision outcomes, when
people are under normal social pressure to conform are likely to
be very different (and of lower quality) than if a position or
several positions of minority dissent are actively taken.

There are some examples in everyday practice. Team members sometimes decide to 'play devil's advocate' and, surely, this
is a useful tactic but it runs the danger, unless it is rigorous, of
merely providing a weak foil to justify already strongly held
convictions. In short, those playing devil's advocate must offer
powerful and challenging dissent. After all, the idea behind
minority dissent is to deliberately disrupt the otherwise smooth
flow of social–psychological interaction.

Those confronted with minority dissent tend to raise counter-
arguments and therefore are forced into consideration of wider
perspectives. Ultimately this procedure raises decision quality
and, owing to people's greater involvement in debate and
inquiry, contributes to enhanced commitment to outcomes or
decisions.

One danger is that those faced with dissent may, in the
absence of conflict escalation protocol or fair fight rules, already
feel committed to a particular decision path. Once hostility is
permitted to rear its ugly head, those in dissent may be sabo-
taged, attacked or shut out of the team. Minority dissent is

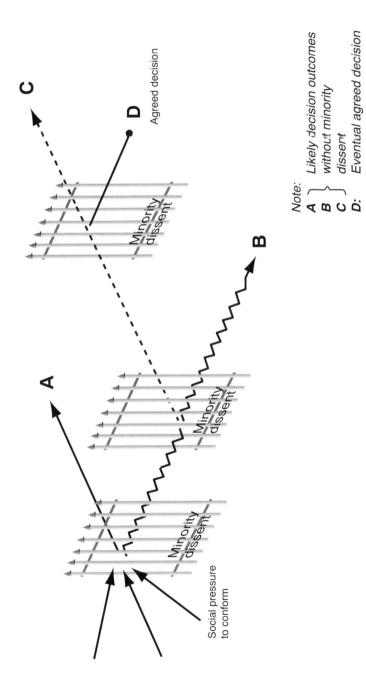

Figure 5.2 Minority dissent gates to counter rampant consensus.

Note:
A Likely decision outcomes
B without minority
C dissent
D: Eventual agreed decision

therefore best used where fair fight protocols are already established as norms or by those with the power or authority to ride out social pressure.

Intervention 2: Implosion

This tactic is most suitable in circumstances where workgroups are under pressure and generally feel exposed or threatened and there is the danger that more effort will be applied to managing the social image of the group and its members than the tasks it is faced with. These conditions occur when the group feel that they are unsuccessful or underperforming and there is a real or apparent threat to their existence – for example, the executive team of a business unit that knows it has been targeted for streamlining or outsourcing.

Implosion is a technique best used either by a clear-eyed team leader or an outsider to the team. The objective is to reduce underlying (but unexpressed) fears and feelings of threat, not by ignoring them or pushing them to the periphery nor by keeping them to oneself, as is usually the case under conditions of social identity maintenance, but by accentuating them. The same principle is at work, as any parent will know, when children are stricken with repetitive nightmares: encourage the child to talk about the nightmare. The fear expressed is the fear reduced. A problem aired is a problem shared. What can then follow is more balanced analysis and decision making on how to resolve or cope with the actual threats. Implosion works well one-to-one but its greatest power is in a social setting – workshops and the like – where the shared experience can be magnified. As in all cases where powerful emotions are at work, the skills of a good facilitator are never wasted.

Intervention 3: Perspective Multiplication

As above, where there is real or perceived threat and the danger of unthinking consensus or simply the frustration of fixed organizational thinking and practice, tactics to disturb the equilibrium and break the narrow pattern are advisable. Perspective multiplication does this by forcing consideration of all stakeholders' interests, objectives and positions, thereby raising debate and points of analysis. Cases in point: Arthur Martinez' invitation to Disney CEO Michael Eisner to speak at a Sears' management conference; Pierre Gravelle's actions to involve during transformation those parties (such as the Canadian Bar Association, industry groups and so on) beyond the bounds of Revenue Canada. Gravelle says:

> I started having round-table discussions with CEOs in the private sector and colleagues in the public sector who had experienced change. We spent the time talking about our respective experiences, what worked and what didn't. . . . At one conference I got a number of people from outside to address 250 of my managers to raise debate and consider external influences.

Intervention 4: Victory or Defeat as Stark Alternatives

When Jan Timmer became managing director of Philips in 1990, the business was in crisis. Its days of expansion and success from its formation in 1891 as a lamp factory had produced 65 000 patents and 10 000 inventions. But Jan Timmer was riding a slow dinosaur, its management and workforce long used to a paternalistic culture and blithely unaware of the changes happening in the outside world, its performance deteriorating and bankruptcy on the horizon. In spite of this, Timmer could see, incredibly, that the warning signs were being ignored. The classic conditions of groupthink and social identity maintenance had become entrenched. Timmer assembled Philips' top 100 managers at a three-day crisis scenario seminar. In dramatic fashion managers were shown the reality of Philips' dire performance and its grim prospects. How? By letting them see a mocked-up article in the *Financial Times* some two years in the future. The article reported Philips filing for Chapter 11 bankruptcy. During the course of an intense and highly emotional debate over the three days, managers were forced to confront the reality that drastic change was imperative. Timmer had successfully raised the level of conflict and refocused managers on the need to transform by presenting alternatives of victory or defeat. There could be no half-way compromise or middle course.

This anecdote demonstrates the power of deliberately raising the stakes around a particular issue. The individuals involved are then less able to retreat to the old context – in Philips' case a matter of muddling through on the assumption that the markets might turn and things might get better. Stark choices sharpen the focus, produce urgency and commitment to action. They also inflict cracks in the edifice of social identity maintenance and, as such, induce emotional reactions. This is no bad thing when groupthink and image maintenance are operating. A temporary escalation of affective conflict can drag the destructive emotional undercurrents to the surface where they can be resolved. However, highly skilled facilitation is crucial when escalating conflict by raising the stakes.

6
Awakening

CRISIS OR AMBITION?

When does big change start? When *should* it start? At Metallgesellschaft, the huge German metals and engineering group, big change was initially and publicly triggered when Deutsche and Dresdner banks (which owned 25% of the company) forced the resignation of most of the management board in December 1993. Confronted by a liquidity crisis, two weeks earlier Metall had called on the banks to stump up over $1 billion to cover cash payments on oil futures contracts in New York. There followed an agonizing January of negotiation and brinkmanship between some 140 creditors and shareholders during which the threat became very real of Metall having to file for the German equivalent of Chapter 11 bankruptcy and claim the dishonourable distinction of being the worst post-war German corporate failure. However, new chairman Kajo Neukirchen, with a reputation as a company doctor, succeeded in steering a safe course with his stricken ship out of the storm. Having secured a financial rescue package, he lost no time in embarking on the disposal of several subsidiaries and taking an axe to the 57 000 headcount. 'When a company is in such a bad state as Metallgesellschaft,' he said, 'there can only be a short-term and not a long-term time frame for job cuts.'

To all appearances, then, Metall's difficulties began with falling oil prices and the resultant impact on the company's hedging arrangements – in essence, Metall bought at the top of the market, then dumped its positions at the bottom. Massive losses were then inevitable. But, in truth, the conglomerate's troubles were much older than that. Overambitious expansion in the early 1990s and a failure to effectively deal with the German recession were the real causes. Indeed soon after his arrival

Neukirchen conceded that something like half of Metall's losses
stemmed from its German businesses. At Lurgi, now one of
Metall's largest subsidiaries, it was clear some time before the
conglomerate's collapse that its affairs would have to be put in
order. The bulk of its senior management, however were, like
those at Sears Roebuck before Arthur Martinez, long-serving
and inward-looking, unused to conflict and unwilling to take
tough action. Some attempts at examining the cost situation
were begun and lay-offs were mooted in the late summer of
1993. Then the crisis at Metallgesellschaft exploded. Chris von
Branconi, who joined Lurgi in 1992, explains:

> The order of magnitude of the transformation that was required in
> Metallgesellschaft in the first instance did not change because of the
> crisis. The underlying reasons for transformation already existed. What
> the financial collapse triggered was a huge impact on the pace and speed
> of actions that had to be implemented and our seriousness in going
> about those actions.

This is a good example of the Transformation S-curve or
trajectory delineated in Chapter 2. Metallgesellschaft, struggling
and overextended, left it too late to begin the big change it
needed. It was already over the top of the second curve and
heading down. The oil futures trading loss owing to bad luck or
management misjudgement (opinions are still divided) was
simply a tough blow that acted as a final, rude but late awakening. The S-curve implies that, in the optimum, executives need
to begin the awakening while an organization is still strong – in
finances, markets, products, culture – and thereby avoid the
difficulties of initiating big change while coping with the threat
or reality of crisis. That would be the ideal. For one reason or
another, of course, this infrequently happens. One major reason
is that managers and employees find it hard to endorse and act
upon change when the *current* need for change is less than
compelling. As Pierre Gravelle remarks, 'The bigger the threat,
the bolder the initiative and the solution, especially if there is a
survival imperative.' It is in the psychology of human beings to
respond this way. The distant threat on the horizon might as
well not exist. Nonetheless, it is also true that some leaders are
distinctive in their ability to do one of two things: either they
materialize the threat by raising the stakes in the manner
outlined in Chapter 5 (in effect, reaching into the future to drag
the threat close enough to cast its shadow upon employees) or

they ignore any threat and instead strive to elevate ambition. Both are hard to pull off. Both require exceptional leadership. But elevating ambition is the harder still.

ELEVATING AMBITION

Levi Strauss & Co., the $7 billion worldwide jeans clothing company started by a Bavarian immigrant to America at the time of the California gold rush, has tried transforming both ways – in crisis in 1984 and ten years later in the USA and through its international operations by raising ambition.

Some background first. From the 1950s through to the early 1980s sales of jeans were hard to hold back. Levi Strauss cranked them out as fast as possible. But the 1980s brought decline as tastes changed and the traditional jeans market began to dry up. Under pressure to arrest falling profits, executives leapt into diversification and introduced a swathe of different lines, but to little avail. On the contrary, as the company pursued each new fashion so its profits suffered. Cost cutting followed. Then, after Robert Haas became CEO in 1984, he and his new executive team responded to the crisis by taking bold action. They disposed of the speciality and fashion businesses, fired 15 000 staff, closed factories and reorganized around the core of the Levi's brand identity – making and selling jeans – with heavy focus on the classic 501s. Smart advertising, initially criticized by industry watchers as excessive (Levi's spent close to $40 million on the campaign), doubled 501s' sales through to 1990. New products based around the jeans core were introduced and, most significantly of all, Levi's developed and published its aspirations statement in 1987, emphasizing values of diversity, teamwork, trust, openness, ethics, recognition and empowerment. Like most organizations' value statements, this one produced deep yawns and little action. Nothing happened until training courses built around and aimed at instilling the values were introduced in 1989. Then, appraisal and compensation systems were installed to enforce the values.

Levi's value-driven culture is now famous in corporate mythology and the company claims that living these values has helped in the buy-in, support and actioning of decisions, even if the process is more time- and effort-intensive than in most Western organizations. It also generates enormous loyalty.

That loyalty was sorely tested when Haas and his team initiated the ambitious plan to transform Levi's supply chain in the USA. Typically, Levi's was hit-and-miss in its service to retailers, often making them wait for deliveries. As much as two months might pass before stores were able to restock empty shelves. The re-engineering project designed to put all this right – to wit, a $500 million expenditure on software, systems and automated distribution centres – unfortunately, got completely out of hand, its cost nearly doubled and the executive team was obliged, embarrassingly, to scale back its ambitions to transform the supply chain. On top of this, the company was forced in late 1996 to look carefully at its overhead cost position in the USA. A few months later Levi's announced that it would taking out some 1000 jobs and trimming $80 million from overhead, and in November 1997 revealed that it would have to axe a further 6400 jobs in North America.

The situation was different in its international units. After 1985 Robert Haas began to see opportunities in making something out of the poorly organized, unprofitable international businesses which in the early crisis had been bleeding and under consideration for disposal. Instead, Levi's executives evolved a strategy identical to ABB – 'think globally, act locally'. So while Levi's US growth saw a respectable but unspectacular 6% per annum, its foreign businesses leapfrogged along at nearer 32% and contributed more than a third of revenues and two-thirds of total profit.

The European operation, which moved some 55 million units and booked around $1.5 billion of Levi's total $7 billion revenue in 1996, showed consistent growth in sales and profits for eight years. Profits were above the industry norms. There was no crisis pushing the company to change, although some threats could be discerned in the level and aggression of competitors and the fact that, just like in the USA, retailers were frustrated by the service levels provided by the company. Some basic re-engineering of one or two processes would have fixed the position. Levi's, however, launched a transformation, tackling six out of seven processes across eighteen countries and twenty production sites, changing most of its major systems and reorganizing jobs. This huge effort was aimed at establishing Levi's as the supplier of choice with its retailers through quality of service, providing a range of products superior to its competitors and securing competitive edge by powerful branding.

Another case of transformation on the wings of ambition, as it were, rather than the rack of crisis, is Novartis, the $29 billion Swiss life sciences company. On 7 March 1996 Dr Alex Krauer, chairman of Ciba, and Dr Marc Moret, chairman of Sandoz, announced their decision to merge the two companies in what they described as a merger of equals – former Sandoz shareholders taking 55% and Ciba shareholders 45% of the new Novartis. Once the approval of the European Commission and the US Federal Trade Commission had been secured, Novartis began trading in December 1996.

Both Sandoz and Ciba were world-class companies but the executive teams at the two were looking ahead at the accelerated consolidation of their traditional business environment. Healthcare, once provider-oriented, was becoming increasingly customer- and regulator-driven because of countries' reforms in healthcare delivery and expense control. At the same time, demand was increasing rapidly from an ageing population in the industrialized nations. The companies were likely to face higher risks as stringent cost-control measures in many national markets made the search for pharmaceutical innovation more expensive and its rewards less attractive. Similar changes were true of the agribusiness in crop protection and seeds products, particularly for the market entry of genetically engineered products, regarded with scepticism if not outright hostility in some European quarters. In short, the success factors of the past would soon cease to guarantee prosperity in the future. For Sandoz and Ciba, to be good was no longer good enough.

The idea of the merger, to combine two already strong players to ensure a place among the top performers, was farsighted but risky. The usual questions arose: why change, why now, why a merger? On the surface those questions were straightforward to answer. Sensible arguments could be advanced. But, as we have already seen, people will not change solely on the basis of rational persuasion. Despite these risks Krauer and Moret were convinced that the merger was the right course. As it turned out, the immediate realization of benefits was excellent. Following the merger, Novartis was ranked number one by industry in the 1997 *Fortune* Global 500, its crop chemicals business dwarfing any of its competitors. But Krauer had a secondary purpose, as he reveals:

> Success is the biggest enemy. Success leads to complacency. Successful organizations need from time to time a revolution – leaving to one side

the need to respond to industry consolidation. Without the dramatic impact of the merger, the window of opportunity for taking actions that were overdue in both companies would never have happened. You can therefore turn destabilization into an advantage. . . .

So, two lessons here. First, a merger escalates conflict – on a grand scale. If handled right, quite apart from the obvious benefits of size, economies of scale and market leverage, it also brings all the benefits accruing from conflict escalation discussed in Chapter 5 – i.e. transformation as opposed to stasis or paralysis. Indeed, Alex Krauer talks explicitly about actively 'exploiting the instability'. Second, and of major interest in our discussions at this juncture, the transformation of the organization is one built on aspiration. Under this rubric, two further points are worth noting.

First, awakening must start when the organization is still strong, even if, as in the Levi Strauss case, ambition turns round and bites you. The costs, in financial performance, market positioning, staff morale and capacity to defend against competitors and predators are much higher and can be fatal if executives wake up too late or recoil from ambition. However, since crisis is by far the most common circumstance to trigger big change we must examine in this chapter examples of awakening in both contextual settings – positions of crisis and strength.

Second, the actions that executives must take during the first transition line to ensure the awakening of the organization are not confined to the initial phase of transformation. Awakening is a transition that carries on over the span of transformation, graphically represented by the sigmoid curve. Clearly, however, there are phases during the transformation where the actions of awakening are more important or occur at higher frequency – for example, in assembling the right executive team or in conceiving and communicating the future vision. Action List 4 sets out the details.

Action List 4   Awakening

1. Raise the stakes: to trigger sufficient motive force for big change in the organization, accentuate a crisis or elevate ambition.
2. Do the groundwork well: assess the need and potential for change; do not be tempted to rush in where angels fear to tread.

3. Create a watershed or turning point: symbolic actions and events are more important than all the strategizing and analysis put together in getting the whole management team on board and committing them at the intellectual and visceral level.
4. Alert managers and employees and then sustain the message of change.

RAISING THE STAKES

During the course of his rapid ascent of the corporate ladder at British Airways, Bob Ayling came to the conclusion that BA could not sustain its performance as one of the most successful airlines in the world by resting on its laurels. Its harsh survival plan in the early 1980s had ensured that it could shift its vision and strategy towards becoming one of the world's leading airlines. Three tactical changes helped build a platform for its globalization strategy: (1) its early productivity improvements (it slashed costs by an annual $500 million), (2) the shift in corporate image to fashion BA as a respected brand and (3) its sharpened focus on staff attention to customer service. Colin Marshall, then CEO, took BA into alliances and franchises with USAir, Quantas, Air Russia, and Deutsche BA to realize his global plans.

Bob Ayling was appointed CEO in January 1996 and hit the ground running. He at once reshuffled the executive team, reducing his top management reports from 25 to 11, chiefly to streamline decision making, and instigated a programme called *Leadership 2000*, intended to get rid of the meetings culture so prevalent at BA and one that he feared was diffusing responsibility. He also acted on his view that even though competitive threats were some way off, BA had reached a plateau, that managers and staff were in danger of becoming complacent – after all, BA was the world's most profitable airline. He recognized that the culture of BA was one in which managers and staff were at their best in a crisis and therefore, when conditions were highly favourable the opposite might hold true. And so, at a time when most observers would least expect it and staff would not be easy to convince, Ayling launched a second transformation of the company. The details are covered in Chapter 4, but the essentials are:

- An extension of the globalization strategy
- Implementation of a Business Efficiency Plan to strip out over $1.5 billion in operating costs over three years
- A shift in the mix of employees, taking on higher-skilled employees to replace low-skilled jobs, and placing increasing emphasis on foreign languages
- A $100 million rebranding of the airline to better appeal to its broad international customer base.

The awakening was therefore both dramatic and rude. Ayling was saying to managers and staff that BA had become complacent and that there was more to play for. He was open with staff, letting them know the challenges ahead and foreshadowing the change he would expect of them and, in doing so, spoke directly to many staff in presentations as well as using broadcasts beamed to staff worldwide twice a day.

The central messages of transformation Ayling had conveyed to staff in the awakening of the organization over the course of his first 18 months in the job culminated in the announcement of BA's new mission 'to be the undisputed leader in world travel', timed to coincide with the unveiling of the airline's colourful new brand images. Reaction to Ayling's ambitions was hardly one of universal excitement and support. Although one of the straplines used in BA's corporate communications was 'the dawning of a new era', investors seemed to prefer the last era. Many were hostile to the new image make-over, remaining unconvinced by chairman Sir Colin Marshall's assertion that the bright new livery had been acclaimed in overseas markets. Bob Ayling himself was heckled by shareholders at BA's annual general meeting. A few months later, even Margaret Thatcher, Britain's transformational leader of the 1980s and now bearing the title Baroness Thatcher, entered the fray. She berated BA executives at a commercial exhibition and, criticizing the firm for dropping the British flag from its corporate image, placed a tissue over the new tail design of a Boeing 747 model on display. The media had a field day. And this was on top of an ugly three-day strike in July 1997, precipitated by Bob Ayling's pursuit of productivity gains – in particular his tough line on cabin crew to hammer through new working conditions which would do away with overtime and other perquisites. More than two-thirds of the airline's flights out of London were grounded. BA lost some $200 million. Suspicions abounded that the dispute was actually about union busting which, of course, Bob Ayling denied, even though BA managers had been talking seriously about the need to reduce wage costs and the likely fall-out for more than a year before the strike. Another consequence of the heavy-handed tactics with staff was that morale fell sharply and an element of trust between managers and staff, forged in the shared sacrifices of the 1980s battle to survive and prosper, died. (Figure 6.1 shows in graphic form the timing and some major steps in the two transformations of BA.)

Bob Ayling's analysis of BA's strategic position and the need to lead a second revolution was basically correct. He took action to raise the stakes by identifying and communicating a new vision, revamping BA's brand to stretch its appeal internationally and facing down the unions to show he was serious about cost reduction: this too was correct. The media judged him critically and sometimes harshly during this period (his first 18 months in the job, in fact). He was accused of bully-boy tactics and being a control freak. Despite his boyish good looks and smiles, many managers and staff found him somewhat cold and mechanical, probably because he suffered by comparison with the inspirational charisma of his predecessor Colin Marshall, himself somewhat remote.

Awakening escalates conflict. Whether it is built on crisis or elevated ambition, it is therefore personally and organizationally difficult for all the reasons given above and because it is necessary to *keep* raising the stakes before the company begins the slide down the second part of the S-curve. Ad Scheepbouwer of $4 billion PTT Post describes this process over the course of the organization's transformation since 1988:

> We wanted to make challenges appealing to people in the whole company. The first challenge was to make a postal company that was profitable, which at the time would be the only one in Europe. Then it was to make it more profitable than our sister organization PTT Telecom. After that it was really to succeed in an international expansion.

Scheepbouwer and his team foresaw that, with accelerating deregulation of postal services after the year 2000, only a small number of companies would provide Europe's postal services. They wanted PTT Post to be the front-runner. To do this,

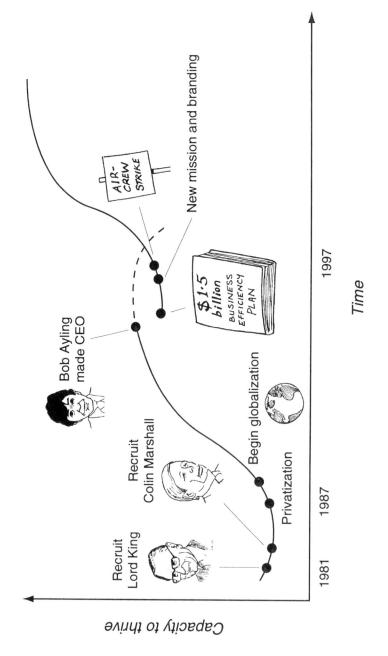

Figure 6.1 British Airways' transformation S-curve.

however, the message both internally and to the market was one of fast growth – both organic and acquisitive – and heavy emphasis on quality, providing an edge by being excellent in logistics and distribution. The additional factor of global interconnectedness (discussed at length in Chapter 1) has not escaped Scheepbouwer's attention. In October 1996 PTT bought $2.2 billion Australian international transport operator TNT/ GDEW as well as a clutch of European distribution outfits across Germany, Austria, Denmark and Belgium. The company's foreign acquisitions had two aims: first, improving the ratio of PTT Post's sales in growth markets and in mature markets and, second, securing a firmer grip on the quality of its cross-border services so that, in effect, it controls end-to-end quality of services both in Europe and elsewhere, most notably Australia, Japan and the fast-emerging Asian economies such as South Korea, the Philippines, Indonesia, Malaysia, Singapore, India and China.

So Scheepbouwer will continue to raise the stakes because he understands the alternative. 'We were privatized in 1989,' he says, 'in the slipstream of Telecom and at that time we were turning over billions and hardly making any money! We aimed to make a reasonable return and to internationalize. That's been achieved. Now we're making a lot of money on our postal business, we've internationalized to 200 countries and we run a world-wide business. But if you want to succeed as an organization you have to go for growth or you end up with no other alternative but organizing and reorganizing yourself silly.'

In short, it is not enough either to drift on, enjoying current success as Ciba and Sandoz might have done, or simply stand still, hoping for salvation from aggressive cost cutting. Awakening is a transition in which the possible futures open to the organization must be explored and executives must raise the stakes, especially when they know this means awakening the powerful demons of conflict.

DOING THE GROUNDWORK

There is a great temptation to get cracking. Transformational leaders are an impatient breed. They want results. More impatient yet are institutional shareholders and increasingly they are vociferous in their criticism and unrelenting in their pressure on corporate boards to recognize, identify and resolve management and organizational difficulties fast. During the mid-1990s the revolving-door CEO arrived on the scene. Robert Stempel survived just over two years at General Motors. Gil Amelio, brought in to transform Apple Computer Inc. was considered a failure after less than a year and a half. John Walter was president of AT&T for eight months. Industry observers, analysts and customers are often impatient too: they create pressure of different sorts. Moreover, there is no doubt that being late to market, especially with new products, can diminish the eventual overall profitability of such products.

So pressure to move quickly comes from all sides. At the outset of transformation, however, this pressure can be dangerous and distracting. A basic rule of transformation runs as follows: *if there is a financial crisis in the organization, fix it fast; once that is done, prepare carefully.* Fixing the crisis creates financial headroom for the organization and the psychological space to contemplate radical change. Starting transformation when the organization is expending all its energy in the agonies of downsizing will mean that executives run the risk of prematurely settling on an ill-thought-out future instead of considering the full range of futures that are possible – including failure. It is equally likely that rushing will lead to unforeseen errors and therefore early programme defeats, thereby further reinforcing learned helplessness. By contrast, the aims of careful groundwork are fourfold:

1. To identify the main drivers of change (e.g. deregulation, competitive threat, financial crisis, complacency)
2. To consider a number of possible futures for the organization, including failure
3. To assess the need for change (what has to be done)
4. To establish the potential for change (the capability of the organization to innovate, manage the risks and transform at the right pace).

British Airways, for example, might have thought itself somewhat immune to challenge. Its enviable reputation for service, its ongoing focus on innovation and efficiency and the fact that it carried more international passengers than any other airline had placed it a long way ahead of most rivals. Its ongoing strategic groundwork, however, was like cold water splashed in Bob Ayling's beaming face. BA strategists reckoned that the industry's rising costs and the fierce pressure from competition that was driving down revenue per passenger would push the company into loss within five years. This did not necessarily mean that cost cutting was the only option, but it was certainly high on the agenda and formed the basis of Bob Ayling's Business Efficiency Plan to rip $1.5 billion out of overhead. However, he refused to believe that BA would be forced into the desperate commoditization battle. It had proved that it could ask customers to pay more for innovations such as arrivals lounges (showers and so on), or in Club (business class) a wide variety of entertainment and 'raid the larder' options for hungry business travellers and, in First Class, the amazing reconfigurable seat that formed a bed or a dining area for passenger and visiting companion. Differentiating on service was therefore desirable and possible. Clarity in this analysis was very important before steaming ahead with the transformation.

Dr Alex Krauer makes the same point about the Ciba and Sandoz merger to form Novartis. 'We had to be very clear,' he says, 'about our objectives before we started to negotiate the deal. Four questions had to be answered: What was our purpose? Was it the right partner? Was the timing right? Were the risks manageable? It was also important that our prospective merger partner – Sandoz – had come to the same conclusions. It would have been a disaster if the analysis we did beforehand hadn't been done well.' In addition to understanding the environmental context that was driving change (set out in the first section of this chapter) key considerations in Krauer's team's analysis, therefore, were about future cost savings the merger might generate and, most critically for organizations in the pharmaceuticals industry, what additional potential for innovation could be injected, both in new products and in packaging and service. For example, the early groundwork pointed to the potential for investment in research and development of around $2 billion, with over 80% going towards healthcare research – at the time the largest budget in the healthcare industry. This would have profound implications for increasing the range of research that could be conducted, the speed with which promising new products could be brought to market and the probability, with pooled resources, of developing more of the so-called block-buster products with potential sales above $500 million a year.

Duncan White of ScottishPower concurs. 'Very early on, pre-flotation,' he recalls, 'Ian Preston [then CEO] and I were working very hard on this with support from other directors. When we put the business in context, this was a single-product company. There were no customers – they were consumers. We were concerned with engineering excellence and keeping the lights on at all costs. The workforce was heavily unionized. There was no competition and we were subject to government policy on investment and prices. Privatization was going to change all that. But while we went through the mechanisms of privatization, the real work was to decide which way we wanted to go.'

Privatization, therefore, was the main driver of change. But what would the organization and the change actually look like? En route to gaining a thorough understanding of this, the executives drew up a map of the change. This portrayed their current position and the desired outcome of change:

Current	Desired
Engineering orientation	Commercial orientation
Diffused responsibility	Ownership and accountability
Oriented to maintain supply	Customer service orientation
Large and centralized	Lean and decentralized
Risk averse	Entrepreneurial attitudes
Electricity only	Broader utility base

Understanding the gap helped the executives to begin to identify what was already in place that would enable them to change and those things they had to get right. A few examples will illustrate this.

Example 1: Entrepreneurial Attitudes

In order to succeed both in transforming the company and surviving as a commercial enterprise ScottishPower would have to be able to draw on entrepreneurial thinking, take risks and expand its conception of business from engineering excellence to an emphasis on shareholder value, earnings, profit and cash. This would require recruitment from outside to significantly raise the commercial skill level of top management. The impact of this eventually was that 17 of the top 20 executives were recruited not only from outside the organization but from outside the industry.

Example 2: Commercial Orientation

The heavily unionized environment and out-of-date working practices were also identified as things that would have to change. A human resource strategy that facilitated greater flexibility in bargaining and setting terms and conditions would be needed. In due course, during the early stages of trans-formation, ScottishPower moved from national bargaining to divisional bargaining, instituted pay freezes and in some cases 30% wage cuts.

Example 3: Customer Service Orientation

Customer service, cost, safety and other standards of perform-ance were either not in place or were geared primarily to maintaining supply. Understanding what these standards should be therefore meant ScottishPower would have to bench-mark against other organizations. As a result, the company started benchmarking against local and American utilities and then, raising their ambition, extended this to companies admired for the highest standards in particular types of activity, such as Federal Express and British Airways.

Example 4: Ownership and Accountability

As a government organization responsibility and accountability were diffused, first across the industry and second across discrete functions, with a strong tendency to centralize and to escalate decisions. A long series of supervisors and managers was signing off decisions or procurements, adding no value and slowing operations. Layers would have to be cut. Responsibility and accountability would have to be driven out through a new decentralized structure and down the layers of organization. The eventual actions: the central service group was rationalized; the original 400 staff was slimmed to 100; the organization was reconfigured into decentralized business units.

This kind of assessment of change needs and change potential provides the basis for the second transition line – detailed vision and strategy (covered in the next chapter). It is also useful to boost the analysis by doing some early benchmarking to establish whether the initial map of the desired organization is sufficiently stretched to create competitive advantage. The caution here is that there are no static benchmarks; you need to take account of the movement of competitors. They too will be stretching their aspirations.

Beginnings . . . and Ends

There must be a beginning of any great matter, but the continuing unto the end, until it be thoroughly finished, yields the true glory.

Sir Francis Drake

CREATING A WATERSHED OR TURNING POINT

In the USA the top six brewers in the beer market together take approximately 93% of the share. North of the border there are only two real players in the Canadian beer market, controlling 90% between them. Molson is number one with just over 46%, closely followed by Labatt with just under 44%. Being in a two-horse race makes for a high level of discomfort: whoever comes second is last. That has implications for acceptance of brands internationally. Being the leader in your home market helps sell brands overseas. Also, in a volume business like brewing profitable growth cannot come from simply cutting costs. It has to come from growing the volume. In the Canadian market there is no growth, so your own volume growth has to come from your competitor. When Molson were reviewing their performance and strategy in the Canadian market one of the most compelling pieces of information, both factually and symbolically, was a chart showing the trend in their perform-ance against Labatt. If the trend continued over the next two years, the chart showed Molson dropping to the number-two slot. The chart was widely disseminated within the management of Molson and its partners, the Australian brewing group Foster's and the US company Miller. 'That one chart was a huge motivator,' relates Molson's Michael Smith. 'It was clear that if we couldn't turn things round before 1998 there would be a whole different group of people doing our jobs.'

Moments or experiences like this are central features of big change. They are symbolic turning points. They signal a shift. They stir people from workaday grind, raise fears and elevate ambitions. They are as necessary for the alignment of the executive team around change as they are for motivating and carrying the commitment of the workforce. They are a watershed: they demarcate a change in direction, past from present, present from future. Almost without exception they are moments of conflict escalation, where old meets new, intellects clash and emotions are shaken. Without watershed events, big change will falter or never start.

At times, such events are thrust upon organizations, in spite of vigilance. Otis, the worldwide elevator company owned by United Technologies Corporation, had, during the 1990s, been driving hard to improve productivity, to ensure faster production, to push up sales per employee and to generally compete more effectively. Likewise, executives were moving the organization to a global footing – for example, no longer would there be American, German or Malaysian products; they would be produced to exactly the same design wherever the factory, although customer service and after-sales support would be localized (elevators require up to 50 years of after-sales service). There was a sense in the organization that they were getting on top of change. Jurgen Reuning, head of Otis Germany, describes what happened:

> We did feel that there were no innovations left to make to elevators. We know a lot about making elevators and we've been doing it a long time. But suddenly we discovered that two of our competitors had come up with brand-new design innovations. You could say we were caught with our pants down!

The shock of this discovery kicked Otis into action on another front. They realized that, just as they had created a quantum jump in quality and productivity, they needed to achieve the same in innovation. They needed to extend their benchmarking beyond elevators and more widely within the metals industry to learn new engineering lessons. They knew they had to push through team-based working on a broader front to begin to attain systemic innovation.

To achieve transformation, the watershed must be dramatic and have immediate impact and consequences, especially when a leader is appointed from outside the business unit or the organization. DERA's John Chisholm uses a nautical analogy: 'You've got to swing the rudder hard over when you arrive. You've got to establish the culture that things will happen. It's about the psychology of change. Most large organizations don't change because the psychology is that's it's not possible. Actually, it's always possible. You've just got to change that psychology.'

Chisholm spent several weeks, both prior to and after his appointment as CEO, talking to senior managers and rapidly building a model of what the transformed DERA would look like, complete with financial projections and costs. During the first two weeks after joining he also made decisions on who among the top managers he believed would be able to con-tribute to the transformation – and therefore who would have to go. Two weeks after starting, on Friday the 13th Chisholm called together the top 70 managers and began his presentation with a sketch of a mad axeman. He then covered the new business model and vision for the organization. Going only this far, however, was not enough. He wanted to be 'deliberately dramatic' and to demonstrate that the change was already underway. Accordingly he announced who among the 70 managers present would be part of the new team and therefore who would be leaving the organization. It was about half. What was the reaction? Chisholm is blunt:

> Obviously it was a shock. But there was a tremendous buzz of excite-ment. They'd been living with this purported change about to happen. All my experience as a manager is that you don't need to tell the people involved that they need to change. They know that better than you do. They'd been living with the illogic of what they were doing for years. Although they feared change, they felt that at least something was happening and there was coherence of direction.

At Siemens Plessey, a similar watershed event was the trigger for real change to begin in the company. Managing director Clive Dolan had tried to kick-start big change in the company on two earlier occasions – without success. 'The sum total of all our efforts,' he says, 'was producing diminishing margins and a growing frustration among the workforce.' Any successes that they did have were mainly due to the strength of an individual project manager who was typically working against the system. Some managers were bold enough to initiate change themselves within their own business units. Even though Dolan encouraged and legitimized their efforts, the force for change was not achieving critical mass. 'Somebody, somewhere,' he says, 'would get in the way and obstruct the things they wanted to do.'

As a result of these frustrations, Dolan began to form a vision of what Siemens Plessey needed to look like. 'While I didn't want to destroy the organization,' he recalls, 'in the sense that it was still capable of providing the skills we needed, I had to find a means to break the power over the way in which we did work and met project goals.' He began to share this incipient vision with his fellow directors, debating how he thought the company should change towards a greater focus on projects and common ownership of individual projects. There was apparent agreement among the directors. They even agreed to Dolan's plan to call this new way of working *Project Focus*. Dolan said to his team, 'Right, this is how it's going to be then. Let's make it happen.' After a few months it was as bad as it had been before.

To get things moving again, Dolan realized that the executive team would have to spend more time together to get to grips with his vision of how the company should operate in the future and to decide on the means to get there. They took three days together off-site to get their thoughts straight – the ostensible purpose being to hammer out a framework to turn the still somewhat hazy vision into reality. They achieved this, but something more important happened. Dolan remembers the moment:

> We bared our separate agendas to each other. We got to know each other considerably better and collectively determined that we would take the company forward. . . . This was our watershed. We held the event at a place called Tilney Hall and ever since then my people talk about the Tilney Hall Agreement.

In short, the Tilney Hall Agreement in November 1994 was a turning point for Siemens Plessey, that allowed the key people to buy into the change and on which they looked back as *the* identifiable moment of conversion. It was at this time that the directors reached a collective commitment to fundamentally change the company.

Why is the symbolism of the turning point or watershed important? There are four reasons which, together, I call the *Failure of Predictability*.

1. Inability or refusal of executives to think outside the box.
2. Exclusive reliance on incremental strategic planning.
3. Preference among executives for personal and organizational predictability – habit, certainty and the plan become all-consuming.
4. Tendency to become complacent and comfortable, to sit still for too long.

The symbolic turning point reverses these failures, the first of which is the *inability or refusal of executives to think outside the box* – as happened with Sears Roebuck and IBM. The experiences of executives narrow over time because their exposure to other ways of viewing the world is systematically curtailed by being insulated (people tell their bosses what they think they want to hear) or by spending almost all their time in other executives' company. Worse still, the internal knowledge circuitry of the organization, with all its filters and processors, can irretrievably distort the picture executives receive – witness Microsoft's early blindness to the Internet.

Second, most organizations have become entirely *reliant on incremental strategic planning*, a process more tactical than strategic and failing, as Hamel and Prahalad have long argued, to prompt the deeper debates of what and how and why about an organization's future. Executives thus suffer from what we might call strategic closure: to them the decisions they must take are merely to do with how to operate in the world as it is – fixed industry, unchanging markets, the same business rules. They are unable to envisage possibilities.

The third failure is quite simply an executive's *preference for personal and organizational predictability*. It is hard to live with uncertainty. Life is much easier when we can see what is coming, when we can plan and we have time to react. It is a truism that people rapidly establish and maintain habits – the same ways of doing things, from those as simple as the way they drive a car to those as complex as strategy formulation. The fact is that there are very few people in corporate life who do not have a preference for personal and organizational predictability.

Finally, executives may just get too *comfortable and complacent* for no other reason than that their personal and corporate world seems secure and enjoyable. There is no compelling reason to question or to change it.

Predictability therefore is an enemy of transformation. That is why the capacity of business leaders to do the unpredictable is so important. The watershed is the kick in the pants, the personal jolt to executives, and it cannot be these things unless it has dramatic and symbolic power, acting at both the intellectual and the emotional level. The objectives of the watershed therefore are to:

- Deliver a personal jolt to executives
- Demonstrate that existing thought and behavioural patterns are unsustainable
- Define the personal and organizational consequences of failing to transform the business
- Build a common understanding among executives and other stakeholders (e.g. non-executive or external directors) of the need to change
- Confirm the CEO and other executives' personal stake in the change.

Many of these objectives can only be attained through conflict-escalation interventions. These are necessary to unfreeze fixed thinking and behaviour, release creativity, bring into the open opposing views and positions and expose executives to the psychology of possibilities. Consequently, no amount of analysis of strategic *content* alone will begin the process of awakening. This restricts change efforts to surface levels, to the logical, technical and rational overlay of transformation. It ignores the underground work – the emotional, the symbolic, the unacknowledged and the unpredictable. As Vernon Sankey says of his own learning from the global transformation of Reckitt & Colman:

> Dramatic action made the difference, signalling that this was not just a series of words but that we actually meant business. The symbolism and the signals were terribly important – are always important. Anybody can do slogans. It's not difficult to do slogans. But to change slogans into reality requires dramatic action.

ALERTING MANAGERS AND EMPLOYEES

The trouble with efforts to awaken the organization is that the messages of big change – which are longer term, organization-wide, and out of the ordinary – are totally unconnected from the everyday, short-term nitty-gritty of organizational life. Consequently, the ardent preaching of executives about transformation, survival, costs, competition, and shareholder value can immediately seem both insensitive to what is happening on the ground and out of touch with the shifting demands faced by the vast majority of employees. At worst, it can seem irrelevant. What is a priority for a large number of staff (e.g. hitting sales targets for this quarter) may override any messages of change that fall from on high.

When Molson Breweries kicked off their big change efforts across Canada, new CEO John Barnett started doing what all CEOs believe they should – getting up in front of people to communicate the big messages of change. 'We started,' confesses vice-president Michael Smith, 'with a lot of broad general messages because we thought it was really important for employees to understand the overall context of the company and the business strategy. So we wanted John Barnett to be in front of people. We wanted him to be articulating his views of the future. But what we have learned is that what is more important for the employees is the relationship between them and their individual boss.'

It became clear that hearing John Barnett talk about the future of the company was important *only insofar as it set a broad context for other communication actions*. The expectation of employees was that executives would take the vision and strategy and translate what it means for employees through the medium of their immediate bosses. Thus, the consistency of message between CEO and more junior managers was important – but the messenger was the key. Employees wanted to be convinced by their supervisor, the person they know best. This was the person with whom they have a relationship, with whom there is a level of ongoing interaction and at least a reasonable degree of trust – all the ingredients that facilitate not only understanding of the intellectual content of the message but also an emotional buy-in to its consequences. A CEO and the executive team can never enjoy this with the mass of the workforce. In a well-argued piece in the *Harvard Business*

Review of May–June 1996, T. J. Larkin and Sandar Larkin reinforce this point: 'Spend 80% of your communication time, money, and effort on supervisors,' they affirm. 'That is a radical recommendation. The traditional approach is to launch change from the top and hope that communication about the change will open like a parachute, blanketing everyone evenly. But frontline supervisors – not senior managers – are the opinion leaders in your organization. Because frontline supervisors greatly influence the attitudes and behaviors of others, they are critical to the success of any change effort' (p.102). As Michael Smith and his colleagues at Molson learned, 'what employees hear from their individual boss is more important to them than what the CEO says. Having him articulate his views of the future was important. I'm not saying you don't need to do it, but the relative emphasis needs to be much more on the relation between each of us and our boss.'

The Larkin recommendations on communicating change are straightforward but powerful:

1. When communicating major change to employees, keep it simple and avoid mission statements and management proclamations – most important, give them the facts; be straight.
2. Introduce the planned change face to face, not through videos, publications or vast, impersonal public meetings.
3. Target supervisors: get senior managers who are involved in the change to brief small groups of supervisors face to face.
4. Do the briefing in two rounds – first, to explain the change and get supervisors' reactions and recommendations, second, to explain any modifications of the planned change based on the supervisors' feedback.

In this way, supervisors are accorded greater power, status and influence by being involved in the change. Moreover, in line with my points in Chapter 4, you create the expectation that supervisors are already on-side (rather than being treated as cynics and antagonists). Added to this, by avoiding mission statements you avoid aggravating scepticism. The same is true, as we discussed in the previous chapter, when it comes to inspirational pieces by the CEO and other executives which attempt to embed new corporate values at a time of turmoil and negative emotion. This is wasted effort. New values are best nurtured on the back of the reality of organizational success and not its promise.

While awakening is happening, managers and employees are likely to be feeling battered and confused, dragged one way by tradition and the oppressive demands of business as usual and pushed the other by an executive team's bright-eyed contemplation of new horizons or brutal determination to make changes. Pierre Gravelle of Symcor relives some of these moments during the awakening at Revenue Canada:

> For a period of a year and a half I brought managers together from across the organization in three-day intensive sessions. I wanted them to be sensitized to the new reality. We did a lot of navel-gazing and staring at a white-board. . . . This was painstaking. It was agony for many managers, because they had lived in a certain mode for fifteen, twenty, thirty years, some of them. So it was gut-wrenching for them to have to confront a new reality, to say to themselves, 'Hey, from now on we behave quite differently.'

Gravelle recalls that he and his senior managers held interminable meetings with employees at local offices across the country. Their key objective was not only to deliver the same messages all the time but also to 'get employees to shift from being passive listeners to active participants', in Gravelle's words. Therefore, they requested advice and feedback, sought out contributions, and asked for people to take on responsibility for particular aspects of the change programmes. The same was true of working closely with the five unions involved at Revenue Canada. Gravelle and his team's efforts were all the more impressive given that the government of Canada decided to freeze wages at the time, holding them static for six long years.

Although Alex Krauer and his executive team were only nine months into the creation of Novartis at the time of writing, they too understood the need not only to communicate during the early days of the merger but also to sustain the message over time. At the outset they set themselves three years to implement the merger but accepted that rumours and gossip would proliferate at times during that period and that the best antidote was to make sure that they 'overcommunicated', setting the proper expectations by telling the truth, factually and consistently, emphasizing the *why* before the *how* and the *what*. Of course, not only did rumour and gossip start but from the first moment that news of the likely merger came out, dozens of arguments were advanced from all quarters about why the merger would be impossible, why it would fail, how it could not be in the best interests of either company and so forth. Such arguments are not always easy to refute and under what can become the overwhelming onslaught of hostile stakeholders, it is very easy to be blown off-course. There are dangers of this kind at the start and throughout big change. Krauer, a tall, serious Swiss, smiles as he comments, 'You have to be cautious not to make compromises or get carried away on account of the reaction. Sometimes it amazes me that it is necessary to keep repeating the same messages, to keep preaching time and time again. Even when you yourself are sick of hearing it, you have to say it all again.'

That is why transformation efforts require more than just ongoing communication. Because the task is so big and usually extends over years, the transition line embodied in awakening runs throughout transformation and is concerned not only with delivering messages (as we typically think of corporate communication) but also with building receptivity to change and the capability to tackle change. For example, Otis launched a series of what they called *Change Seminars* in their European business to sensitize managers to the challenges confronting the organization and to get them asking questions such as 'Why change? What should we change? How should we change?'

7

Conceiving the Future

WHEN YOUR ENEMIES ARE YOUR ALLIES

Bank of Montreal, Royal Bank and the Toronto Dominion are fierce competitors in the Canadian retail banking market. In the mid-1990s the three banks had all realized that, with declining volumes of paper transactions and escalating unit costs, there was a need to make changes that would enable them to stay competitive and maintain productivity. Between them, the three banks were handling about 50% of the bank processing work in Canada, which amounted to some 170 million cheques as well as 18 million statements, 96 million pages of reports, 9 million credit card sales drafts and 4 million remittances – every month. Separately but simultaneously, the banks were searching for solutions to lower the overhead cost they were carrying while improving customer service – a difficult trick. Outsourcing was a solution that was attractive and trendy but meant walking away from previous substantial investments in people and technology. In essence it meant asking someone else to fix their problems. An alternative was co-sourcing. This would mean creating a joint venture with one or a number of banks, thereby sharing costs and risks in preparing for the future. But it would also retain the motivating force implicit in having each partner in the venture keeping a vested interest in the conception and implementation of the solution.

Having been awakened to the need to change, there were then two questions each of the banks needed to answer: Do we want to go into a co-sourcing alliance? What attributes are we looking for in that alliance? Dedicated teams in each organization examined these questions. The answers were revealing. None of the three banks in question held a competitive advantage in the field of volume processing, therefore none would be surrendering a position of strength by choosing to cooperate with the enemy. All had basically the same technology plans and objectives, and each had roughly the same structure in cities across Canada. Co-sourcing therefore might make sense. What was also self-evident was that developing the strategy and creating and maintaining the technological architecture to stay ahead of the wider North American competition would be both expensive and time consuming and that the investment in imaging technologies on the scale envisaged in just one of the banks was going to be enormous. It would be difficult to justify for any single institution. The pooling of resources between the three banks therefore began to look quite attractive.

On 15 August 1996 Symcor Services Inc. was formed. Lloyd Darlington, Chief Technology Officer of Bank of Montreal and the new chairman of Symcor, commented in a speech a few months later:

> We are, as we have always been, serious competitors, dedicated to drawing off each other's best customers. If any of us had found a cost-effective way to keep large volume document processing in-house, we would not have joined forces. . . . It was only in the absence of such an alternative that Bank of Montreal, The Toronto Dominion and Royal Bank of Canada began to consider going into business together. Economics, like politics, also makes strange bedfellows – especially when we are talking about the economics of survival.

The future business context the three banks wanted to create was one in which imaging technologies would replace the physical handling of paperwork. Pierre Gravelle, having completed the transformation of Revenue Canada, was asked to take on the leadership of this new organization, Symcor, and to turn the idea of co-sourcing into the reality of competitive advantage for the three banks. 'The executive team at Symcor,' he declares, 'has a favourite term which we like to apply when talking about the early days when Symcor was nothing more than a concept and a bunch of enthusiastic people. . . . That term is to know *what the prize is*. You have to have a prize in mind. In our case it is multiple. Increased shareholder value, greater customer service and satisfaction, access to better technologies, cost reductions, revenue and market share enhancement. So we identified the prize and then we went for it. . . . When Symcor is fully phased-in two and a half years from now it will employ more than 2700 people, making it one of the largest companies of its kind in North America.'

The transition line called *conceiving the future* is concerned with knowing what future you want to create and how to get there. Vision and strategy are obvious key elements. So is knowing what the prize is, for the organization, shareholders, executives and employees. It is not a one-off event at the start of transformation, even though it is very important to get coherence of direction early on and to stick with it. The future, however, is contingent upon experiences now. In other words, strategy merely serves vision and should be continually refreshed by the acquisition and analysis of knowledge – rich knowledge about the market and industry fracture lines that drive change and that is not accessible if it remains the preserve of senior executives or a small corps of strategists. Moreover, far too many organizations think of strategy as a linear extrapolation from today – this is a route to eventual commoditization. Even vision needs to be challenged from time to time in the light of contemporary movements in the market. Things change. Tastes wane. Markets move on. Technology accelerates. Three competing banks become unlikely bedfellows. Truly one's enemies become one's friends.

PURPOSE

So, if conceiving the future is about knowing what future you want to create and how to get there, it is, at its heart, to do with *purpose*. Increasingly, over the last two decades of the twentieth century concepts of vision, mission and strategy have come to be used in ever more complex and sophisticated – i.e. confusing – ways. A good deal of angst and fruitless debate could be set aside if executives reminded themselves that it behoves them to be as clear as possible about the organization's *purpose*. Purpose is a powerful motive force for people and yet in large organizations it has become badly eroded or is entirely missing – in the sense that firms' current pronouncements on mission and values have become disconnected from the world in which they are supposed to be operating. Here is a good example.

On 26 July 1997 the US Central Intelligence Agency turned fifty. The CIA was a product of the early tensions with the former Soviet Union and the still-fresh memory of the American fleet being taken by surprise at Pearl Harbor. In the late 1940s and for some time thereafter it was an elite organization, perfectly in tune with its times, trusted in general by the American public and good at its job. The disaster of the Bay of Pigs invasion, authorized by President John F. Kennedy in 1961, to overthrow Fidel Castro's Cuba brought embarrassment and criticism. Then a string of scandals involving clandestine interference in other countries, support for coups and intolerable alliances with dictators began to break down support for the agency. Newly unclassified documents released in 1997, for instance, revealed CIA proposals for assassinations and the agency's direct involvement in the 1954 *coup d'état* of democratically elected President Jacobo Arbenz Guzman of Guatemala. With the end of the cold war, the demise of the Soviet Union and the collapse of any obvious or serious threat to the USA, the CIA was left bereft of purpose. A series of five directors, none of whose tenure exceeded two years, oversaw its self-conscious stumbling through the early 1990s. The US media speculated on the need for such an organization. Former directors bemoaned its weakness and confusion. Politicians considered its future. Without a purpose it was doomed. It had, we can see, long passed the top of the lifecycle curve and was in serious decline.

The CIA case vividly demonstrates the damage that lost purpose brings. Any organization may face this. Therefore, examining and re-examining purpose is perhaps the single most important task of executives. When Richard Sears founded and built the early business of Sears Roebuck in the late 1800s its purpose was clear: it was a mail-order retailer for farmers. Richard Sears' successor, Julius Rosenwald, who bought the company in 1895, formalized and systematized the development of the organization and it was he who introduced the 'satisfaction guaranteed, money back' policy. The purpose of Sears had not changed, even with the introduction of the regular mail-order catalogue. By the 1920s, however, the world had moved on and the boss of Sears, Robert E. Wood, recognized that the company would have to change too. The traditional target market of farmers, isolated from stores, was disappearing. With increasing wealth and access to towns through the spread of cars, farmers were becoming more similar to middle-class city folk. Wood recognized that the business would only prosper in this new world were its purpose to be adjusted: Sears became a store retailer.

It remained a department store retailer until the mid-1990s, even after the earlier crises leading up to 1992, discussed in

Chapter 3, brought Arthur Martinez through its doors. Initially, in 1992 he too was caught in the spell of linear extrapolation from the past. He cut the famous catalogue, he chopped out huge costs, he changed people at the top, he provided urgency – but the purpose of Sears was still the same. It was still a department store retailer. And it was a purpose unsuited to the times. It was a purpose that was wrong, that could not win in the future. By 1996, however, Martinez and his team were beginning to emulate the process their illustrious predecessors had been through in re-examining Sears' fundamental purpose. Martinez was crafting a new vision for the organization. He was doing this because he realized that 'all' he had achieved from 1992 to 1996 was a corporate turnaround: he had fixed the finances. He knew he also had to transform the organization. The first time he discussed this publicly was in April 1997 in an interview with *Fortune*. Martinez's vision was becoming clear, as the article revealed (p.108):

> Two years ago, in a *Fortune* interview, Martinez defined Sears as 'a moderate-price department store retailer.' Now he says, 'As we thought about it, we realized that's a very limiting definition.' So he's changing the definition. Martinez' new plan is to transform Sears, the retailer, into a top-echelon consumer-brands and services company. To do so, he is rejecting all retail models of how to run a company. He is copying – unabashedly – key strategies of standout consumer companies like Coca-Cola, Walt Disney, General Electric, and General Motors' Saturn division.

Two things are striking here. One, Martinez recognized that financial turnaround was not enough for Sears' future prosperity – transformation was necessary. Two, the purpose he and his team began to envisage for the giant organization's 300 000 employees required deliberate *discontinuity* (a break from what had gone before), hence the emphasis on 'changing the definition' and the 'rejection of current retail models'. The temptation to engage in simple extrapolation from current purpose to future purpose is – in most cases – insufficient for transformation. It cedes no advantage. At best it is a holding pattern.

Organizations may be slowly awakened by early warning bells of difficulties to come (as was the mammoth $128 billion Royal Dutch/Shell by its endemic management indecision on how to grow the business) or rudely awakened by sudden changes in their environment (as was Otis Germany by competitors' innovations) or they may awaken themselves (as did

Sandoz and Ciba when they formed Novartis), but whatever the case, if they choose to transform, they must re-examine their purpose. Where firms have attempted to transform but have neglected their future purpose, the reasons for failure are discernible. Together I call these reasons the *Failure of Purpose*, i.e.:

1. Mistaking the things you do for the thing you should be
2. Linear extrapolation from current to future purpose
3. Unwillingness of CEOs to drive changes in the top team
4. Inconsistency between executive behaviour and word.

The first of these, *mistaking the things you do for the thing you should be*, is typical of organizations struggling with big change for the first time and whose horizons have been limited by years or even decades of one fixed way of looking at their world – at best from within the bounds of their industry, at worst from within the narrow confines of their organization. When I have worked with executive teams like this, it is clear that their instinct is to examine what they currently do, include everything and exclude nothing. As they debate the purpose of their organization, they find it hard to see what is important and what is not. If one executive is bold enough to describe their purpose succinctly, others at once interject, 'But what about this? And we can't leave out that!' They are also frightened of contemplating pulling the plug on current commitments that are really extraneous to the essence of the business. The thinking of most people is fixed in the present; we have difficulty stepping into the future. The business world, in any event, is generally inimical to imagination, so executive teams of this sort can be forgiven for not possessing the capabilities that would help them see beyond the present. Left alone, what generally emerges from days and weeks of hard-fought dicussion and argument is not a purpose, but a consensus-driven mish-mash of overly inclusive *activities*. They mistake the things they do for the thing they should be.

Linear extrapolation from current to future purpose is probably the most common failure. In the example above we showed that even with its recent history of crisis and decline and a new CEO in the corner office, Sears' executives were still thinking about the organization as the department store retailer it had been for decades. Although many tactical and operational features were challenged and changed, it was only after a couple of years of awakening that Sears began to seek deliberate *discontinuity* – to break from the historical business logic of what had gone before. Martinez wanted to change the definition of what the organization was about while rejecting current retail models. For most organizations confronting the need to transform, the temptation to engage in simple extrapolation from current purpose to future purpose is very great. As we shall see later in this chapter, mechanisms to challenge the old and create the new must be deployed to avoid this trap. Such mechanisms, however, will not be acceptable or workable unless the social–psychological capabilities of leadership, systemic innovation and conflict escalation are at least partially embedded in the organization.

The third reason why firms fail to define their purpose is *unwillingness of CEOs to drive changes in the top team*. As DERA's John Chisholm remarks, 'One of the things that causes most chaos is lack of unity at the top . . . Change of the scale that we were envisaging could only be done through an absolutely committed top team. And it could only be me who would be in a position to decide whether they were committed or not.' In the course of building a new purpose, CEOs are required to make the difficult judgement of who in their team has the ability and willingness to help to frame the purpose but without reducing the team to clones who have only one perspective. The objective here is to escalate cognitive conflict (intelligent, informed debate about the future) but smooth affective conflict (unify around trust and common points of view). In Sears, British Airways, DERA, IBM, Reckitt & Colman and many other organizations that have launched successful transformations, the new CEO has always made changes in the people at the top.

Inconsistency between executive behaviour and word is the fastest way to destroy purpose. It has been said many times before and it will be said many times again: executives must learn to walk the talk. When you change the purpose of the organization, when you create a new vision that you expect other people to work towards, you must in some ways change yourself. Indeed, as we discussed above, in some cases it is impossible to fundamentally change the purpose of the organization without appointing new leadership from outside. That is because inconsistency between behaviour and word is an issue of credibility. John Chisholm again: 'Change of this scale is almost impossible to lead if you've been part of the old system. It's to do with just not carrying the credibility if you've been leading the troops in one direction to suddenly swing round and lead them in another. You simply don't carry credibility.' In other cases it is possible for executives to lead the change when they have been part of the old system but, when the organization has struggled to redefine its direction, it is galling to find that the authors of the proposed change cannot change themselves and become obstacles to change instead.

Perhaps the biggest mistake is to make the assumption that once you have done what seems to be the hard part of wrestling with the vision and strategy, you will automatically behave differently. Getting what you preach and what you do in alignment takes effort and time. 'My first attempt to change the business,' says Reckitt & Colman's Vernon Sankey, 'wasn't successful, but it was a great learning experience. I said to myself that the important thing was to get the change going, but I found that I was part of the blockage. And you know what it's like – everybody is always busy changing other people. So if you really are going to try to get through to other people you had better change yourself.'

With these failures in mind as due caution, let us proceed to the key actions for conceiving the future set out in Action List 5.

Action List 5   Conceiving the Future

1. Force discontinuity of purpose: make a deliberate break from the historical business logic that has carried the organization this far.
2. Articulate the new context: devise a simple, powerful 'story' that encapsulates where the organization has come from, where it is now and what its future is; if transforming from crisis, avoid grand visions.
3. Convert purpose to strategic action by deciding what pragmatic activities will bring the organization to fulfil its new purpose.
4. Deploy a discontinuity search strategy: systematically survey the environment to identify possible discontinuities (both threats and opportunities).

FORCING DISCONTINUITY OF PURPOSE

'An outsider,' says DERA's John Chisholm, 'has tremendous advantages when he first arrives because at that stage big change is possible. The system hasn't yet developed the defence mechanisms which hold off change. The system doesn't know how to defend against you.' When new leaders take the reins, they have an opportunity of short duration in which the old ways of thinking can be most effectively challenged, when managers and employees are psychologically at their most receptive. People will accept the escalation of cognitive conflict and even affective conflict because it is being triggered by someone unknown to them, who is objective (being an outsider) and in authority. This is the fastest way to set the context of discontinuity. In DERA's case, Chisholm announced the break with the past within two weeks of his arrival at the first gathering of senior managers, the same one in which he identified who of the 70 managers attending would remain part of the team and who would not.

Chisholm had quickly realized that the history of both work and culture in the old organization was intimately bound up in the physical infrastructure and facilities across 50 different sites. The thinking of scientists and support staff was driven by a mainspring of pride in accomplishments which they believed only the impressive laboratories and experimental facilities would enable them to sustain. 'This is what differentiates us,' they insisted. To Chisholm's eye, of course, the organization was out of synch with its customers and the reality of competition. At the senior management gathering Chisholm told them: 'It's what we carry in our heads that is important and not the physical infrastructure we're standing in.'

Chisholm knew that a sea-change in technology had made much of the research and experimental work swing away from physical apparatus to experiments conducted via computers. The comprehensive site infrastructure was therefore not only costly but also, crucially, was conditioning the way people thought about the purpose of the organization and the way it should work. Too much effort and attention was being directed to struggling to keep up the infrastructure (in fact, of 12 000 employees some 6000 were dedicated to 'non-earning' work). Chisholm was looking for a quite different mode of behaviour. In short order he disposed of much of the old infrastructure.

Several years later he comments, 'Now, for instance, on one site where we have 1700 scientists we have 6000 computers.'

To some extent, Chisholm was fortunate that one key decision about the old organization had been taken prior to his arrival. This was the decision by the British government to change its status to an Agency and therefore to clarify its role. At the time there were four fundamentally different roles it could have played:

- Inventor of advanced systems for the British Ministry of Defence (MoD)
- Provider of technology to the defence and aerospace industry
- Contract research and technology organization in any profitable field
- Intimate technical advisor to MoD to enable it to be an intelligent customer.

Only in the last role was continued public ownership appropriate and this was the role that the organization took on. 'The importance of this clarification,' declares Chisholm, 'was that not only did it provide a *raison d'être* for the organization, it also put it into a proper customer–supplier relationship with those in the MoD who gained value from its services.'

But although the formal role clarification had been resolved at a governmental level, this would have meant nothing without the forcing of discontinuity at the management and organizational level. The enterprise and its employees were still working to the old historical logic. What emerged from all the above was the bringing together over four years of the MoD's four principal non-nuclear research establishments into a coherent and single organization. The mission became: 'To harness science and technology to UK defence needs.' The ongoing vision: 'To be recognized as the world's foremost defence science and technology organization and thus be a source of pride to our owners, our customers and our staff.'

Chisholm's initial action at the first management gathering had made it clear therefore to managers (and later to staff) that there was a disconnection between the old and the new logic of the enterprise. Precisely the same need applied at Revenue Canada. It was clear that the organization would have to change, with the federal government during the 1980s seeking to modernize public service management, reduce central agency control over line departments and, despite budgetary constraints, maintain most programmes and services by doing more with less. All this was driven by government fiscal pressures in the Western world; this in turn had led to a rapidly evolving expectation that democratic governments in general and the Canadian government in particular would have to be more modest and the services they provide more client-focused. This was a huge challenge. We must remember that public institutions of this sort are responsible for enormous transactions: in one year Revenue Canada collects nearly $200 billion in revenues for federal and provincial governments. The challenge of transforming Canada's Revenue Adminstration fell to deputy minister Pierre Gravelle.

Gravelle was convinced that the change required at the Revenue would have to be a radical one. 'I had inherited,' he reflects, 'a very traditional, hierarchical law-enforcement-oriented organization, highly structured and working in solitude in their own silos. Within a year and a half we managed to realign our thinking and change the compliance paradigm from one of enforcement and public oppression to one as trustees of the public interest.' One of the chief ways Gravelle and his team did this was through what he calls 'a sustained challenge to the *status quo*'. This started with action to set out very clearly what compliance with Canada's laws and regulations actually meant. Basically, it was clear that Revenue Canada's purpose was 'Helping people discharge their obligations and avail themselves of their rights'. This purpose could be interpreted within the old compliance paradigm as a matter of balancing service with enforcement. The assumptions which drove all structures, strategies and behaviour in the organization were therefore that:

- Compliance with laws and regulations is best ensured through rigorous enforcement actions (audit and investigation, fines and other penalties, prosecutions and so on)
- Enforcement programmes, if provided with adequate resources, could single-handedly achieve maximum compliance
- Laws and regulations must be enforced rigorously, uniformly and without exception
- The general public does not appreciate the regulatory responsibilities of government for the common good, and

is unreasonable and demanding in seeking to advance personal interests
- The effectiveness of enforcement actions is impeded and often compromised by the influence of special interest groups
- The ultimate goal of compliance measures is to catch and convict all those who attempt to avoid their obligations.

The old paradigm is best summed up in these comments by Gravelle: 'I recall that, in taking on the expanded Revenue Canada portfolio, I remarked that the Customs legislation we were then administering still included a provision whereby Customs officers, duly appointed by the Crown, were empowered to fire a warning shot across the bow of any vessel that did not present itself for inspection at a Customs port of entry.'

In building and articulating the new purpose of the organization, Gravelle made it clear that the old paradigm was now dead. It was too simplistic for the complex modern environment. The new compliance paradigm emphasized Revenue Canada's role as a service provider not a public oppressor. Compliance, in this new view, would be best achieved through accessibility to information and services, fairness in applying the law, transparency and consistency of decisions. Emphasis would therefore shift to:

- Public education and awareness
- Client information and assistance
- Facilitation and self-assessment opportunities
- Accessible and responsive services
- Simple, streamlined administrative requirements
- Due process, including accessible and transparent appeals and redress mechanisms
- Fair, responsible and effective enforcement.

In summary, Gravelle and his team intended that the ultimate objective should be to optimize yield through voluntary compliance, rather than through costly, intrusive, burdensome enforcement. The purpose of the organization therefore had been redefined through his 'sustained challenge to the status quo', showing the clear discontinuity with things past and emphasizing that the old way was, in Gravelle's words, 'now dead.'

SETTING A POWERFUL, SIMPLE CONTEXT FOR THE FUTURE

Howard Gardner, Professor of Education at the Harvard Graduate School of Education, argues a simple but powerful thesis about great leaders in his book *Leading Minds* (1995). His thesis is that the key to leadership is the effective communication of a story, a story whose common core clarifies for people their personal and group identity. Specifically in the business environment, I referred to this in *The New Leaders* as 'imposing context' – interpreting the world for employees, saying clearly where they have come from, where they are now and where they are going to. The context is concerned with concentrating attention by slicing through the countermanding managerial and organizational noise, by saying what matters and what does not. By implication, the context must be consistent and repeated and is not confined to the simplistic statements of mission or vision found in formal corporate pronouncements. Rather, the context is imposed by being part of everyday experience for managers and employees – all modes of communication are essential, including the moment-to-moment decisions and behaviour of executives (as discussed in Chapter 6 as part of the Awakening transition line). Our concern in this section, however, is with the articulation and immediate delivery of the context.

In DERA, at the outset, John Chisholm was striving to do two things: first, to give immediate coherence of direction and, second, to change the employee psychology of 'it's not possible' to a psychology of 'it is possible' (i.e. to shift the culture of learned helplessness). The second of these was a longer-term goal which could be set going but would take time and would depend on changes in executive's expectations of employees, re-engineered processes and empowerment of staff. For the first, though, on the basis of the agency's purpose as 'harnessing science and technology to UK defence needs', he announced at the first management gathering three simple key objectives: customer care, cost efficiency, and total quality. Chisholm explains why:

> They needed to be simple and communicable to everyone in the Agency. They needed to capture the main levers I wanted to pull. And they needed to be issues on which everyone could unite. Our thinking has

developed since then and today's management team has elaborated its own version of this crude initial statement of objectives. But I don't regret the original simplicity and I believe the early articulation of the message was crucial to setting the Agency on a path of recovery.

In short, Chisholm was making an unambiguous statement of context, appropriate to DERA's current and future needs, amounting to: this is where we are and this what we are going to do. The same was true of IBM when Lou Gerstner arrived to rescue it. Its profitability was in tatters, its direction unclear, the value of its shares had collapsed by some $75 billion, it declared a loss of $5 billion in 1992 before Gerstner came aboard and almost $1.7 billion during his first year in 1993. Revenues had declined 13% the same year. One of Gerstner's first actions, however, had been to impose his own context on IBM and its future, widely discussed at the time. He said in a press conference in July 1993:

> There has been a lot of speculation that I'm going to deliver a 'vision' of the future of IBM. The last thing IBM needs right now is a vision. What IBM needs right now is a series of very tough-minded, market-driven and highly-effective strategies that deliver performance in the market-place and shareholder value.

Analysts wanted a vision. Gerstner refused to give them one. A year later, analysts were still seeking a vision and Gerstner still would not oblige. Instead he spent his time reducing costs and creating what he called 'global solutions' to provide sales to multinational customers as a single IBM entity, instead of through the traditional product and geographic organization structure. He also reshaped its 70 000 person worldwide sales force into vertical marketing groups focused more intimately on particular industry sectors as well as getting the industry teams more closely involved in product innovation and development – thereby linking new products more directly to customer needs.

One of the lessons here is that organizations that seek to transform from a position of crisis will lose credibility and impact with managers and employees if they devote time to grand visions of the future – no matter what the analysts and anyone else might say. The instincts of leaders like Gerstner and Chisholm are right: be clear about the context of the business and immediate objectives; articulate the context in powerful but simple terms; leave grand visions to later. Gerstner only returned to the vision issue in 1995 when the transformation of the company had progressed to a point where it made sense to start getting people in the organization to think more deliberately about the future and to focus their efforts or, as Gerstner put it in a gibe at the selfsame media that had harangued him for visionless wandering, 'it's with an enormous sense of irony that now, almost three years later, I say this: What IBM needs most *right now* is a vision.' The strategic vision articulated that year placed IBM at the heart of a networked world that transforms the way people work, interact, learn and do business. The vision was spelt out this way:

> IBM will lead the transition to network-centric computing by:
>
> - Continuing to create the advanced products and technologies needed to make powerful networks real; and
> - Working with our customers to help them fully exploit these networks.

Looking back on this time, in his 1996 letter to investors Gerstner recalls:

> I said our vision wasn't some slogan or a flashy-but-improbable dream. Rather, it was our view, grounded in decades of experience, of where technology and commerce around the world were headed, and that we would help our customers use network computing to improve what they do and how they do it.

In essence, Gerstner and his senior executives were tying the firm to the concept of network computing, both intranets and the Internet – offering both hardware and software solutions as well as services in consulting, systems integration and education in what IBMers were calling 'e-business' or electronic business. In a sense, there was nothing very dramatic or ground-breaking in setting out this vision; Gerstner and team were merely following a powerful trend (as were Gates and Co.). What was cleverer was making the connection to enterprise computing, rather than personal computing. In the mid-1990s IBM databases already managed some 70% of the world's business information. Merely sustaining that veritable stranglehold on global business information transactions in a rapidly growing worldwide market would deliver long-term, impressive results. Of the transformation journey IBM had made since its spectacular fall in the early 1990s, Gerstner is characteristically blunt and to the point. 'We understand,' he affirms in IBM's 1996 annual report, 'that leadership is not a birthright. There is only one way to claim it – or reclaim it – and that is to take it.'

Somewhere between the extremes of crisis and elevating ambition was Revenue Canada. Pierre Gravelle's early task had been the delineation of the old and the new paradigms of organizational life – that is, how compliance could be viewed within the laws that Revenue Canada was bound to uphold. The notion of a service ethos was hardly new. This had been the avowed dedication of the organization for decades, but it had come to be re-interpreted and actioned within a new context. This new context was what Gravelle in a speech in 1995 to the External Advisory Committee on the Public Service in Canada referred to as 'the realities of the current political, social and economic environment, not the least of which, the prevailing fiscal reality.' The new paradigm (i.e. new context) of client-centred service provision to facilitate voluntary compliance became an engine to drive the Revenue's new strategy, actions and behaviour. Gravelle and his team expressed this new paradigm as fundamental service principles, enumerated as:

- Consulting those we serve – both direct and indirect clients
- Developing, communicating and achieving realistic client service standards
- Monitoring and resolving client complaints and
- Sustaining our commitment to continuous service improvement.

All service initiatives followed this set of principles and Revenue Canada's service-compliance strategy (discussed in the next section) was founded on this overall context of client-centred services.

For those organizations in the category of elevating ambition, where managers and employees cannot automatically see a compelling reason to change, the need is slightly different: a powerful future vision is a priority. The reasons for the change are more complex. And the temptation is to offer complex arguments, as if rational persuasion will carry the day. But even here the requirement for simplicity and power in the new context so that it appeals to the mass of employees is vital.

British Airways' new context was about global reach, being the undisputed leader in world travel. Bob Ayling and BA's executives knew it must appeal not only internally to 55 000 staff but to its 32 million customers. After a year and a half of messages to staff about the need to change, with emphasis on business efficiency and globalization in particular, BA's second awakening was in full flow. Then in mid-1997 Ayling revealed the new mission to staff and media at the same time as the colourful changes to BA's livery were being slapped on tailfins, corporate literature and airport lounges. The branding and imagery around 'the world's favourite airline' were replaced by a distinctive ambition:

Our New Mission, Values and Goals

Mission: To be the undisputed leader in world travel.
- Undisputed because we intend to remain clearly ahead of the field, setting standards for others to follow and alert to challenges for the leadership.
- Leader because we intend to be first through innovation, best in serving customer needs and delivering the best financial performance in the field.
- World travel, reflecting our focus on international routes and our intention to build global alliances and because this frees us to diversify into other world travel-related areas, moving away from just an airline to a world travel business.

When it came out few managers or employees could repeat this mission – never mind the values and goals – and still cannot. But the juxtaposition of powerful brand images with the aspiration had all the grandeur of a world-class organization at the cutting edge of its industry and the emotional kick to inject intense feelings of pride and commitment. The distinctive features of 'global', 'leader' and 'world travel' came through loud and clear. Employees understood the 'context'. Sustained over time, this is more than adequate both to outweigh the ill-feeling generated by the airline's entanglements with the main aircrew union and the three-day strike that followed and to take managers and employees with Ayling into the new future.

CONVERTING NEW PURPOSE TO STRATEGIC ACTION

The primary driver of change for ScottishPower was privatization and the coming liberalization of Britain's energy markets. Executives had begun to describe and understand what the future organization and the change actually would look like (see Chapter 6). This early groundwork, in the terminology employed in this book, fits within the Awakening transition line and directly feeds into those actions to do with Conceiving the Future – forcing discontinuity of purpose and setting the new context. The initial groundwork portrayed their current position and the desired outcome of change:

Current	**Desired**
Engineering orientation	Commercial orientation
Diffused responsibility	Ownership and accountability
Oriented to maintain supply	Customer service orientation
Large and centralized	Lean and decentralized
Risk averse	Entrepreneurial attitudes
Electricity only	Broader utility base

The early analysis provided the means to articulate the discontinuity between the past and the future and to define precisely ScottishPower's ambitions. There was a real danger, however, at this stage of letting purpose and ambition run beyond the real reach of the organization – that is, chasing the moon before the launch platform was securely built. 'We were a newly privatized utility,' says Duncan Whyte. 'We said to ourselves: "Don't let your ambitions and your ability get confused. Concentrate on what you know, stick to your knitting and become best-in-class." By that we meant best-in-class in the world. Only then would we have earned the right to consider geographic expansion or diversification.'

The clarification of ambition to become 'best-in-class' before fulfilling other elements of their desired future concentrated efforts among executives. It was now apparent that they should convert purpose to both an initial corporate strategy, focussed primarily on their home operation (set out below), and then a longer term strategy. The initial corporate strategy became:

Step 1: Improve efficiency and cut costs.
Step 2: Exploit assets and skill base to the full.
Step 3: Broaden utility base – Gas and Telecommunications.

ScottishPower proceeded to implement the initial strategy, cutting costs, restructuring, recruiting new talent and getting human resources policies right. Later this would be followed by an increasing focus on identifying value-creation opportunities (see next section) and refining the strategy, if not the purpose of the organization.

At Revenue Canada, the new purpose was 'to optimize revenue yield through voluntary compliance' and the underlying theme that would embody this became 'client-centred services'. Pierre Gravelle and his team used this theme to create and to test their new strategy. This was made up of three major elements:

- *Market Segmentation*:
  - identifying distinct clients and stakeholders based on analysis of service needs;
  - responding to distinct client needs with tailored solutions and services;
  - offering alternative service options wherever feasible; and
  - employing risk analysis and targeting in providing services.

- *Simplification and Streamlining*
  - modernizing legislative and regulatory frameworks;
  - reviewing and revising forms, guides and other information publications;
  - simplifying administrative requirements and transactional processes; and
  - reducing red tape and paper burden.

- *Technological applications*
  - using technology to improve service by reducing processing times and increasing responsiveness;
  - offering clients electronic access to programs and services;
  - realizing operational economies through automated systems applications and integrated databases; and
  - reducing costs for both the Department and its clients.

Gravelle speaks about the process of converting purpose into strategy in very practical terms, but with obvious passion for the subject. 'You have to take a commonsense approach,' he says, 'albeit a very rigorous approach. Discipline is important because what you're doing is creating a case for action – concrete and meaningful action.' It was important that Gravelle and his managers move quickly once the vision and plan for the future were articulated, or these would be seen as having no connection with the reality of people's experience in the organization. At the same time, the articulation of purpose and strategy cannot be done in a pure setting, experimenting with them for a time and then modifying or abandoning them in favour of something better – an obvious point, it must be conceded, but one which some executives implicitly make by failing to communicate and properly act on strategy. 'This is not a test-tube environment,' Gravelle declares. 'We had to be prepared to move quickly once we made a decision and immediately make management teams accountable for implementation and results.'

In summary:

1. *Let the organization's new purpose provide focus for strategic decisions*: purpose should not be a sterile, watered-down mission statement, offensive to no one, but instead a clear articulation of the new context – what is now important in contrast to what once was important. (Remember what St Luke's mission connotes, in Chapter 4: 'To open minds – by creating fascination in ourselves and in our clients.') As such, purpose provides focus by setting the question 'If this is our purpose, what must we do now and in the future to fulfil this purpose?'

2. *Be pragmatic and execute fast*: Vernon Sankey of Reckitt & Colman makes the comment 'There's nothing complicated about strategy and if there is, it's probably not a very good one'. The only reason for strategy is to create action. There are many strategy tools that can help but, bear in mind, endless analysis and refinements or overly sophisticated formulation distract rather than inform. The key is to be practical and uncomplicated and then make management teams accountable as quickly as possible for execution.

DISCONTINUITY SEARCH STRATEGY

I have made the case in this book (Chapter 1) that the organizational world is accelerating into a highly integrated global market of increasing specialization, manifest in 'chunking' and 'modularizing' of what were once core work activities and processes. Knowledge will be distinguished essentially in two forms – (1) *information* that can be specified, programmed, or engineered in precise terms, a process built for it or around it, and then outsourced to suppliers of highest quality, lowest price; (2) *rich knowledge* that is reliant on individual psychology (judgement, experience, trust) and that is most effectively leveraged by firms that take action to access and integrate different knowledge clusters worldwide and manage the inherent complexity. It will also, largely because of the global dissemination of smart information technologies and their knock-on impact, be a world of unremitting speed – *Faster, Faster* as Chatham House Forum's Dr Sparrow puts it.

Other changes are also likely but on the strength of these two alone – the changing nature of knowledge and the speed of business life – discontinuities will appear on organizations' horizons more rapidly and from unexpected directions. The world will be a turbulent one – at least by comparison to our experience now. Thus, it will be a foolish executive who does not begin to put greater and greater effort into the systematic search for and early detection of discontinuities in the business environment.

A good example of this is the growing likelihood in the major industrialized economies, especially those equipped with a very high standard of engineering skills spread throughout industry (Japan and Germany), of a rapid return to further development and deployment of robotics. As far back as 1985 it had been argued (but in general sceptically dismissed) that widespread application of robotics in the manufacture of steel, machines, heavy equipment and textiles could again make serious business sense in those industrialized economies which had lost such industries to cheaper labour in the developing countries of South-east Asia and elsewhere (Carnoy, 1985). In his future history *Preparing for the Twenty-First Century* (1993), Paul Kennedy makes this salutary point (p.93):

> The final irony – and an awful future possibility – is that low-labor assembly plants established by foreign companies in Southeast Asia may one day be undermined by an intensification of the robotics revolution in Japan.

Or Germany. Germany's famously high wage costs over the late 1980s and 1990s drove basic and, increasingly, high-quality metals and engineering work out of the country. In fact, according to *The Economist*'s monitoring (27 September 1997), German firms themselves increased their overseas employment by more than 50% between 1985 and 1997 while leaving their employment in Germany almost unchanged. For example, much of the detailed engineering work associated with plant engineering and contracting traditionally done by employees at $1.5

billion Lurgi slipped through German fingers into countries like neighbouring Poland where labour costs for good engineers were one-eighth of Germany's. Similarly, a swathe of jobs from Mercedes Benz was relocated in the USA.

Rolf Renke, of ABB Germany's Calor Emag, noticed, however, a looming discontinuity. Competition in the form of lower wage costs and rapidly improving engineering skills in Asia and southern Europe had forced the company over the years to ratchet-up the quality of all its operations, from development through production to sales of its prime products in power transmission switchgear and substation components. Calor Emag were playing the *Faster, Faster* game of commoditization. Higher quality meant a narrowing of product range. Narrowing the product range meant competing in niche products. Competing in each niche meant diving deeper and deeper into the niche, with a further narrowing of product range, progressive loss of economies of scale and the concomitant need for higher product prices. With a small range of products the possibility of automating processes reduced while labour content increased. 'That was just the wrong way!' Renke says. 'We were allowing the commodity products – that means the mass production work – to go to outsiders in Taiwan, or China, or India and reserving for ourselves the high-quality work.'

Renke and his managers realized that the complex, tailor-made products could be manufactured anywhere in the world. Rising levels of education and improved training had equipped developing countries with the skills to do this work to quality standards and at *low cost*. Competing on this basis was foolhardy. Any niche ABB Calor Emag occupied this year would disappear next year, or the year after. It was simply a matter of time. Renke concludes:

> Now we've changed. We deliberately try to give away the high quality, tailor-made, low-volume work and we are trying to solve the labour cost problem by investing in automation. For example we are building an automated factory in Dusseldorf to realize this aim.

IBM also could see discontinuities in the way organizations would function in the future. Having sorted IBM's cumulative mess of the late 1980s and early 1990s, the executive team under Lou Gerstner began spending more time actively pondering the future of business in general and IBM's role in this in particular.

Like many others they saw intranets and the Internet as key
mechanisms facilitating global business. More and more a company's day-to-day, hour-to-hour or minute-to-minute operations
would be dependent on the rapid assembly, deployment and
disbandment of teams from within the organization, its partners,
suppliers and vendors, and often right across national
boundaries. Electronic tools for conferencing, mail, scheduling
as well as using the Web would draw people together across
time zones and borders. Firms would set up store-fronts on the
Internet, offering their services to a vastly expanded marketplace of billions of potential buyers.

IBM's opportunities lay squarely in the jump that many
industries and organizations would have to make from the
old way of business to the new electronic or e-business as
IBMers liked to call it. Gerstner and his executives were realistic
about the speed at which this jump would happen – disavowing
the breakneck explosion of electronic commerce that others
in the industry envisaged – but were nonetheless convinced
about the enormity of the market and its suitability to many of
the traditional strengths of Big Blue. As Gerstner says in his 1996
letter to investors:

> Our industry is about to crack the trillion dollar mark. We see the
> industry growing by about $400 billion – to $1.2 trillion in the next four
> years. About half of that growth – $200 billion – will be driven by
> network computing. And the majority of *that* growth will be in solutions
> and services. Those are big stakes.

On a somewhat different scale but with the same intensity of
ambition, ScottishPower, having set off down the track of its
initial strategy, focusing on efficiency, costs and exploitation of
assets in the home business (described in the previous section),
began to broaden its business scope. Against the axes 'territory'
and 'business', it looked to expand both its UK utility business
and diversify into other utility businesses (Figure 7.1), promptly
gobbling up Manweb, another regional electricity company, and
then Southern Water in a bid to be a major cross-sector player. It
was also keeping an eye on electricity opportunities in the USA,
South-east Asia and Australia.

Executives had also begun to formulate a sharper definition of
their early strategy to 'broaden the utility base into gas and
telecommunications.' The concept of multi-utility, announced in
May 1996, was greeted by analysts with what the *Financial Times*

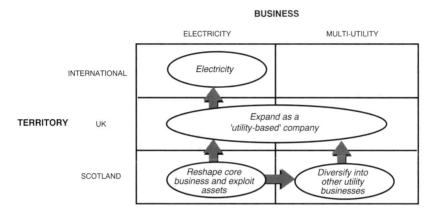

Figure 7.1 ScottishPower's overall strategy.

called 'interest, tinged with scepticism'. They fussed that multi-utility meant diversification and, among utility businesses, diversification ended more often in failure than investor delight. ScottishPower, meanwhile, denied that multi-utility equalled diversification, insisting that it played to the company's core strengths in the management and control of large asset bases and capital expenditure and in customer service. Indeed executives could see a potential discontinuity, as the customer research displayed in Table 7.1 shows: it was telling them that customers were interested in buying more than one utility from an electricity supplier, that a single point of contact for utility services was attractive, particularly the hassle-reducing idea of

Table 7.1 ScottishPower: in search of discontinuity

Customer wants	Multi-utility could deliver
Price benefit	
• Lower	• Share of cost synergies
• Fairer	• Single fixed charge
Service and convenience	• 24-hour, single point of contact
	• Flexible, multi-product billing
	• National payment infrastructure
	• Automated meter reading
	• On-line transactions
	• Energy/utility management
One company/reputable supplier	• Recognized brand
	• Understands wider customer needs
	• Service infrastructure
	• Safety

receiving a single consolidated bill, and that higher-income customers were the demographic group most interested (and most attractive to ScottishPower). The nature of the utility service offering, therefore, could be changed. It could move into telecommunications and retail gas supply, stepping foursquare into the markets of British Telecom and BG (British Gas) and mobilizing its new businesses from its existing customer loyalty. ScottishPower, the electricity company, was in effect challenging its own and others' business logic.

British Airways has relied on future-oriented scanning to identify what might be distant threats. Bob Ayling and his strategists were assembling the pieces of the future industry jigsaw when the airline was at its strongest. Their analysis showed that with the industry's rising costs and with fierce competitive pressures driving down revenue per passenger, the company on trend would slide into loss within five years. The current, highly successful way of running the business would therefore rapidly become the old, out-of-date way. What was a relatively new business logic now would actually imperil the organization in five years' time.

This part of Conceiving the Future connects closely with the Awakening transition line, feeding into key actions which enable the organization either to make ongoing readjustments to business as usual or, if future turbulence and discontinuities are assessed as offering sufficient threat (as in BA's case) or opportunity (as in ABB Calor Emag, IBM or ScottishPower), to reawaken and make the leap to a new transformation S-curve.

The way I have described it here perhaps makes the whole effort look easy. It is not. More often than not, executives fail to see the discontinuities, or neglect to act on what information they do get, or choose the wrong business logic, or simply cannot envisage a new paradigm. They may also act too late or too soon. Igor Ansoff (1987) makes the observation that the relative aggressiveness of firms will determine their success in identifying and grasping the opportunities that arise from discontinuities. Many firms' executive teams are insufficiently aggressive in seeking and acting on discontinuities and therefore lag behind, permanently playing catch-up and never reaping the benefits of being first to market or, worse, being destroyed by the industry sea-change. But others are quicker, sometimes too quick. Ansoff gives the example of Henry J. Kaiser, of the American Kaiser Aluminum Co., who recognized the need for the compact car in the USA and pioneered its development. He was, however, 20 years ahead of the American public. The market was not ready for it and Kaiser became what Ansoff calls one of the 'dead heroes' – a business leader whose aggressiveness exceeded the environmental turbulence.

Apple Computer Inc. got it right. Steve Jobs and Steve Wozniak noticed the discontinuity in the computer industry in the mid-1970s: technology was available to pack the computing power of the big mainframes into desktop models. Jobs had the vision, Wozniak the engineering genius. The personal computer was born. Their timing was right. In Ansoff's terms their aggressiveness in response to environmental turbulence or discontinuities was exactly right – ahead of the crowd but not way out with the dead heroes.

Twenty years later, in the mid-1990s, the same could not be said (Figure 7.2). Apple had missed its chances for a second awakening. There were no transformations. With its revolving-door CEO problem – Sculley, Spindler, Amelio – and with co-founder Steve Jobs invited back to act as a board advisor but refusing to step into the leadership slot, the organization had been searching for elusive solutions for years. In August 1997, Jobs was talking openly about 'a new paradigm' for the company, but without articulating clearly what this might be. Would it be low-cost network computers? A refocus on innovative software? Did the man who brought the world the user-friendly personal computer, complete with idiot-proof clicking mouse, and trash-can and file-folder icons, have a mould-breaking operating system up his sleeve? Or would it be cunning use of the famous Apple brand? A week later he revealed to breathless Mac devotees (and the world in general) the great news. Yes, you guessed it, far from a new paradigm the old enemy had infiltrated the Apple citadel: the predatory Bill Gates had paid $150 million to get his teeth into the Apple. Why? Apple, by then, was a spent force with negligible market presence. What could Gates gain? *Time* ran ten pages of moment-to-moment reporting of the story (18 August 1997) and concluded:

> Industry wags swiftly dubbed Microsoft's Apple alliance 'antitrust insurance,' and with good reason: spending millions to ensure his rival's very survival should stymie the government's urge to halt Gates' long march toward market dominance. . . . His $150 million has also won him several subtler victories. Saving the Mac maintains his $300 million share

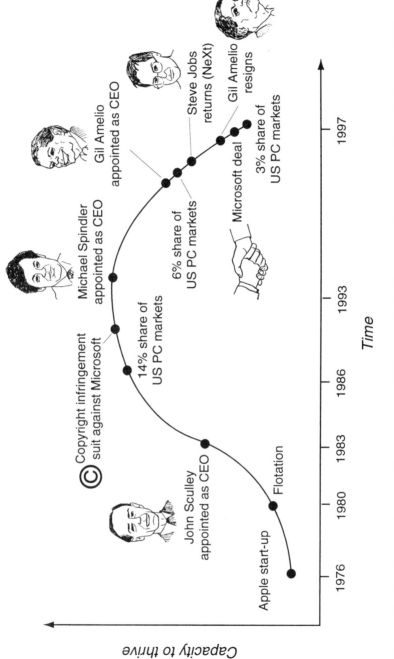

Figure 7.2 The S-curve for Apple Computer Inc. Whither now? Whither away? (Data source: *Time*, 18 August, 1997)

Capacity to thrive

Time

1976

Apple start-up

John Sculley
appointed as CEO

Flotation

1980

1983

© Copyright infringement
suit against Microsoft

Michael Spindler
appointed as CEO

14% share of
US PC markets

1986

1993

6% share of
US PC markets

Gil Amelio
appointed as CEO

Steve Jobs
returns (NeXt)

Gil Amelio
resigns

Microsoft deal

3% share of
US PC markets

1997

of the 20 million-strong Mac-user base while increasing Apple's reliance on Microsoft software to keep the public hooked on its computers. . . . Gates' richest prize may be Apple's intellectual property. . . . [and l]ast week's deal, which commits Apple to developing a Java platform with Microsoft (Apple is also free to partner elsewhere), was an attack on the Sun/Netscape/Apple alliance that would use Java to fight Microsoft for control of the Web. (pp.42–3) © 1997 *Time Inc.* Reprinted by permission.

Transformation? No. Survival – just – for Apple. Swift recognition by Gates of profitable discontinuities and a damned good deal. Another victory for Microsoft. A kick on the shins for Microsoft's competitors.

So what should executives do to get a Discontinuity Search Strategy emplaced? Four actions are necessary:

1. *Recognize that the current business logic is never forever.* If periodic environmental analysis shows that the strategies that worked in the past are less likely or unlikely to work in the future, then it is crucial to begin to question the current logic. Occasional strategy away-days are a good start but not enough. Conflict-escalation tactics (discussed in Chapter 5) should be brought to bear to raise the level of critique and intellectual analysis and to instil a pervasive ethos of strategic challenge rather than unquestioning adherence to 'what is'.

2. *Involve a wider body of people in both strategy making and understanding current strategy.* This means setting in place the infrastructure for managers, external or non-executive directors (preferably from other industries) and even staff to be engaged by strategic debate. Employees who are far from the top but closest to customers and suppliers see their organizational world in a very different way – this perspective is of incalculable value, if it can be *directly* tapped rather than through the distorting filters and screens of normal organizational information flows.

3. *Broaden environmental scanning to industries beyond your own.* Refocus–redesign–benchmark–converge: the danger is ever present. Strategic intelligence from competitors in the same industry has declining value as each year goes by. New entrants are more common. Cycle times are shorter. Industries are being transformed faster. Competitors rarely provide answers to your problems: they think *you* have the answers.

4. *Invest in rich knowledge and complexity management.* Knowledge creates ideas. Capital and machines were the core of
   the old business paradigm. Ideas are the new wealth creators
   of the organizational world. Rich knowledge is power but is
   inherently complex and needs to be managed. Getting access
   to knowledge is but half the challenge; pulling it together
   from its multiple sources, interpreting it and using it is the
   other half.

8
Building the Change Agenda

LEVEL 1 AND LEVEL 2 CORPORATE CAPABILITIES

The reconsideration of a firm's purpose and historical business logic, that springs from the transition lines of Awakening and Conceiving the Future, generates broad sets of actions. It is easy to underestimate the effort and resource implied by such actions and just as easy to be put off when you realize the scale involved. Reckitt & Colman's CEO Vernon Sankey comments: 'Transformation has to be holistic. You can't do it in bits. It's the enormity of understanding how the thing fits together and looking at it in its totality that is truly difficult. The whole thing has to be coherent, or it will not work . . .'

Totality and coherence are words oft uttered at this stage of transformation. The attempt to transform an organization is complex and confusing and requires considerable effort and resource. To change the purpose and direction will make demands on the business that stretch its capacity – chiefly to sustain business as usual while strategic analysis and planning draws off resource. But transformation also makes demands for a whole different tranche of actions that have to do with how the organization functions. When both these sources of demand are simultaneous – as is typical in transformation, particularly when it is crisis-driven – the total demand can seem overwhelming, but its main difficulty is not in the effort required, considerable as this may be, but in the complexity of the agenda for change.

We can make a start at easing this complexity by usefully dividing the overall action sets into two levels of corporate capability. Level 1 capabilities have to do with direction setting and decisions on where and how to compete. Thus the actions that emerge might involve needed changes in the business portfolio – e.g. the disposal of businesses that do not support the organization's new purpose, the acquisition of businesses that help balance geographic coverage or exposure – or in the way the organization approaches its markets – e.g. using market intelligence and product expertise globally to develop new products and to open new or build existing markets. Level 2 capabilities have to do with how the organization operates, with those elements that provide the organization with the where-withal to shift towards selected new directions. The actions here, therefore, are to do with its structure and assets, systems and processes, technologies, its management talent, the quality of human resources and HR practices and the prevailing social–psychological ethos. Specific actions might include the intro-duction of high-speed, high-volume image-processing tech-nology to improve responsiveness to customers and reduce costs or integrating resources on a global platform to take advantage of product development, advertising and production economies of scale.

So Building the Change Agenda is focused on the translation of strategic decisions made during the previous transition line, Conceiving the Future, into a sensible programme of change as well as developing a detailed blueprint of the new organization. In order to draw out the key elements and practical lessons, it is essential to examine a specific case not only from the point of view of building the agenda but also to show the evolution of future purpose through strategy development to agenda. The case we shall use is Reckitt & Colman's global transformation.

A GLOBAL LEADER IN HOUSEHOLD PRODUCTS

Transition Line 1: Awakening

Reckitt & Colman is a household and over-the-counter (OTC) pharmaceutical products company that manufactures and sells famous brands such as Lysol, Dettol and Disprin to more than 1 billion consumers every year. Sales in 1996 were $3.8 billion. The company operates out of smallish headquarters in Chiswick, West London, but with a history reaching back to 1814 it has extended operations to 120 countries, in the past typically in devolved and decentralized growth through the autonomy given local entrepreneurs to exploit the brands or diversify into profitable but, as it often turned out, sideline businesses. By the 1980s Reckitt & Colman executives were beginning to think about their international business in a more coherent way and a number of acquisitions followed, but it was becoming apparent that 'the only thing that sustained it was the acquisitions,' as CEO Vernon Sankey puts it. 'The core of the business was not getting the attention it needed because resources were going elsewhere.' This was reflected in the stock price, which had languished, and the ongoing scepticism of analysts who saw the company's main European and North American markets as mature or shrinking while bloodthirsty competition from rivals such as S.C. Johnson and Clorox was unremitting and likely to intensify.

After his appointment as CEO, Vernon Sankey realized that he would have to make radical changes to the way the business was run or it would not survive. It was clear that a number of factors were driving the need for change. Later, as the transformation began to be communicated throughout the organization, executives used the following factors to position transformation as a requirement for the company's survival:

- Our consumers and customers are increasingly sophisticated and demanding. We need to ensure that Reckitt & Colman continues to offer products which will support future growth.
- Existing initiatives such as Continuous Improvement and Manufacturing Excellence are already improving our business. However, we now need a *real* step change to move forward.
- The range and diversity of our product categories makes it necessary to focus our efforts on fewer key categories to achieve our growth targets.
- Our competitors are all facing the same challenges but they are already on the way to finding a response to them.
- Our staff and shareholders expect us to lead the way in the industry, not follow, in order to provide greater security and rewards for everyone.

Transition Line 2: Conceiving the Future

Impatient to make things happen, Sankey was nevertheless to be disappointed. Big change was not going to be as straightforward as pushing a button to set it going. 'My first attempt,' he recalls, 'was a thing called Vision 2000, a wonderful document supported by a video – all invented by Vernon Sankey! It was quite clear who had written it. Anyway, off it went round the organization, with roadshows and support, but when I looked round six and nine months later to see what was going on, it was clear not too many people were doing anything at all. The trouble was that no one had been a major part of putting the vision together: I had done it pretty much on my own. I had to start again.' This time there would be no 'Vernon's Vision', as Vision 2000 had come to be known, rather dismissively, by managers. Sankey put effort instead into change leadership development for the top tiers of the organization and, as part of that, brought a group of people together over a four-day period to tackle vision specifically. The idea of global coherence emerged, as did the concept of 'think globally, act locally' – a theme that several companies have struck upon, including ABB and Levi's, to name but two. Reckitt & Colman's vision read: 'To be an outstanding global company with leading brands and exceptional people that together really make a difference.' The vision statement itself, however, was much less important than the turning point or watershed that the event created – everyone there signed the piece of paper on which it was written (it is now framed on Sankey's office wall). 'Yes,' concedes Sankey, 'it is a relatively banal set of words, but it *wasn't* for the people who put it together.' Moreover, the way of working that had produced the vision pioneered the teamwork approach by which all the principal changes – whether concerned with structure, process or values – were subsequently undertaken throughout the global business. The teamwork approach, in essence, called for a senior group of individuals to come together to produce radical ideas and solutions whose only constraint was that these remained in alignment with the vision and strategy.

The vision enabled executives to begin to ask searching questions about the strategy that must follow. 'The vision required us to be able to compete globally,' says Sankey. 'That meant that we had to look closely at what we had which really makes a difference. The answer was household products, OTC pharmaceuticals and probably *not* food. Next, taking just the household business, it meant that if we really were going to compete globally we had better build a stronger and bigger business in the States.' The formal strategy was agreed in December 1994, redirecting the company towards building on its heritage, leading brands and geographic reach, but making the household products business the core of Reckitt & Colman's portfolio with pharmaceuticals as the second leg. Three specific strategic objectives were identified:

- To create a powerful US household business
- To establish a global organization, focused on consumers and customers, capitalizing on worldwide strengths and resources and
- To intensify activities in developing markets with their higher potential for future growth.

This would mean selling off businesses that were not in line with the strategy, ruthlessly cutting products that were not number one or number two in their categories and intensively supporting the market leaders that remained. The organization was unused to such direct and brutal action. Sankey, however, was determined. A dramatic signal that he was in deadly earnest about change came in the form of acquiring, from Kodak, L&F Products, the owner of the famous Lysol brand in the USA – thus realizing one part of the strategy to build the US presence. It also created for the company a more balanced geographic spread, with a third of the business in the USA, a third in Europe and a third in the rest of the world. On the other hand, but even more dramatically, Sankey's team disposed of what was, in some employees' minds, half of the company's heritage – the Colman's of Norwich part of the business – but in doing so signalled forcefully that the organization was getting out of foods. Apart from these high-profile moves, however, the list of current, ongoing and future actions required to make the transformation happen and maintain business as usual was growing by the day. To streamline priorities and bring coherence to the global transformation plan, Sankey's executive team established what amounted to two transformation agendas:

1. The 1995 Business Priorities, in line with the overall strategy and
2. An overall Global Transformation agenda.

Transition Line 3: Building the Change Agenda

Sankey and his team knew that they could not achieve their global transformation goals quickly and, therefore, the '1995

Business Priorities' were a way of systematically meeting their short-term financial objectives (i.e. business as usual) while tackling the longer-term transformation priorities. The Business Priorities were:

- The development of an organization design to support the aspiration of being a global company
- The successful integration of L&F with Reckitt & Colman Inc. in the USA and the subsequent transformation of the combined businesses
- The restructuring of the European business through a programme known as Transformation Europa
- The implementation of a worldwide cost-reduction programme
- The clear establishment of an overall global transformation agenda
- The simplification of the firm's product portfolio in line with the strategy of focus on household products and OTC pharmaceuticals that were number one or number two in their categories
- The establishment of leadership programmes to support the vision
- Regional restructuring programmes
- The transformation of the global pharmaceuticals business (which amounted to 11% of total revenues).

Some of these priorities, of course, spoke directly to the longer-term global challenge. New organization design, for example, was identified as the top priority. Reckitt & Colman's structure (and the thinking and processes that went with it) had evolved over time to generate profit and cash from a large number of national businesses, very loosely connected. Local managers were really entrepreneurs, reacting independently to local consumer and customer needs, who listened politely to what head office executives had to say, then ignored them. Synergy between national firms was limited, to say the least. The existing organization design would never enable Sankey and his team to implement global strategies and therefore become a global leader. Organization design would underpin everything.

Design, however, meant more than simply structure. It would also mean processes and, crucially, *mindset*: the beliefs about how employees succeed in their working lives, what must be done, how to do it and who to work with. The primary changes that executives wanted to deliver were through a gradual rebalancing of the old emphasis on geographic accountability with a new focus on global categories, research and development and supply. Reckitt & Colman, in the future, would have to be able to see opportunities and threats from a single, coherent worldwide perspective, create economies of scale and avoid duplication, but stay close to individual markets and transfer best practice and knowledge across the whole organization. The organization design would have to allow fast reaction to competitor threats: thus, switching resources from one area to another would have to be a key feature.

Another move the executive team made was to use the European business as a test-bed for designing the agenda and implementing transformation worldwide. This was known as Transformation Europa. It was clear that the European operations would throw up many of the issues that the firm would face globally and that work here could therefore offer a model for the worldwide transformation. It would also be an opportunity to get a core team together from other regions such as the USA and Australasia in order to share learning about the change process so that lessons would have been learned for the longer-term roll-out – creating, in effect, a pilot in one-third of the organization. Mike Kay, the project director for Transformation Europa, pulled together a core team and spent 12 weeks analysing the requirements for change, based on the global vision and strategy. Five workstreams emerged, as shown in Table 8.1, overlaid by a project management and integration framework.

The Transformation Europa programme of work was, however, to be overtaken by wider global developments in the business. Having grappled with vision and strategy, executives had begun to realize that, at the highest level, there were three key elements of the business that needed to be reinvigorated and aligned with one another. These were structure, process and people. At its most simple, then, Reckitt & Colman's global change agenda was focused on these three elements, but under each was a series of workstreams to transform the firm's corporate capabilities. Global transformation, therefore, was launched, its day-to-day work led eventually by Tim Vernon, appointed as Head of the Transformation team, focusing on the three primary elements that would deliver big change.

Table 8.1   Reckitt & Colman: 'Transformation Europa' workstreams

Workstream	Workstream objectives
Organizational Development	To ensure a new organization structure for Europe is designed, implemented and supported by the required skills and reward system as well as effective communications
Demand Generation	To support the growth objectives necessary to close the value gap and to design world-class processes for Category Management, Key Account Management and Product Innovation
Supply Chain	To implement new supply chain management processes to support the requirements for the European business to become cost effective and responsive to customers
Business Planning and Performance Measurement	To develop and implement a performance measurement system and planning processes which are aligned to the strategic objectives
Systems Implementation	To implement information systems which will support the new processes and structure for the future European business

Structure

The work that the organization needed to do to create a global structure involved modifying what existed as a patchwork response to local and regional conditions that, overall, was part international, part parochial, into one that was globally coherent and based on function and region. This would necessitate not only the creation of new geographic regions (ultimately seven, in place of three, and geared much more to consumers and customers) but also the wholesale restructuring of the executive team to become a Global Leadership Team. Below this they would have to build global teams based on key areas of the business, with a global leader and regional representatives – their responsibility to ensure implementation at a local level of global strategies, rapidly transferring ideas and resources around the world.

Process

Early work had identified five key processes – multidisciplinary, cross-departmental, cross-functional and transnational. These defined the way that Reckitt & Colman in its projected global incarnation would invent, develop, manufacture, sell, launch, deliver and support its products to consumers through customers. The five processes were:

1. Service the customer
2. Generate consumer demand
3. Supply chain
4. Human resources
5. Business planning and finance.

The essential next step in setting the transformation agenda was a High Level Process Review, completed in March 1996. Starting from a 'blank sheet' mindset, the review team used three criteria to guide their thinking and analysis:

1. What do we have to do in order to be successful – to deliver better value to customers and consumers – in the future?
2. What needs to change in order to make that happen?
3. Which of these changes should we work on first?

This examination of the key processes pinpointed the required priority workstreams or projects, kept strictly to a manageable number, despite the temptation to over-include. The five processes and the subsidiary projects are shown in Table 8.2.

People

Executives realized that structure and process would provide them with the design and mechanism for achieving their goals, but that the people dimension would, in Vernon Sankey's words, 'make the whole thing run.' It was also recognized that this element of the global transformation agenda would be the single most difficult aspect to tackle. Goal setting, reward, recognition, career planning, skills development and training would all have to be overhauled. A number of initiatives were planned, those central to the transformation effort being:

- Appointing people with the right skills to the new positions of the organization, including some from outside the business

Table 8.2 Reckitt & Colman: Global Transformation Priority Projects

Service the customer
- Customer Satisfaction (identifying and satisfying needs); Sales Force Effectiveness; Key Account Management/Retail Category Management
- Trade Marketing (encouraging customers to stock and display products)

Generate consumer demand
- Brand Management (establishing a Reckitt & Colman way of managing brands) and Consumer Insights (generating information on the wishes, lifestyles and activities of consumers)
- Product Development Process (developing a consistent global way of using research and development to create and then bring innovative products to market)

Supply chain
- Global Procurement (ensuring better worldwide supplier deals and using suppliers' innovations to Reckitt & Colman's advantage)
- Harmonization (eliminating unnecessary complexity and therefore concomitant cost)
- Manufacturing Resource Planning (MRP II: improving the linking and managing of activities to ensure complete and on-time delivery to customers)
- Sales & Operations Planning

Human resources: key enablers
- Communications (building understanding and commitment to the business strategy through skill and information enhancement)
- Organization Development
- Performance Management

Business planning and finance
- Regional/Global Information (providing appropriate information for decision making throughout the new organization)
- Strategic Planning and Focus (clarifying how to compete in the future)
- Allocations of Resource (using resources to reinforce and support strategy)

- Establishing the core values by which people should work in future
- Implementing a leadership development programme, especially concerned with the leadership of continuous change
- Implementing high-performance team working through widespread training
- Devising mechanisms to align individual and team objectives to ensure delivery of strategic objectives.

The Workstream Management Structure

Sankey's earlier abortive experience with Vision 2000 held lessons not only for commitment building but also for the way in which major projects should be managed. None of the agenda workstreams would make much progress without a coherent overall project management structure. Executives wanted to bring focus to the transformation efforts. Four roles were defined:

1. *Process Owners*, who would champion the change within their specific process stream (all would be members of the Global Leadership Team)
2. *Process Stream Leaders*, who would manage process change and the improvement programme on a day-to-day basis
3. *Project Leaders*, who would manage the projects on a full-time basis
4. *Project Team Members*, who would carry out the project work (all in multidisciplinary teams drawn from the regions).

The whole was also backed-up by a Global Transformation Team, charged with creating momentum for change. Their remit included monitoring progress and ensuring smooth entry of people involved full-time with the transformation and their subsequent return to normal duties. Critically, this Global Team were positioned to have the best possible overview of the transformation effort, providing not only cohesion for the numerous initiatives worldwide but also *context* to interpret individual activities and projects within the larger, strategic whole.

So a number of actions are involved in building the big change agenda, summarized in Action List 6.

Action List 6   Building the Change Agenda

1. Stocktake the total of programmes, projects and initiatives by any other name: find out what projects currently exist, who owns them and what their objectives are.
2. Set priorities and ensure coherence of the big change agenda: there must be a hierarchy of purpose, context, strategy and then action sets or workstreams that will deliver change to corporate capabilities and therefore transform the organization.

3. Identify and name workstream sponsors, champions and programme coordinators: there must be a clear workstream management structure – multifunctional and, in larger organizations, multibusiness.
4. Cull projects not on the critical path: anything on the periphery, no matter how important the history of the project, will simply use up the available transformation firepower.
5. Deploy monitoring mechanisms and programme management skills: complexity management requires very high skill levels in designing and implementing programmes of action; the same applies to the monitoring tools needed to keep transformation on track.
6. Devise the blueprint of the new organization: expand the original vision of what the organization will look like into detailed specification of how it will work.

STOCKTAKING ALL INITIATIVES

In the postal sector worldwide, change has been happening apace. In the USA the US Postal Service (the largest employer in the country, with some 887 000 staff and $56 billion revenues) underwent the most dramatic change in its history as Marvin Runyon, Postmaster General and CEO since 1992, laid into everything from simplifying regulations to improving delivery times, keeping postal rates steady, and getting financial stability. Persistent rumours since 1992 charged that Runyon would also privatize the USPS, but the rumours came to nought. Elsewhere, as we have already discussed, PTT Post of the Netherlands under managing director Ad Scheepbouwer made rapid progress to consolidate its privatized status, conferred in 1989, by transforming into a much more business-oriented enterprise and grabbing a string of acquisitions across Europe, Australia and Asia – most notably TNT, the logistics and transport company. Postal services in Sweden, Denmark and New Zealand had also restructured under the framework of company law to allow them enlarged commercial freedom. The German postal service likewise was being prepared for privatization, ready to join the fray in deregulated European postal markets.

In Britain, for a decade and a half the Conservative government privatized, largely with great success, virtually anything it could lay its hands on – British Airways, British Telecom, British Gas, railways, the water and electricity utilities – and established trading fund status or similar for those it could not, such as DERA. When it came to the Post Office it lost its nerve, concerned that the British public regarded it as a privatization too far. After all, it was the most profitable mail organization in the world with annual revenues of $10 billion and had made subsidy-free profits for 20 consecutive years, profits that since 1981 had contributed nearly $2.5 billion to government finances. Bill Cockburn, the CEO of the Post Office, could see the way the world was going and had lobbied long and hard for privatization so that he could raise money in the capital markets for diversification and compete on an equal footing in the coming deregulated postal market in Europe and worldwide. He became so frustrated by the government's about-turn that he resigned in October 1995 to take up a transformation challenge elsewhere (at retailer W. H. Smith). John Roberts, an avuncular, more introspective chief executive than his blunt, no-nonsense predecessor and who had joined the Post Office in 1967, became the new CEO. His personable nature notwithstanding, he got his team to face reality at once. 'The fact,' he says, 'that privatization had gone away did not mean that the market had gone away. The whole of the market was changing and we took the view that we had to change – to focus on how we made the Post Office as commercial as we could within the constraints our shareholder, the government, placed on us at the time.'

The 190 000 employees of the Post Office, meanwhile, had breathed a collective sigh of relief, glad that the uncertainty surrounding privatization had been resolved. To them the whole business had been unsettling and confusing. John Roberts and his team, by contrast, were looking closely at the market and the competition. Change was still very much on their agenda. Still, they knew that it would be difficult to carry employees, convinced that change (i.e. privatization) was now behind them, along a path of significant upheaval. Undeterred, the executive team decided on a new awakening for the organization, committing themselves initially to answering a number of key questions:

- What was really happening in the marketplace?
- What new products should the Post Office be introducing in the next 5 years?
- To what extent was technology (Internet!) a threat or opportunity?
- How was the Post Office going to grow, assuming it was granted increased commercial freedom by government?
- What sort of capabilities did the business need among its people?
- What was the strategic direction of the business and what changes might flow from this?

The executive team then set in train two primary actions that, ultimately, would start to concentrate the effort of the four major businesses of the Post Offce onto key priorities. These were:

1. A Review of the Corporate Centre, known as ROCC, which was intended by John Roberts as a deliberate signal of strong changes at the top and
2. A redefinition of the Post Office's purpose, direction and values.

The ROCC programme stripped out people from a bulky 3000-person group headquarters, reducing it to 100 and clarifying its purpose as an 'activist centre' concentrating on strategic imperatives. 'Of the 100 people,' says Roberts, 'something like half are in the Corporate Treasury Department and Press Office. For the other 50, we defined very clearly what the reserved powers of this activist centre were to be – around setting strategic direction – then freed up everything else for the four businesses to tackle. So this was a big change and a way of signalling that further changes would come.'

Underpinned by the redefinition of purpose, direction and values, the ROCC programme in its impact on the four businesses also began to flush out numerous issues that would need attention. For example, the new activist focus of the centre meant that it began to push the businesses hard, in line with the overall corporate plan, to build their own business plans. Roberts began to see a pattern coming back. 'In getting them to build their plans,' he says, 'we were getting them to start to expose the initiatives they had on the go. So we did a stocktake of these initiatives right across the organization. It was clear we were in danger or perhaps were already suffering from initiative overload. Therefore, there was much tightening and focusing to be done to get people to concentrate on the real things that we had to do.'

It is characteristic of organizations, large and small, to launch multiple projects and initiatives – sometimes leading to what John Roberts calls 'initiative overload'. Project proliferation acts as a palliative to stressed-out executives because the sense of action and general busyness in the firm makes them feel progress is being made. Of course, nothing could be further from the truth. In a typical large organization facing external threats or crises, it is not uncommon to find that the CEO and every member of the top team is each the sponsor of ten or more major business projects. Given a top team of ten, that amounts to at least 100 major business projects running simultaneously and absorbing time, effort, organizational resource and huge budgets. Closer inspection will show that each project is legitimate, there are sound reasons for its existence and, if completed, it would probably make a positive contribution to the organization.

These initiatives generally come into being because the organization is fire-fighting or is in the earliest stages of awakening. Projects are launched to put things right. When things don't come right, more projects are launched to bolster those that are failing or to prop up key business activities that are not getting the support they expected from the original projects. Project proliferation, of course, is hard to discern when you are in the middle of it. And the tendency is much worse when an organization has tumbled into crisis. Crisis creates a fog that reduces executives' perspective. What is missing, of course, is the overarching connection between all these initiatives – not just programme management, although this is important, but purpose. Project proliferation comes to substitute for purpose. Transformation agenda setting requires that Awakening and Conceiving the Future have gone before it. Clarity of purpose informs the agenda for action, ensuring that peripheral, out-of-date and irrelevant organizational actions are no longer working at cross-purposes.

But how can you tell if the organization suffers from project proliferation? A good rule of thumb is to check for duplication. Proliferation without guiding purpose begets duplication. Two or three different projects will be pursuing similar aims. That pattern will be repeated, resulting in massive duplication of effort and cost. An objective snapshot across all the major projects, as John Roberts actioned in the Post Office, will soon show duplications. Projects should not spring into being unless they can satisfy the question: 'How will this project serve the attainment of the organization's fundamental purpose?' In short, the proliferation of projects and initiatives is both a clear sign that there is no guiding purpose and a constraint on attaining such a purpose. Before any initiatives are kicked off to make transformation happen, executive attention must be redirected to the clarification of purpose or its proper communication. Assuming, however, that the main actions of the first two transition lines have been successfully initiated, building the change agenda can begin.

SETTING PRIORITIES AND ENSURING COHERENCE

Maintaining business as usual and then adding a series of projects to modify and enhance the capabilities of the organization places strain on the same set of finite corporate resources. Consequently, agenda setting must deliver priorities. Similarly, the resulting action sets or workstreams must be coherent – i.e. driven by the same purpose. Of course, making this happen in a precise, logical order when you are dealing with a large corporate body with multiple business units is almost impossible. But the penalities of not trying are much worse, as Chris von Branconi of Lurgi found out when Metallgesellschaft was in the early stages of trying to save the company:

> You need a certain consistency and persistence in priorities to really get people moving along a change track. With the exception of a few people at Metallgesellschaft board level and mainly Mr Neukirchen, everybody was bringing in new priorities and confusing the whole change process – kind of 100 projects and 150 priorities and one not fitting the other. Senior managers were always generating more questions, therefore more projects, therefore more priorities. There is a limit to this game! Even the most perfect manager can only manage a limited number of priorities at a time.

This is not to say that sudden changes or adjustments should not be taken into account, but that the speed and impact of big change will be reduced if some priorities are not dropped when others are added. 'It would be very nice,' says John Roberts of the UK Post Office, 'to stop the world and work through a beautiful, logical order, but of course there are new issues hitting you all the time. You can't do that but what you can do is to ensure that you have a hierarchy of purpose, direction, values, and strategy.'

In other words, purpose and strategy should provide coherence and the first mechanism for establishing priorities. A useful way of doing this is to agree the primary corporate capabilities that will be required in the future organization – i.e. the new paradigm – then measure the organization as it currently stands against those capabilities. Remember, you are measuring the organization against a future state (the future purpose, context or vision), although information on competitor profiles will undoubtedly form part of the data used to construct both the future state and the detail behind each item in the list of corporate capabilities. These capabilities then become the critical success factors – i.e. those strengths and weaknesses that most critically affect the organization's future success. An example is given in Figure 8.1, that I have developed from an idea of Professor Igor Ansoff (1987). This provides:

1. A target list of the primary cross-organization capabilities.
2. An early (and ongoing) measure of the gap between current capability and required capability and thus the relative emphasis or priority that must be accorded efforts to change, modify or enhance each capability.
3. An indication of the workstreams that must be launched to bridge the gaps between current and future capabilities.

Together, this information tells executives what the likely total programme of change will be to shift the organization from old to new paradigm. The key workstreams emerge directly from the capability gaps. For example, we discussed in Chapter 6 the circumstances driving Siemens Plessey to transform. The organization was facing more demanding customers requiring largely unique solutions in commercial air-traffic electronic systems, military surveillance and air-defence systems, as well as tactical communications systems for armed forces worldwide. The firm had long been organized in a traditional functional structure which meant that managers and staff were continually breaking down incoming customer work to fit Siemens Plessey's structure, rather than having the flexibility to do it the other way

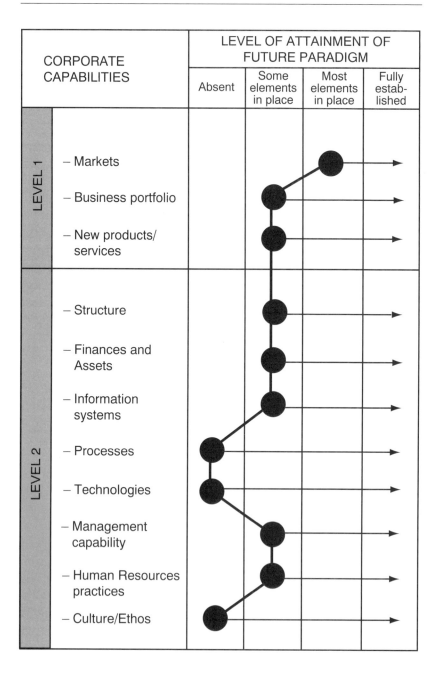

Figure 8.1 Paradigm shift: bridging corporate capability gaps.

round – in fact, most of the work was non-repetitive and the structure was getting in the way of achieving results.

Managing director Clive Dolan began to share his incipient vision of the way he wanted the organization to work with his fellow directors, debating how he thought the company should change towards a greater focus on projects and common ownership of individual projects, called 'Project Focus'. Once he and his team had taken time out to work together on the vision and to commit to transforming the organization, they began to devise the change agenda, intending it to be an ambitious and all-embracing undertaking. From the outset it was designed to address the full breadth of the processes in the firm and to engage as many people as possible in generating solutions to shape the future. Within Siemens Plessey the change agenda became known as the 'remedy framework' (Figure 8.2). The corporate capabilities (called 'remedy themes') were thus the high-level workstreams that the organization would need to execute to close the gap between current and future capability:

- Leading the Business: concerned with building the longer-term vision of the firm and new behaviour at executive team level and throughout the business (for example, creating trust through open communication)
- Manage against Processes: remodelling (i.e. re-engineering) the main business processes and establishing and then institutionalizing 'process thinking'
- Make the Weight: designing and installing priority based budgeting as well as taking action for ongoing functional improvements
- Controlling the transformation programme: developing appropriate performance metrics for each initiative – later absorbed as the normal business performance control approach.

As a subset of each workstream or remedy theme were the detailed actions or initiatives to deliver Dolan's original vision of 'Project Focus'. The initials below each initiative designated which executive team member would act as the main sponsor for each initiative.

At DERA John Chisholm took a similar approach. The only difference was that the organization faced a more immediate crisis and survival was at stake: therefore Awakening,

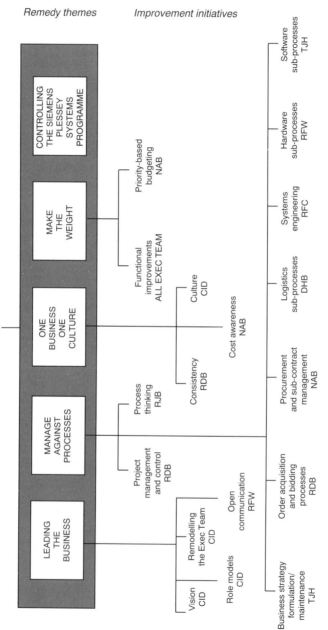

Figure 8.2 Siemens Plessey: big change agenda.

Conceiving the Future and Agenda Building were happening in tandem. Chisholm explains how the executive team got on with agenda setting:

> This first plan was to take a view of the total scope of change needed and to assess what resources would be required to make the organization viable. . . . We set targets as to what level of performance was required to make the Agency a self-sustaining competitive organization. We then modelled what changes were required in the overall shape of the organization to reach these goals over a five-year transition period.

The top-level agenda for change was not needlessly complicated. Chisholm and his team were working to just five agenda items, the first of which Chisholm had actioned within two weeks of his arrival (see Chapter 6). The agenda specified that senior managers should:

1. Choose a top team who were committed to the task.
2. Set some guiding principles.
3. Improve the organization's teeth-to-tail ratio.
4. Re-engineer processes to change from bureaucracy to world-class scientific service organization.
5. Re-equip through investment in people, science and systems.

The *guiding principles* (item 2) were straightforward, captured the main levers that Chisholm wanted to pull to make rapid improvements in the Agency and were issues around which everyone could unite. They were: customer care, cost efficiency, and total quality. They were communicated early and right across the organization and Chisholm used customer-satisfaction surveys to reinforce the message, pointing out that staff and technology were rated well above average but delivery was seen as poor.

Reforming the teeth-to-tail ratio was going to be more difficult. The teeth of the organization – essentially scientists in customer delivery roles – were equalled in number by support staff. The beast that owned too few teeth and too much tail was not, therefore, well adapted to its environment. This was the obvious product of a history that had bequeathed the organization some 50 sites, nearly all of them too large and mostly expensive to maintain because of long years of inadequate investment. The large numbers of support staff were mainly dedicated to this task and not to any kind of value creation. Most of the facilities and infrastructure were the inheritances of a different era and could never be economic in the current circumstances. A rationalization programme was required. This would be complicated because laboratories and equipment are much more difficult to move than staff and offices. Nonetheless, the programme aimed at rationalizing duplicated laboratories, abandoning unnecessary facilities, preserving essential environments and cutting overall support costs. The projected cost was calculated at nearly $400 million – sizable, given the organization's revenues of $1.3 billion (now nearer $2 billion) – but the payback, at around $170 million a year, would make it an excellent investment. (Ultimately, the numbers of staff in support roles were reduced by two-thirds to 2000, with a parallel two-thirds increase of scientific or knowledge workers to 10 000.)

Re-engineering processes was going to be equally difficult. The vehicle DERA decided to use was called Total Quality Process (TQP). It would involve re-examining everything people did in the organization, starting from Chisholm's desk down and analysing from an input/output and customer/supplier point of view. The eventual aim was to untangle the complex layers of bureaucracy that had been steadily encrusting the organization over the years.

Re-equipping through investment in people, science and systems was the final change agenda item. This would mean reform to the nature of jobs (from inflexible, hierarchical posts to responsive design around customer need, projects and skills), reworking of personnel practices (from fixed-grade hurdles and career channels to internal markets) and focused training timed to coincide with the introduction of major change programmes. It would also be necessary to identify and invest enough in the various technical, scientific capabilities needed for DERA to be at a world-class standard – to the extent that the advice drawn from them would be worth having. That would mean ensuring a minimum critical mass in each capability at times when the normal sustenance provided by projects for customers was not available. Finally, the Agency needed to overhaul its information systems and invest heavily in new ones. But in the course of launching this workstream, Chisholm believed it would be better to gain as much experience as possible with paper-based systems, despite the resentment of employees. Why? 'Automating poorly thought-out or badly understood processes,' he maintains, 'is far worse than no automation at all.'

Thus, the change agenda should cover all capabilities measured against the organization's future state (the future purpose, and context or vision), thereby creating critical success factors for the workstreams to systematically address.

NAME WORKSTREAM SPONSORS, CHAMPIONS AND PROGRAMME COORDINATORS

It is very important, at this point, that the workstreams also have in place named sponsors (responsible for providing ownership, focus and public support) as well as programme managers (dedicated to making the workstream actions happen) and in many cases programme coordinators (accountable for managing the integration of the workstreams). At Siemens Plessey, for example, the workstream actions began with the appointment of an overall change agent, Bob Barton, who was installed as a full-time member of the executive team. Workstreams (called 'initiatives' in Siemens Plessey) were launched by appointing a specific director as overall sponsor, who then selected a specific change agent to undertake the workstream action (such as process re-engineering). These initiative change agents each formed a cross-functional core team, who then engaged various task or project teams, as appropriate. Each team underwent a mobilization process to ensure that they were fully conversant with the overall programme of change and possessed the necessary skills and techniques. Bob Barton, the overall change agent, was responsible for ensuring that the separate workstream teams were adequately supported and equipped throughout the transformation. Figure 8.3 shows the overall workstream management structure.

A similar workstream management structure was used in the UK Post Office. John Roberts had confirmed four programmes as the top priorities for the organization as a whole. These were *Developing the Product Portfolio, Harnessing Technology, Competitiveness through People*, and *Competitive Overhead Structure*. A number of projects and sub-projects ran below this cross-business agenda, but in the case of each of the four programmes there was a named programme line manager, programme champion, and programme coordinator as well as a central

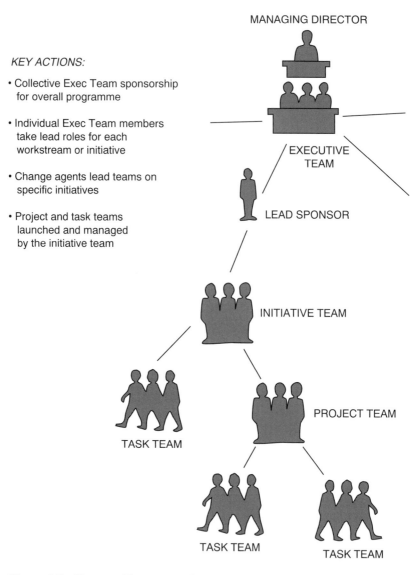

KEY ACTIONS:

• Collective Exec Team sponsorship
  for overall programme

• Individual Exec Team members
  take lead roles for each
  workstream or initiative

• Change agents lead teams on
  specific initiatives

• Project and task teams
  launched and managed
  by the initiative team

MANAGING DIRECTOR

EXECUTIVE TEAM

LEAD SPONSOR

INITIATIVE TEAM

TASK TEAM

PROJECT TEAM

TASK TEAM

TASK TEAM

Figure 8.3   Siemens Plessey: workstream management structure.

programme integrator to ensure strategic oversight for the
workstreams and provide support to the coordinators. This sort
of programme management structure need not induce a
ballooning central function. On the contrary, the workstream
management structure should obey the rules of any effective
team, remaining small enough (around 12) to be workable while
at the same time ensuring that the combined impact of the

programmes moves the organization towards the attainment of the new purpose and paradigm.

For the workstreams and even some of the sub-projects themselves, another key rule is to staff them with a multi-business or multifunctional mix of people. This pre-empts the not-invented-here syndrome so damaging to later implementation as well as yielding the benefits that accrue from escalating conflict as a result of bringing differences and dissent into the equation – for example, making underlying issues open and explicit, engendering a sense of corporate-wide urgency, improving decision quality, sharpening understanding of cross-business interests and goals and enhancing mutual understanding between subsidiaries, groups or functions.

This was certainly the experience of Gurhan Çalkivik, vice president of Corporate Management Information Systems (MIS) of Koç Holding, the huge $12 billion Turkish conglomerate, headquartered in Istanbul. Koç comprises 98 companies and some 41 000 employees working in everything from the automotive industry, household appliances and consumer goods to energy, construction, financial services and tourism. In addition to its domestic operations, Koç has been pursuing an internationalization strategy under its chairman Rahmi Koç, with a push into Europe in household appliances and penetration of the emerging markets of Russia, the Caucasus and Central Asia, as well as a number of acquisitions in the USA. Gearing up for this has meant some major changes within the organization, not least an accelerated use of information technology (IT) for competitive advantage. Gürhan Çalkivik began to introduce new IT for a variety of purposes across the conglomerate. There was a central feature to the structuring of the change programme, as he indicates:

> We used a team concept that involved mixed groups of people from different companies as well as corporate management in the working groups. That was a way of giving them ownership and involving them from the very beginning almost in every aspect of the project. If you want to make change acceptable, there is no other way. Even the central project group consisted of representatives from different companies in the group and from different sectors.

Even so, there were difficulties. Getting multibusiness and multifunctional teams together was hard work and time consuming. To make sure that team members in the various projects would work well together in strong cohesive teams, Çalkivik invested in training in team concepts right at the start. In spite of this, there were disappointments and failures. 'Some of the guys,' Çalkivik relates, 'had to leave their projects because they could not really adapt to working in a totally foreign team outside their own company environment. So we had a big problem with some of the people.'

CULLING PROJECTS NOT ON THE CRITICAL PATH

We have discussed at some length the proclivity of organizations to launch initiatives, even to the point of project proliferation, duplication of effort and what John Roberts calls 'initiative overload', a tendency from which the British Post Office had suffered. 'What I don't think we've done critically enough in the past,' says Roberts, 'is to examine initiatives closely and, if they're off-plan, to stop them or demand that their owners provide a very, very good case for proceeding. Gradually now we've been pulling people back and getting them to look more carefully at this whole area – asking questions especially on why the initiative should go ahead, its relative importance against cross-business programmes, and how it fits in with an individual group's finances for the next two or three years. So we are getting better at taking what I think is the toughest decision: saying no.'

Saying 'no' does not have to mean escalating decisions of this sort to the most senior levels. Roberts actively attempted to push decisions of this sort down the management hierarchy, encouraging a culture of critical examination and personal accountability for tough decisions. Instead of introducing new initiatives on the back of those that had been successfully launched (such as new products), Roberts got managers to challenge this view, showing that in the past the organization tried it but did it badly, failing to underpin the original projects because attention and effort was redirected away to the new initiatives. Now the emphasis moved to concentrating on getting benefit out of a limited number of initiatives or as Roberts put it to his managers: 'Let's finish what we've started before we move on.'

By implication, this approach necessitates tough action to consider all projects and cull those that do not promote the objectives of the core change agenda items, as well as those that duplicate work elsewhere. Such tough action is not possible while the support framework has not been emplaced to allow managers to terminate projects without the political fall-out of loss of face, diminished respect or permanent career damage. Mechanisms to build this support framework start with communication of purpose and strategic direction, tying all the main programmes to this overarching focal point. This provides the *reason* that justifies why a project is no longer relevant or off the critical path – rather than leaving a default implication that a responsible manager has failed or is somehow to blame. A second mechanism is CEO and senior executive legitimization of saying 'no' to new projects or terminating the old, a tactic John Roberts successfully employed. A third mechanism is acting quickly to pull the plug. The longer the decision is left, the more likely project sponsors and team members are to make some sort of rough fit with the legitimate agenda – producing a fatal compromise or fudge that will retard overall progress. Their action will spring from the normal human need to attach value to their everyday work. Rapid acknowledgement, after a project stocktake, that a number of projects are now no longer appropriate and should be merged or terminated is the task of effective leadership. Finally, the project stocktake with its resulting determination of duplications and targeting of projects for termination is an activity best handled by external consultants. Objectivity is critical here.

DEPLOYING MONITORING MECHANISMS AND PROGRAMME MANAGEMENT SKILLS

Alex Krauer, Chairman of Novartis, makes the point: 'There are no perfect solutions, only timely ones.' In the merger of Ciba and Sandoz (and any other merger, to be sure) speed is of the essence. Indeed, the longer that integration drags, the greater is the risk of failure. Apart from the concern about speed, the other substantive lesson is to do with how perfect one attempts to make the solutions or sets of action that are intended to deliver big change and how far one should go in resourcing them. Krauer advocates erring on the side of timeliness rather than perfection. At stake here is progress. At a gross level that should be the prime measure of stage-by-stage success. Transformation is a big undertaking, easily sunk by undue emphasis on getting the ideal rather than the best in place. Reckitt & Colman's Vernon Sankey ponders this question with his usual candour:

> Nothing is completely resourced in the way it ought to be. Nothing. Everyone, given their full requirement of resource and time for the project in hand, will simply bankrupt the business. The real question is: at what stage and to what extent does it become detrimental? More important too is getting the whole lot going at the same time. You can't say, 'Oh, we'll do this bit later.' If you do, you'll find the whole lot stops.

Siemens Plessey's Clive Dolan makes a similar point. 'In a sense, the priorities and your rate of progress are set for you by the business-as-usual needs, the genuine availability of people and their willingness, and your own energy.' Therefore, the workstreams emerging from big change agendas are inevitably going to end up with 80% resource and time and most probably 80% solutions. This should not be a worry if the original purpose and vision have forced stretch goals on executives – BHAGs, or Big Hairy Audacious Goals, as Jim Collins and Jerry Porras call them in *Built to Last* (1995). BHAGs help to push up organizational ambition and mean that, even if only an 80% solution is attained, it is 80% of an enhanced goal.

Ensuring that goals are achieved, nevertheless, requires a framework for accurate and timely information on planned and actual performance. Such a framework should also have built-in mechanisms for developing and communicating realistic performance and service standards for all workstreams. The entire monitoring framework is best coordinated through the overall workstream management structure described earlier – i.e. sponsors, programme managers and programme coordinators and a central transformation team. In Reckitt & Colman's case, for instance, the Global Transformation Team, made up of a core of between five and ten members dedicated full-time to transformation, were charged with creating the momentum for change. Their remit included monitoring progress and ensuring smooth entry of a wider range of people involved full-time with the transformation and their subsequent return to normal duties. From their central position, this Global Team had the best possible overview of the transformation effort, providing not only cohesion for the numerous initiatives worldwide but also *context* to interpret individual activities and projects within the larger, strategic whole. As Vernon Sankey remarks, 'While I could only devote a proportion of my time to transformation, I could rely on a full-time team giving 100%.'

As to measurement of progress and effectiveness, Siemens Plessey, for example, initiated a programme-control process which eventually became absorbed as the normal performance control throughout the business. Each of the main initiatives conceived its own measures based around the balanced score-card approach outlined by Kaplan and Norton (1993) with metrics covering four distinct perspectives:

1. Financial
2. Customer
3. Process and
4. Innovation and learning.

Control and monitoring depends very largely, too, on project management. Siemens Plessey executives realized that they needed a radical change in the way managers controlled and managed not only the transformation agenda workstreams but also the business-as-usual service to customers. For years the organization had been attempting to achieve the appropriate project emphasis within a matrix structure, but one damaging outcome of this was functionally bound thinking which seriously impeded the flow of work and information. There had gradually been an erosion of project management skills and an inability to achieve on-time delivery. Managing director Clive Dolan introduced the concept of Project Focus, based on the premise that the people necessary to effectively staff a project would be drawn from the various functions and placed under the direct control of a project manager. A distinction was also made between 'project-retained staff' and 'function-retained staff' to ensure proper management and career development. The same distinction made explicit where accountability lay for detailed project actions – i.e. with a particular function or with the project team. Most important, the new approach emphasized project critical success factors, shifting the focus of attention and effort to *achievement*, rather than *activities* – the what before the how. Time was devoted during project start-up, using multi-functional team members, to consider what achievements or outcomes were required before determining how to achieve them. The resultant goals were then transferred to a top-level milestone chart to form the basis for ongoing measurement and control of project progress.

DEVISING THE NEW ORGANIZATIONAL BLUEPRINT

As Siemens Plessey began to move forward along the change track, they formed a team to improve understanding of the way that key work activities were performed in the company. This team began to model business processes – that is, they started to devise a blueprint of how the organization should work. As they currently stood, the key business activities could be divided into:

- Marketing
- Pre-bid work (e.g. developing prospects into customers)
- Development of relationships with specific suppliers and partners in order to open up new markets
- Bidding for and winning contracts (both new and in-service support contracts)
- Implementing contracts
- Formulating business strategy
- Maintaining capabilities, products and infrastructure
- Developing capabilities, products and infrastructure.

This was too complex and produced unnecessary complications because some of the processes depended on each other in a much more integrated manner. One of the most salient objectives of Clive Dolan's executive team and the blueprint team was to minimize the complexity of the interfaces between the main business processes. For example, in considering the front-end activities of the firm – usually called 'marketing' – the team decided that a wider scope was needed, involving any aspects of pre-bid work (such as developing a prospect into a customer to whom the firm would offer a formal bid) as well as development of relationships with specific suppliers and partners to enhance the company's chances of opening up new markets. This process would not necessarily be one that led to a detailed and binding commitment to produce any deliverable – thus, it could be separate from any downstream processes. In the blueprint of the new organization it was termed *Developing Siemens Plessey Systems Markets*.

Conversely, the team found that the process of bidding for and winning a contract for a particular customer requirement does result in making a commitment. If this were separated from the implementation process, it would be likely to cause the kinds of difficulties that Siemens Plessey often experienced – most notably, business proposals and solutions that were, in practice, hard to implement or, worse, underestimated. Consequently, the bidding and implementation activities could neither be assessed nor operate in isolation. From the blueprint perspective, therefore, it was right to avoid any separation of the two activities. The work involved in bidding for and winning a contract and then implementing it, if disconnected, would result in communications breakdowns, sometimes of a serious nature. The two were therefore joined together as a single process, defined in the blueprint as *Win and Implement Systems Contracts*.

A similar logic was adopted to cover the processes of winning and implementing in-service support contracts. Although support aspects were, in the normal course of work, often contracted at the point of the original sale, the blueprint team identified that there remained a significant wider opportunity to win and implement service contracts outside the scope of the main contract and even beyond Siemens Plessey's own product range. The blueprint team termed this new process *Win and Implement In-service Support Contracts*.

These three new processes defined the core of the new organization and were those processes most visible to customers. Moreover, from these processes would come the primary source of income for the firm. As such, the three processes were identified as the *core business processes*. Behind them, however, it was clear that a number of enabling activities, aimed at supporting the three customer-focused processes, were essential. Therefore, two *core enabling processes* were defined. The first concerned the mechanisms by which the longer-term direction of the firm was determined – in short, how to *Formluate and Maintain Business Strategy*. Nonetheless, on its own, business strategy could not effectively enable the core customer-facing processes to flourish over time and changing circumstances without a process to systematically develop the firm's skills and capabilities. This core enabler was termed *Maintain and Develop Capabilities, Products and Infrastructure*.

Siemens Plessey, therefore, had designed the core business and the core enabling processes for the new organization. These things, however, define only the rational, technical overlay of big change. 'We realized,' says Clive Dolan, 'that change is an organic process. It is not a binary or one-shot event.' Executives knew that real change would mean fundamental changes in behaviour, sustained over time. At this point, therefore, in line with new mission and vision, the firm also defined its values and backed them up with a comprehensive training programme in four streams:

1. Making the culture work: learning the importance of behaviour and values
2. Change management skills: understanding how to handle change, particularly difficult transitions
3. Life skills: basic skills to support the new processes (such as coaching, feedback, creative problem solving and team working)
4. Process-specific skills: the technical skills needed in each of the core and enabling processes.

9
Delivering Big Change

BIG BLUE'S BIG CHANGE

Between 1993, the nadir of the company's fortunes, and 1997 IBM's market value had grown by more than $50 billion. The pain and the palpable sense of dislocation experienced in the dark days of the early 1990s had been washed away in the wake of the new tough, no-nonsense chairman and CEO Louis V. Gerstner Jr. Big Blue was riding high once more. The business was growing, it had a new strategic vision focused on the networked world, managers were hiring tens of thousands of new people and Gerstner was able to speak of reclaiming industry leadership. Nevertheless, the transformation, as Gerstner conceded, was far from over.

Still, basking in the glow of record revenues and steeply rising market value, it must have been easy to forget that the word 'survival' had cropped up innumerable times in previous years or that Gerstner had spoken of bringing 'IBM back from the brink.' In IBM's 1995 annual report Gerstner said, 'I think it's fair to say, however, that the question about IBM is no longer one of survival. We've stabilized the company financially and, beyond that, strengthened it. IBM is back, and we're here to stay.' IBM, we should remember, transformed from crisis.

But what were the main features of the transformation that had brought the company from crisis to the wholesale implementation of change throughout the organization? Examined from the perspective of the transformation S-curve, the characteristic transition lines are clear. At the time of writing, the balance of effort devoted to the first four transition lines had decreased and IBM was beginning to shift physical, financial and psychological resources away from the large-scale implementation of solutions and new ways of working (i.e.

Delivering Big Change) and concentrate on mastery of the changes and the new business logic. 'Even as we grow,' says Gerstner, 'we are relentlessly continuing to fine-tune our operations to improve our efficiency and productivity, mostly through our re-engineering efforts.'

The pattern of IBM's transformation, leading up to the delivery of big change, is worth examining in some detail. Using the S-curve model shows the progression of key actions over time and in particular the iteration between the different transition lines – for example, actions to do with scanning the future, vision and strategy do not simply occur as a major effort at the outset; they recur, are reconsidered and refreshed in dynamic interrelationship with the progress being made on each transition line. Let us follow the IBM transformation along the S-curve.

Awakening

Lou Gerstner joined the company in April 1993. The immediate goal was clear: IBM would have to be turned round. Gerstner set out the obvious priorities to executives, employees and shareholders: 'IBM must be profitable. IBM must be more competitive. IBM must increase shareholder value. IBM must grow.' He was equally clear about the reasons for IBM's demise: the firm had failed to keep up with the rapid changes in the computer industry. IBM was beginning to wake up to the fact that, like many large companies, it had become overly bureaucratic and self-obsessed. Research and development staff were still creating magnificent technology, but it was getting to market too late. Competitors were consistently beating IBM. IBM's new executive teams had begun to realize that, in Gerstner's words, 'one of the unusual things about this industry is that a disproportionate amount of the economic value occurs in the early stages of a product's life. That's when the margins are most significant. So there is real value to speed, to being first – perhaps more so than in any other industry.' It was also apparent to Lou Gerstner, who had been a customer of IBM and other IT vendors for a couple of decades, that there was an endemic industry habit of making promises about products, technologies and due dates and then failing to deliver. He believed this ranked number one on customers' what's-wrong-with-this-industry list.

Gerstner and his executives correctly diagnosed IBM's problems as largely of its own making. Getting into this sorry state was inexcusable – although depressingly common, as we have seen elsewhere – but because *they* had made the problems it meant that IBMers could do something about them fairly rapidly. This was not to pretend that the transformation would happen overnight. Gerstner made it clear in countless communications that the transformation would be a multi-year commitment. His communication efforts were also marked by candour about the difficult actions that would need to be taken, particularly the necessity to fire tens of thousands of employees in a bid to reduce costs. The tone of Gerstner's communication changed during the course of the transformation. At the outset, it was blunt, tough and to the point, exhorting hard work and sacrifice in order to ensure the company's stability, if not survival. Then, it was about growth and ambition as the change took hold, never letting employees forget that the transformation had to be sustained.

Conceiving the Future

Gerstner's famous statement in July 1993 at a press conference that 'the last thing IBM needs right now is a vision' set the clear context for action at IBM. The press thought otherwise, worrying about a visionless IBM, lost without a direction. Gerstner and his senior executives, however, knew they had to fix the financial problems first and set out four priorities for the 1993 fiscal year:

1. Right-size the company rapidly, avoiding the uncertainty and ongoing discomfort of salami-slicing costs quarter after quarter. This would mean further big workforce reductions (some 35 000 on top of 45 000 the previous year) and an $8.9 billion write-down.
2. Restore employee morale, especially through a high level of sustained communication, saying candidly what would need to be done in the company. Gerstner himself communicated personally with many thousands of employees.
3. Get closer to customers and avoid the charge of arrogance that had come to so bedevil IBM in its dealings with the market. Gerstner was convinced that the customer needed

to be put back centre-stage and listened to. He wanted employees to be obsessed with satisfying customers.

4. Begin setting the important strategic directions for the company, designated at the time as:

    - Continuing to be the leader in technology
    - Placing greater emphasis on delivering solutions (value, ease of use and manageability)
    - Becoming the leader in open distributed computing, known as client/server.

A year later, as these initial priorities of the transformation were beginning to show results, Gerstner and his team were able to fine-tune the dozen or so business and technology strategies they had been working on (emerging from priority 4 above) into six 'strategic imperatives' – what Gerstner referred to as 'our roadmap for IBM's near-term future.' These were:

1. Exploiting our technology.
2. Increasing our share of the client/server computing market.
3. Establishing leadership in the emerging network-centric computing world.
4. Realigning the way we deliver value to customers.
5. Rapidly expanding our position in key emerging geographic markets.
6. Leveraging our size and scale to achieve cost and market advantages.

These strategic imperatives would be the drivers for what later amounted to the agenda workstreams (described below) and, as these workstreams began to be implemented, Gerstner returned in 1996 to what he calls 'the V-word'. Convinced both that network-centric computing would be the next phase in the development of computing demanded by customers and that new technologies were becoming capable of properly supporting rich interactive information sources like video, high-resolution images, voice and music, Gerstner set out the new IBM vision:

IBM will lead the transition to network-centric computing by:

- Continuing to create the advanced products and technologies needed to make powerful networks real; and
- Working with our customers to help them fully exploit these networks.

He also made the point in IBM's annual report that 'for the first time in nearly 30 years, we have the opportunity to align virtually every part of IBM in a single direction. Network-centric computing has emerged as our integrating strategy – the vision guiding our investments, products, services and our people.'

Building the Change Agenda

The six strategic imperatives articulated in the second year of the transformation, after the initial efforts to stabilize the organization were seen to be working, were aimed at launching a broad set of workstreams to change the organization and to ensure its growth. Some of the workstream actions that formed the agenda for change are outlined below each strategic imperative:

1. *Exploiting IBM technology*: getting new products out of the R&D labs and into the marketplace fast, forging technology agreements with other companies, building up technology licensing and selling more IBM products to other manufacturers.
2. *Increasing IBM's share of the client/server computing market*: further developing services around open systems in a number of countries and improving the way products from IBM and other vendors work together.
3. *Establishing leadership in the emerging network-centric computing world*: first, defining the new market and the new model of computing, for example through building IBM Global Network (a worldwide data network), embracing the Internet, and working with telephone and cable TV companies on interactive services to consumers and businesses.
4. *Realigning the way IBM delivers value to customers*: restructuring the organization on a more global footing as a worldwide sales and services firm, organized by industry and technology specialization.
5. *Rapidly expanding IBM's position in key emerging geographic markets*: opening new subsidiaries as well as assembly plants and research laboratories in targeted countries and regions.

6. *Leveraging IBM's size and scale to achieve cost and market advantages*: improve efficiency and continue to reduce costs through the creation of common technology 'building blocks' for hardware products, and consolidate purchasing and supply and office space.

In addition, if the company were to achieve its goal of building a new IBM – 'new culture, new directions, new spirit', as Gerstner put it in 1994 – it was clear that considerable effort would have to be devoted to changing the old corporate culture. For instance, this would mean establishing mechanisms for gaining better and faster information on what was happening outside IBM, in its markets, among customers and within competitors. Speed of decision making and execution would also have to become the norm, replacing the hierarchical, convoluted and bureaucratic decision making of the old IBM.

Delivering Big Change

By the fourth year of IBM's transformation, the key strategic imperatives and workstreams were advancing apace. This was manifest most gratifyingly for the company in its strength in the businesses that represented the best long-term potential for growth. For example, professional services in systems integration, outsourcing customers' data centres and the like were leaping ahead, as were the firm's hardware lines in mainframes and new desktop networking computers. The problems in the PC business, which had been in the doldrums for some time, had been resolved and IBM was shipping much-expanded volumes and taking share. The company was also fast exploiting its position as the largest software house in the world, especially as the intranet application Lotus Notes (Lotus was acquired in 1995) began to be used more widely under the IBM banner. IBM had, moreover, succeeded in building up its operations in China (becoming the largest PC vendor), Russia, Central Europe, South Africa, India and other parts of the Asia-Pacific. After setting out the company's progress in transforming the business in a letter to shareholders in IBM's 1996 annual report, Gerstner commented:

> Now, it's at this point in annual letters to shareholders where a CEO might be tempted to announce some bold new direction. I'm going to

resist the temptation and report to you that I believe we should stay the course. To be sure, our transformation is far from complete. We must and we will pick up the pace and intensity of everything we do.

Indeed, perhaps this sums up best the nature of the delivery transition line – in organizations large or small. Much effort (and probably pain) has gone before. The organization's performance has benefited from the early and arduous work to right the company: cost has been stripped out, the financial highlights look impressive, managers and employees are energized and excited. Now's the time, now's the temptation to be distracted and diverted and strike out in ambitious new directions or, alternatively, to relax in the celebration of victory – too soon. Persistence, singlemindedness and sustained execution are critical factors in the delivery of fundamental big change.

'EXECUTION: *THAT'S* WHERE PEOPLE GO WRONG . . .'

'I believe we should stay the course,' says Lou Gerstner. His comment is echoed by Ad Scheepbouwer of PTT Post: 'Like everything else, large-scale change is 1% creativity and 99% hard work. Execution: *that's* where people go wrong.' This is partly about dogged persistence, partly about the need to overcome the inclination to keep analysing and planning, and partly about letting go of the old ways of working and old business logic. The delivery of big change is the time when the break with the past must become real. Much of the preparatory work in the first three transition lines is intended to create turning points, to force discontinuity of purpose and embrace the new context. Without these things, scale change is not possible. But organizations do stumble when it comes to execution, attempting to prepare everything perfectly before taking that agonizing step into the future. In this regard, the caution of Symcor's Pierre Gravelle is worth heeding:

> You cannot have a pure setting. This is not a test-tube environment. We had to be prepared to move quickly once we made a decision and immediately make management teams accountable for implementation and results.

This can be daunting. In effect, the delivery of big change is the same as letting go of control. As a CEO or senior manager, all of a sudden you are almost totally reliant on the (sometimes vast) organization around you. You are, as Siemens Plessey's Clive Dolan acknowledges in his comments below, 'unleashing a complex writhing organization into the unknown' but, with the benefit of having seen through a number of years of the transformation, he also makes an additional salient point at the conclusion of his remark:

> At its heart, launching change like this means having to take the risk of letting go of the reins at some point. And that means that you are unleashing a complex, writhing organization into the unknown. You know that at any one time all the parts of it aren't working perfectly, but that's the only way you learn what does work and what doesn't . . .

The delivery transition line involves all the actions which begin to put the new business logic into place. This often involves the migration of solutions and blueprints – for example, cross-functional processes – developed off-line by dedicated teams into each business unit, the adoption of new technologies, or targeted acquisitions and disposals. It usually entails a high volume of training in new ways of working, in managing the process of change and possibly new approaches to day-to-day management and leadership. It may require the gradual but wholesale redesign of jobs, career routes, remuneration structures and training and development provision. All these things must be delivered if transformation is to be achieved. Which brings us to the main actions required to deliver big change, as outlined in Action List 7 and discussed in the rest of this chapter.

Action List 7   Delivering Big Change

1. Stay the course: start the delivery of change and complete it; persistence and singlemindedness to avoid diversions are vital.
2. Ensure the sustained sponsorship of transformation agenda workstreams.
3. Generate a critical mass of change across a broad front: communication and commitment building will not work without conflict escalation; most resistance to change is a *precondition* for change.

4. Implement change fast: the longer delivery of change drags on, the greater is the risk of failure.
5. Acknowledge mistakes fast, fix them and learn from them: there is always a danger of creating or returning to a culture of learned helplessness.
6. Construct the critical enablers of behavioural change: prompt, measure and reward the appropriate day-to-day behaviour that will deliver and sustain the new business logic.

STAYING THE COURSE

The first three transition lines set the occasion for big change. They are the antecedent conditions that provide the context and trigger for transformation. Leadership provides the prime motive force. Therefore, if the antecedent work has gone well, big change should begin – at different rates and with varying success, but it should nonetheless begin. Starting change initiatives is less of a problem than finishing them. 'If there's one thing we learned,' ScottishPower's Duncan Whyte acknowledges, 'it's to make sure you don't take your foot off the accelerator and you see it through to completion, because it's too easy to start initiatives and not complete them. At one stage we kicked off TQM [Total Quality Management] which we used as a change mechanism, but we probably left that in limbo and there wasn't follow-through. Also a couple of things we started with senior management development: there wasn't follow-through in terms of changing people's roles in jobs, expectations weren't met and there were some detrimental effects as a result. So we learned that completing things was very important.'

Although the danger of starting initiatives and not finishing them is characteristic of an organization in crisis or in the earliest stages of awakening, the same tendency may become apparent during the delivery of big change. (Project proliferation once more, as discussed in Chapter 8.) Workstream projects are launched, but make slow progress. Managers lose interest or slip back into dealing with business as usual. Smaller, fire-fighting initiatives are triggered. Or managers identify other interesting opportunities, putting a different spin on current workstreams, even to the extent of changing their direction. Later, when the transformation is clearly off-track, projects are launched to bolster those that are failing or to prop up key business activities that are not getting the support they expected from the original agenda workstreams. The net effect of all this is the gradual erosion of the overarching connection between all these initiatives – everything that had been constructed during the first three transition lines, linked carefully and directly to organizational purpose. The false sense of action that arises from project proliferation comes to substitute for purpose and progress. Diversions, distractions and peripheral and irrelevant organizational actions begin working at cross-purposes with the transformation agenda.

In innovative cultures the tendency towards diversion and distraction is natural. Bright people who value change, difference and novelty can get bored quickly with the dogged pursuit of a singleminded goal and the execution of long series of carefully planned actions. Even a small organization, packed with highly creative people and dedicated to creativity like St Luke's (see Chapter 4), needs considerable effort applied to direction setting, focus on each client and constant 'formation of the culture into bite-sized chunks', as chairman Andy Law puts it. So much greater is the challenge at organizations the size of IBM or British Airways. BA's S-P Mahoney makes the point: 'We've not always been good at following through. We've started to learn that, while often we have good ideas, many times in the execution of them we don't stick with something long enough to make it work.' Mahoney relates some of the problems the company faced in launching its subsidiary Deutsche BA, noting in particular the danger of distraction and diversion from the original decision:

> There we were, back in the late 80s and early 90s thinking France and Germany are important European markets, they're just in our backyard – let's try something. We had a really good objective – which was to be the second domestic airline in Germany – and we aimed to challenge Lufthansa and make it work. But we lost sight of what we were going for and as a result Deutsche BA started to take on some international flying, some charter flying, and lots of other things that actually distracted from the core business and therefore from being successful. Now, after a major review, we're keeping Deutsche BA and we're turning it round. But we will not be deviated this time. Deutsche BA will be the second domestic airline in Germany. We'll keep our focus.

Follow-through has crucial implications, not only for making progress but also for gaining commitment from employees. It is self-evident that if actions or workstreams are seen to be forcefully driven through by senior managers, any waverers are more likely to stiffen their resolve and resistors to acknowledge that the way things are moving might leave them behind. The responsibility on senior management, in the fist instance, to stay the course and be seen to stay the course, is very demanding. 'There is an enormous need,' Reckitt & Colman's Vernon Sankey sums up, 'to be very singleminded about this. You have to grit your teeth and repeat and repeat the messages and keep going, keep going, keep going. It requires a tremendous amount of determination.'

ENSURING SUSTAINED SPONSORSHIP OF TRANSFORMATION

Even with the right workstream management structure (see Chapter 8), the motive power of implementation can be diminished by failures in the sponsorship of transformation efforts. It is very hard to focus attention on changes lasting several years, absorbing large amounts of executive time and energy and often in apparent conflict with the everyday running of the business. Ensuring that sponsorship is sustained requires:

1. Training in the sponsorship role and duties
2. Periodic refreshing of the precise sponsorship remit for particular workstreams and projects – especially in line with adjustments to the direction, pace or objectives of workstreams during delivery
3. The appointment of new sponsors from time to time (or the reshuffling of sponsorship responsibilities) to ensure that energy is maintained.

In Chapter 3 we described the experience of Molson Breweries, an experience which cuts to the heart of sustaining sponsorship over the life of transformation. In anticipation of a more competitive beer market in Canada, Molson had embarked on a big change programme whose early phase was aimed at massive rationalization and cost reduction. In the process, of course, like many organizations worldwide, Molson slimmed down its middle-management workforce. With the best of intentions, as Michael Smith, Vice President, Organization Effectiveness, concedes, 'we spent a great deal of money and time on those we fired, making sure we treated them sensitively and with full support. Meantime, for those managers who remained and who were helping to lead the brunt of the change and for whom the change was most profound, we did nothing to help them make the change.' Now, Michael Smith has launched targeted leadership development for this group and acknowledges, 'We should have got it running earlier so that the change message was cascaded better and earlier . . .'

Change agents are the facilitators of behavioural change throughout the organization. Usually, because they are few and far between at the start of transformation and because of the novelty and importance of their efforts at that time, they receive substantial support from executives who realize their worth. The danger is later on when it is natural to assume, because of the massive effort applied over months and years, that change has been embedded in the organization. At this juncture, it is easy 'to take your foot off the accelerator', as ScottishPower's Duncan Whyte confesses, and through oversight or by declaring victory too soon to 'put people in positions where you leave them abandoned'. In ScottishPower, they have learned this lesson and invest heavily in training, education and support.

Gürhan Çalkivik, Vice President of Corporate Management Information Systems of Koç Holding, the $12 billion Turkish conglomerate, headquartered in Istanbul, faced similar difficulties. The steering committees for major projects were disbanded after the planning and design work and at the start of implementation. 'That was a mistake,' says Çalkivik. 'The implementation continued for two years, with a lot of new issues coming up. We needed sponsorship and direction, even during implementation. Somebody should lead, somebody should steer from the top so that you are covering the strategic needs of the projects.'

Likewise there is the counterpressure, emphasized by Lou Gerstner, of needing to do 'everything we can to focus everyone here on what's outside IBM – markets, customers, competitors.' Before Gerstner, IBM had been an organization self-absorbed (not to say self-obsessed) and arrogant, less inclined to listen to its customers than its competitors. IBM's turnaround and subsequent transformation might have sucked managerial and employee attention and efforts inwardly to the myriad tasks that big change demanded. But Gerstner, with his 'customer-is-king' predeliction, knew that profound *internal* changes to the business could only come about through a committed *external* focus.

In similar vein Novartis' Chairman Dr Alex Krauer talks of 'keeping in mind that there is a business to run'. With the stresses and strains of merger between Ciba and Sandoz, employees were distracted and inward-oriented during the integration, their attention not entirely focused on the market and the business, but on what was going on internally and how things would turn out for them personally. 'That is the time to make sure,' continues Krauer, 'that results are monitored closely.'

GENERATING A CRITICAL MASS OF CHANGE . . . OR USING RESISTANCE EFFECTIVELY

Despite the palpable sense of crisis and need for change felt within Metallgesellschaft and its largest subsidiary Lurgi, following the 1993 catastrophe, convincing people to change was not an easy task. There is a widespread but, to my mind, inaccurate assumption in organizations that crisis somehow instantly triggers change in people. The more likely reaction from people faced by crisis is to freeze, sticking sometimes absurdly to the old, 'normal' patterns of behaviour, since it is through these behaviour patterns that the experience and feelings of self-efficacy have been strongly established. This is often accompanied by cognition and behaviour characteristic of learned helplessness – 'there's nothing we can do; we can't make a difference'. At best, crisis provides the context and argument for change. But people need to become aware of what, to them, are virtually unconscious ways of doing things, no longer appropriate to the organization's changed circumstances. This is sometimes referred to as 'unfreezing', followed by change and then 'refreezing' (stabilizing the new behaviour), to use the nomenclature of Kurt Lewin (1947), one of the earliest researchers into the human dimension of organizational change. For Lurgi's Chris von Branconi, this was clearly evident, as he describes:

It depends a lot on the patience and consistency with which you demand change from people. It takes quite some energy to convince people to do things differently. The real problem is that you cannot automatically trigger their conviction. You can tell them to do it, but until they start thinking by themselves and understanding the idea behind the need to change, it will be very difficult to change behaviour.

Thus, von Branconi talks of opening an ongoing 'dialogue' with employees. Initially, in von Branconi's experience, this simply raised the temperature. 'People feel attacked,' he says. But the dialogue is a way of escalating cognitive conflict through challenge and critique of business and task-related issues while de-escalating affective conflict – i.e. surfacing common goals, values, norms and ensuring that people feel they are working, in common, together. ABB Calor Emag's Rolf Renke makes a similar point to do with communication, but describes its operation not in terms of crisis-driven transformation but as a normal part of delivering and mastering change. 'I think,' he says, 'one of the most important things is to set targets, communicate these targets and get the targets accepted by a wide range of not only managers but also employees. . . . The target setting is my task, but we try to encourage the other managers to communicate in teams and to discuss the targets in their teams and possible ways of achieving them.' So communication and target setting is never a one-way process. Managers and employees are *involved*. They are able to contribute, raise objections, and get frustrations out in the open. Renke goes on to describe the details of getting a critical mass of employees committed to the change:

> The point is *not* to *tell* them. The point is to *communicate* with them: that means in groups of 10 to 15 people and normally we use what we call in German a 'snowball' system – a cascade – through the opinion leaders first because they are most influential, then on to others. If we don't get a reaction or any hard discussion, then we know the change will not work. They have just said yes, but are not committed.

Two points emerge here. First, the cascade of communication is initially through the opinion leaders, so that senior management have a chance to build critical mass in bite-sized chunks. This also enables them to leverage off the sustaining sponsorship of such opinion leaders more widely in the population of employees and further down the track if change gets bogged down. The second point is that the commitment building is always in teams or groups of a size where debate and discussion (task-related conflict) can take place and are manageable. In short, a critical mass of commitment will never be generated without conflict escalation – the airing of differences, divided opinions, good ideas, criticisms and the like. The necessity, quite clearly though, is for those facilitating such commitment-building events to understand the counterintuitive nature of conflict and to possess effective conflict-escalation skills.

Embedded within the above discussion is an assumption that so-called resistance to change is no bad thing. The notion of conflict escalation turns the traditional view of resistance on its head. If you do not get resistance – that is, some level of conflict – then transformation will, at best, underdeliver on your expectations or, at worst, get nowhere, sparking smouldering cynicism and feeding the roots of a culture of learned helplessness. This is actually made worse by some prevailing notions of 'participation' in the workplace, where participation is equated with smooth interaction (for this read 'the suppression of conflict') or with senior management requesting 'ideas' from employees but not criticism or debate. The position I take in this book is one which exhorts the active escalation and management of conflict (see Chapter 5).

IMPLEMENT CHANGE FAST

Novartis regard themselves as the world leader in the science of life – pharmaceutical products dedicated to humankind's problems. The name Novartis was conjured from the Latin *novae artes*, meaning 'new skills', and both organizations that made up the $29 billion Novartis enterprise – Ciba and Sandoz – knew that the prize for getting the merger right was the global leadership position in their industry. But it was necessary to make the transition quickly: most mergers do not deliver on their promise of transformation; they fail to create the anticipated value or do so too slowly. Chairman Alex Krauer contends:

> We had to be fast. We were in a race against operating problems, competitors, employee complacency and those who resisted the change. One of the basic lessons in a merger is that the longer integration drags, the greater is the risk of failure.

The question, of course, arises: How fast is fast? In the British Post Office, CEO John Roberts' initial efforts to get 190 000 employees to understand that they had not reached a plateau and could now stop changing, became too threatening. The result was strike action and disruption. 'A lot of that,' declares Roberts, 'was us trying to move change faster than the union and staff were prepared to go. This is a hard nut to crack. If we could have been better able to predict the amount of change that we could have got through without triggering disruption, that would have made life a hell of a lot easier. The whole thing would have moved forward a lot faster. With hindsight, there are probably ways we could have done it better.'

Plotting and adjusting the speed of change is an executive judgement call. It is however, facilitated by robust information channels and communication of the sort described by Rolf Renke and discussed in the previous section – communication that engages the critical faculty of employees and is attuned to problem solving and therefore commitment building, *not* conflict suppression.

Success in delivering change at speed is also directly dependent on the sense of *change overload* experienced by employees. Big change is, by its nature and intent, broad and deep, affecting the entire organization. Combined with the pressure to move quickly and to sustain the ongoing business, such significant change can rapidly approach overload. Employees will start to off-load those activities that in their estimation are not priorities – usually anything not constantly demanded or scrutinized by their immediate bosses. If overload increases, a climate of reactivity will be engendered, employees concentrating less and less on the organization's transformation agenda priorities and more and more on immediate demands and on the *appearance* of action. Employees feel overwhelmed and increasingly helpless. High work rates disguise directionless activity. These conditions and the feelings produced by them can become generalized across the business. Each part of the organizational entity affects and depends on others. This reciprocity is not confined to positive interaction. Disruption in one eventually produces disruption in others. Severe overload can tip the organization into the culture of learned helplessness. ABB's Rolf Renke has learned this lesson. 'One of our mistakes in the past,' he recalls, 'was to have too many things changing at the same time. If you overload the organization, you confuse people.'

Another important action here is to judge carefully when to increase the velocity of change. There comes a point during the implementation of big change when all the data and feedback filtering through to senior management will indicate that the new business logic defined and amplified in the efforts of the first three transition lines and in the early part of delivery are not only properly understood but also have become the accepted way of thinking about the business. At this point, managers and employees are ready for an acceleration of change and disruption (on the grounds of emotional resistance) is likely to be minimal. Reckitt & Colman's Vernon Sankey speaks of the timing for accelerating big change and extracting maximum value from the transformation:

> We are in a much better position now. Whatever the future holds, we are in a much better position. But the transformation is not over. The train has left the station and most people who need to be on it are on it and there is no question about the train going back. However, the implementation in order to really capture the benefits of global transformation is in its infancy. It is worth, in monetary terms, hundreds of millions of dollars and we may be capturing 20 to 30 million currently. So the next three years are about actually implementing transformation as opposed to designing and getting the pieces in place. The concept is well understood and well accepted. It is irreversible. The train has now got to move at a much faster speed . . .

ACKNOWLEDGING MISTAKES AND LEARNING FROM THEM

There exists an implicit danger in implementing the streams of actions determined by new organizational purpose, strategy and agenda. The danger is that the workstreams and projects become prescriptions carved in stone, never to be altered. One of the contradictions leaders of transformation face is the need to be singleminded and relentless in delivering change, but simultaneously open to the lessons from changing circumstances, mistakes and failures. To strike this balance is the task of leadership. What can help is making an explicit commitment to each other in the executive team to acknowledge mistakes quickly, make the necessary changes and then move on. Making this explicit prevents the inevitable difficulties later on of embarrassment, losing face, blaming and concealment. Apart from anything else, there is the simple truth that, no matter how well conceived, planned and executed the transformation, 'you cannot,' to use Clive Dolan's phrase, 'think it all through beforehand'. Dolan goes on to describe his conception of the Siemens Plessey transformation and the recently announced decision to sell the business:

> My mental image of the change is of a marching army; now there is a column approaching from right field and that is slowing the army. But we can't just stop the army. We have to absorb and reassemble on the move.

Problems lying in wait can be created at the outset but only rear their heads during implementation. So, for example, with 100 000 staff in 60 countries, the announcement of Novartis as 'a merger of two equals' brought with it the danger that during implementation managers and staff would interpret this as implying a 50/50 split in everything. 'This can be a serious pitfall in mergers,' asserts Alex Krauer. 'It's tempting to talk about it like this in the early days, but when it comes to implementation it can become dangerous if it is interpreted as a strict 50/50 right to be applied when choosing people or designing structures and so on. So we use it as a guiding principle, but apply it in a constructive way – each side has to be sufficiently generous to make compromises. And that means providing leadership at every level, instead of playing politics.'

Being able to see and then do something about mistakes and difficulties requires leaders to have developed both the skills and the mechanisms that enable them to *disconnect* from the everyday delivery of transformation. By disconnection I mean the capacity to stand outside the detail and progress of big change and view it warts and all. In a sense this is both hardest and easiest for chief executives – hardest because they are the individuals feeling some of the greatest pressure to understand the fine detail of every aspect of the transformation, thus they may fail to see the wood for the trees; easiest because they have the authority and corporate altitude to be able to view the whole picture without constraint, without the boundaries that encircle the perspectives of most other managers and employees.

A failure of leadership is to have feet of clay, to concentrate on delivering workstreams that may gradually have become cosmetic and irrelevant, or to get too involved in the politics of the situation, thereby losing objectivity. To gain the freedom, the release from internal political constraints, the opportunity to stand back and dissect the workings of the organization with dispassion, is an ambition worth striving for, if transformation is to be achieved.

CONSTRUCTING THE CRITICAL ENABLERS OF BEHAVIOURAL CHANGE

People are profoundly influenced by the environment in which they live or work. Talented individuals may devote hours each evening and over weekends to a complex hobby and become experts in a subject unrelated to work; at the same time in the organization that demands most of the waking hours of their adult life, they may only do enough to pass muster; they may be disenchanted and unable to contribute more. Why this disparity between home and work? The environments are different. One is set up to encourage and reward interest, involvement and positive contribution, the other to control, to schedule and to constrain.

'As managers,' says Symcor's Pierre Gravelle, 'we are always tempted, in a logical and Cartesian way, to deal with the things that are most appealing – i.e. a technology plan, streamlining, re-engineering and so forth. We tend to leave for later the people dimension. This has to be pursued at the same time. You must give as much, if not more, attention to the people dimension.' Executives who also pay close attention to the critical enablers of human change will deliver transformation faster and more smoothly. We are not concerned here with communication – despite its huge importance – but with the mechanisms that support adoption and maintenance of the new business logic: clarity about what behaviour is relevant, measurement of it, and rewards to build and sustain it.

At IBM, for example, executives laid out clearly what employees should be focusing on. The company had been inward-oriented for a long time and this would have to change to consistently view what was happening outside the business, in its markets, among customers and at competitors. Speed of decision making and execution were also priorities as the lifecycle of computer products dropped steadily from eighteen months to a year to nine months. Lou Gerstner had awakened the company to the fact that customers had slipped from centre-stage and had to be put back. On-time delivery in fulfilment of expectations was a key objective in the transformation. This could not happen without a new emphasis on speed of decision making and fast action by managers and employees. IBM's old culture of approval hierarchies and 'that's-the-way-we've-always-launched-products' had to be swept aside.

IBM underpinned these behavioural changes with a complete overhaul of the entire compensation system. Managers looked at how competitive the current system was in the job markets and designed and implemented new incentive-based elements of the compensation framework to pay better rewards to those people who were star performers within the new IBM way of working. Likewise, a series of new training programmes focused on relevant skills and career development was started. Moreover, to fuel growth the company began hiring new employees – more than 60 new executives in early 1994 (to bring new perspectives and as Gerstner put it, 'quicken the process of transformation'), plus another 15 000 through the rest of the year, some 26 000 in 1995 and 16 000 in 1996.

Attention to the critical enablers of behavioural change is especially important where the change itself is well outside employees' normal experience, i.e. where the gap they must leap is wider and more challenging – in short, frightening – than anything they have previously experienced. The transformation at Revenue Canada, for instance, profoundly affected the content of jobs through a combination of cost reduction and consolidation as well as automation of many of the operational and delivery processes. Of course, some of the old types of work were eliminated altogether in the blueprint and its implementation, but new technology and the process re-engineering also created more complex work and enabled the Revenue to handle much higher volumes.

Pierre Gravelle and his management teams sketched out the details of the expected behavioural changes. Managers and administrative employees would have to behave in very different ways. For managers the main headings for the behavioural descriptors were:

Before	*Now*
	Change agent
	Mentor/coach
Planner	Holistic visionary
Organizer	Communicator
Controller	Facilitator
	Innovator
	Coordinator
	Team leader

For employees, the shift would have to be from administrative support to *knowledge worker* and the headings for the knowledge worker skill set were:

- Analytical
- Problem solving
- Versatile, adaptable and greater mobility
- Continuous learner and responsible for learning
- Decision maker
- Team player
- Communication and interpersonal skills

It was obvious that training and retraining would have to be integral to the roll-out of new technology and re-engineered processes. Indeed, implementation is largely dependent on the delivery of training and the absorption of new behaviour by a critical mass of employees – both technical knowledge and especially the new skills identified in the descriptors above. There was no naiveté about the difficulty of making the adjustment towards these behavioural descriptors, however. Gravelle and his managers were convinced that only some staff could adapt. Others would not. 'Training,' declares Gravelle, 'cannot help those who can't adapt or whose skills cannot be ungraded. In some cases it may be better to buy or recruit the skills required rather than to invest in the training.' Recruitment therefore became geared towards assessing for and hiring adaptive, continuous learners while also raising the entry-level skill requirements.

Even with mammoth efforts across recruitment, training and rewards, building and sustaining the change can still be difficult. Siemens Plessey's Clive Dolan was surprised by the personal effort and commitment he needed to make in addition to the changes to the human resources enablers that were required. 'We humans,' he laments, 'are very good at taking in the signals from our environment and thus subconsciously being shaped in the way we do things. I don't believe we realize just how programmed we are. We think we're open-minded, adaptable and resilient. But when you start a change programme like this, you realize it's a myth.'

With this new learning in mind, Dolan's ultimate goal was to get managers in particular to understand that *their real job now was to make change happen*. When it came to the delivery of change it was obvious that too many managers had a vested interest in maintaining the old organization and *status quo*. They had, in actuality, grown strong because of it. 'I had begun,' admits Dolan, 'to understand the way that reward and recognition systems, the measurement processes and the artificial boundaries of the organization influence the way that people behave.' These would have to change if the new business logic was to be set in place and properly embedded. But for the enablers of behavioural change – new behaviour descriptors, measurement and reward – to be embedded required that they be *personalized*. Dolan explains what he means:

> I could regard changing my business as a duty, but I don't: I have a conviction. I can tell you it burns away at me. It's what I have to do. And you have to transfer that conviction to those who work for you by personalizing it. You can't avoid this. You have to put new measures on people to change their behaviour patterns and when they don't meet those measures, you have to be prepared to push them hard. Equally, you have to be prepared to sing the praises of somebody who has gone against the in-built constraints of the organization and employees, or who has gone out on a limb to make the required changes happen. You have to resist the instinct to criticize mistakes. You have to say, 'We learned from what you did and we can be better because of it.' And if, just once, you nail someone for efforts to change which turn out badly, you've nailed your whole change programme.

10

Mastering Change

MAKING IT STICK OR RUNNING FROM CHANGE

In March 1997, reviewing the change efforts of $38 billion Sears, Roebuck and Co., Chairman and CEO Arthur Martinez made the comment:

> While we have made good financial progress and have solid growth plans, we have not yet achieved fully the kind of transformation that we seek for the business. Transformation requires a work force, from top to bottom, that is committed to embracing and fostering change, not running from it. Associates must think like owners if we are to keep the process of continuous reinvention alive inside the company. We will continue to accelerate the pace of change inside Sears. The best retailers are constantly improving their business. There are no final solutions. The question is, how do we improve our business today to make it better tomorrow?

Mastering change begins from the premise that there are no final solutions. But Martinez's ambition for the Sears' workforce to embrace and foster change rather than run from it defines a level of organizational functioning to which many will aspire but few will attain. St Luke's, the $110 million, 80-person advertising agency discussed in Chapter 4, has a powerful underlying philosophy and culture that comes close to the Martinez ideal. But while Martinez talks about Sears' associates needing to 'think like owners', St Luke's managers and staff *are* owners. This difference is pretty fundamental. It affects not only the way people think and behave but also the way the business operates. Information and responsibility are not held or trapped at more senior levels; information flows directly to frontline workers and vice versa; responsibility is taken rather than offered. Moreover, the idea of ownership is not one based purely on financial considerations but rather common purpose. In fact, chairman

Andy Law expresses the ambition of St Luke's as being the transformation of the advertising business, away from ego and greed and towards something durable. Honest, ethical advertising is the company's purpose. Employees talk about the company's 'Total Role in Society' – how it interacts with all its stakeholders, whether shareholders, employees, clients, competitors, the environment or consumer groups. Though small, St Luke's offers lessons for larger organizations, especially those in knowledge-based industries, but more widely for all organizations attempting to grasp and leverage individual creativity and business innovation and most especially in elevating the mastery of change to a higher level, as we shall see later in this chapter.

Larger organizations whose workforces do not run from change may nonetheless subsequently and suddenly fail – a fear expressed by Novartis' chairman Alex Krauer. 'Success is our biggest enemy,' he worries, 'because it may lead to complacency.' John Roberts of the British Post Office is also less than sanguine about the issue. 'One thing I've learned about change,' he says, 'is that whenever you think you've made it stick, you probably haven't. You have to reinvigorate and reinforce.' In a sense, though, the ambition to master change, to challenge all employees to embrace and foster change and therefore take transformation to its highest point of achievement, is more important than its attainment. For it is the habit of *struggling* for victory which gives an organization the power to continue to transform. One of the ways to launch an organization into the next inevitable big change trajectory – a second transformation S-curve – is to have embedded the chief driving forces of that struggle for victory deep within the organization: these are systemic innovation, the tools for conflict escalation and the capacity for transformational leadership. So the transition line mastering change, at the very least, must ensure that these elements are in place.

Mastering change is concerned with two primary goals:

1. Consolidating gains and extracting maximum value from the new business logic.
2. The pursuit of constructive instability – i.e. searching for internal and environmental pressures to deliberately force the organization to progress and improve in the *absence* of real threats.

The first of these is to be expected and it will be driven, in many organizations, by pressure from shareholders for optimum performance. It is about raising the game, drawing value from what will have amounted to a major investment in the transformation, consolidating positions in new markets or using and defending newly acquired core competencies. In businesses, like IBM, Sears and British Airways, it will mean fine-tuning the capacity of the firm for commercial exploitation of its assets – financial, human, physical and knowledge-based. In state or not-for-profit organizations, like DERA and Revenue Canada, it will mean continuing deployment of service enhancements for, and jointly with, clients and stake-holders.

A number of actions are identifiable under both of the goals set out above and are shown in Action List 8.

Action List 8   Mastering Change

Consolidating Gains and Extracting Maximum Value

1. Exploit transformation breakthroughs: big change will have produced one or a number of major advantages or defensive capabilities which must not be allowed to languish in the afterglow of having changed the organization – it is no good declaring victory after the battle, only to lose the war.
2. Accept nothing less than ongoing consistency of behaviour in alignment with the new business logic: measure behaviour and business performance accordingly.
3. Continuously build and reinforce a culture of personal responsibility for change.

The Pursuit of Constructive Instability

4. Aggressively invest in the improvement of all corporate capabilities, in preference to seeking the easier option of stabilizing the organization.

5. Actively seek exposure to external pressures
   and competition, even if such threats seem
   avoidable: aim to build superior organizational
   strength and capability *as a matter of course.*

CONSOLIDATING GAINS AND EXTRACTING MAXIMUM VALUE

Exploiting Transformation Breakthroughs

Transformation should deliver an overall business performance improvement, such that the financial ratios look more impressive than before or outshine those of competitors. Many organizations will be tempted into strategic errors at this point: easing back or concentrating effort on the way things are now, growing the business on the assumption that a kind of plateau has been attained through the transformation. Certainly improved financial performance is a desirable outcome, especially if this means that the firm has created both an infrastructure and culture of low cost: in itself this is a competitive advantage. But by no means is this the best payback for the cost and disruption of big change efforts.

Significant gains will be made by organizations that focus their efforts on exploiting a few critical breakthroughs achieved during the course of the previous four transition lines. Such breakthroughs may be many and varied. A firm may so effectively transform its customer service throughout the organization that it succeeds not only in winning custom and loyalty in its market but leverages this to magnify and strengthen its brands, creating a positive feedback cycle between customer service and brand – something Sears attempted to achieve in its transformation. Alternatively, an organization may boost new product development by globalizing the process, cutting back on the number of initiatives and focusing resources on a smaller number of priority projects. This has the benefit of cutting duplication and therefore reducing cost, most certainly. But it also may increase the probability of real excellence in a focused range of global products. This has been a feature of the transformations of both IBM and Reckitt & Colman.

The most desirable transformation breakthroughs, however, come from building a *defensive capability not subject to simple replication by competitors*, and it is this that is the chief prize of transformation – a topic discussed at length in Chapter 1. Further, in a world where increasingly (perhaps exponentially) the use and application of information, knowledge and ideas have the potential for vast wealth creation, harnessing knowledge to new ends will be the most powerful of defensive capabilities.

Of course, no defensive capability will be forever, but this kind of breakthrough generates powerful advantages for the firm and high barriers to competitors. The greatest advantage to a firm is *time*, time to exploit existing or new markets and invest in the future, time to see and respond to new entrants and non-traditional competitors sweeping in on your flank. The most critical barrier to competitors is the cost they will have to pay of regaining parity and relatedly the risk of stifled opportunity and sub-optimal growth that comes from playing in the second rank. Reckitt & Colman's Vernon Sankey, for example, talks about 'owning a distinctive position', recognizing that the weaker companies in the industry are disappearing and the strong are getting stronger. This distinctive position, carved out through transformation efforts, is something that is defensible and can be protected. But, as Sankey remarks, 'you have to own a position that gives you a year or eighteen months'.

At the same time as Sankey and his team were actively embedding the massive changes to the business, not least the strategy of embracing what was a dispersed international collection of autonomous businesses into a focused global organization, they were also looking ahead to the breakthroughs. This was particularly relevant in attempting to drive growth into the new global business. What Sankey and his team wanted to do was gain breakthroughs from the dynamics of pooling world-class ideas and expertise between global teams – both on a day-to-day basis through the new structure and coordinated communication and by transferring skills and expertise where they could be most effective. This was in addition to integrating product innovation and development activities globally to speed the launch of new products or using buying power on a world scale. As Sankey contends, 'In a global company, transferring good ideas more rapidly – that's worth a lot of money.'

So is the voice with which the organization speaks to its markets, the more so in this globalizing world economy. The old IBM, for example, when Lou Gerstner took the reins in 1993, was running more than 100 advertising campaigns through a plethora of ad agencies in different countries and regions. As part of the IBM 'global solutions' approach, all this was consolidated into a single voice conceived and administered by one worldwide agency.

Finding and exploiting transformation breakthroughs are therefore crucial to making the most of the time and effort devoted to big change.

Accepting Nothing Less than Ongoing Consistency

Successful, purposeful behaviour change in organizations requires complex adjustments at two levels:

1. Employee understanding of the intended change and willingness to adopt the change
2. Modification of the organizational environment within which people work (i.e. structure, processes, norms).

The organizational environment supports a particular range of behaviour patterns. For example, a functional structure will tend to limit cross-business working; a process structure will emphasize team work; a culture of hierarchy and formality will create ponderous, risk-averse decision making and so forth. Changing these environmental elements necessitates some kind of change in people – but what emerges may not always be what was intended. Thus, communication and commitment building (especially through conflict escalation) are critical actions in getting the right change to happen. Nevertheless, organizations in transition are just that – in transition. The environmental frameworks that trigger, support, reward or rule out certain behaviour are not properly established. Nor can they be established simply by management diktat or heavy doses of communication. The organization is a social–psychological system and the new frameworks governing much of employees' behaviour will be bedded down by the employees themselves. This is a crucial point. People establish the new social–psychological system by functioning within it; there is no shortcut.

However, the behavioural system will tend to revert to its previous forms or to construct variations of it if it is allowed to do so. In short, disciplined, categorical management of the behavioural system is needed, in addition to communication and commitment building. Any inconsistency in this management will be picked up by employees and behaviour will adjust accordingly – out of synchrony with the intended transition. This is why the notion of 'values' has become so popular in the management media. Values represent a firm-wide way of establishing and reinforcing behaviour under myriad day-to-day working conditions, ostensibly without close management control. US retailer Nordstrom, for instance, has established a core value of 'satisfying the unreasonable customer' and this is clearly articulated in its corporate literature. It does seem to focus and channel employee behaviour. British Airways also has powerful values but staff do not go around with the new mission in mind, nor are they able to articulate on demand a set of formal values. But the values are there nonetheless: safety, security, proactive and spontaneous goodwill to the customer, excelling in a crisis.

Much money has been spent on devising corporate values and teaching them to employees – most of it wasted. Why? Usually because the new values are aspirations totally unconnected from the reality of organizational life – i.e. what employees know and understand about the way the organization really is.

As pointed out in Chapter 5, values must be built on the reality of organizational success, not on its promise. This usually means that values either emerge naturally from what the organization becomes or are successfully grafted onto organizational life only following massive changes to what DERA's John Chisholm calls 'the underlying reality' – the processes of the organization, the way the organization works. It is the overt victories of transformation that are the foundation for expressing and spreading new values throughout the organization. When the underlying reality has changed and people witness its success, that is the time to link new values to the emotional experience of winning.

So there is a timing issue to do with building and using values. Moreover, making sure that the emerging behavioural system (which includes the value set) reinforces the appropriate behaviour depends exclusively on the capability of leaders and managers to install and then *consistently* manage those mechanisms that encourage and reward appropriate behaviour and rule out the inappropriate. This must be vigorously pursued as Siemens Plessey's Clive Dolan confirms:

> It takes a long time to create change in an organization. Change is really about producing consistency. Change becomes real when regularly, patiently, everyone in the organization behaves in a way consistent with the new values.

Attaining this means fine-tuning the behavioural and performance measures of the business constructed and rolled out during the delivery transition-line (Chapter 9), so that there can be no misinterpretation of what is required by the new business logic and no backsliding to outmoded ways of working.

Building and Reinforcing a Culture of Personal Responsibility for Change

There is something of an in-built contradiction in encouraging consistency of behaviour, as detailed in the previous section, and building a culture that expects people to embrace and foster change. Yet this is what some organizations do achieve. British Airways' empowered culture is a case in point. This means that employees use their brains. They make decisions on specific actions. They try things. They are individually responsive to other individuals, whether colleagues, customers, or suppliers – anywhere in the value chain. Multiplied up from the individual to the business as a whole, this generates enormous motive power, especially where BA employees come up against the unexpected or the non-standard. Yet, what BA have discovered is that empowerment is not a one-size-fits-all. A different sort of empowerment, along the lines of factory process empowerment, is required in the main process-driven chunks of the organization (see Chapter 5). So the apparent contradiction disappears once we apply a higher magnification to the problem.

At ABB this culture of personal responsibility is articulated in the statement of values and reinforced through the constant management messages about action orientation, acting decisively and managers being the driving force for change. Indeed ABB Calor Emag's Rolf Renke can envisage no other way to work; the culture of personal responsibility is ingrained, as he describes:

> The responsibility for changing processes or anything else is not down to me or a Board member or some special guy. We all target the changes we have to make. That is participative. Then, depending on what it is, many different people are responsible for making the change.

But getting to this state does take time, constant communication of the same messages about change, and good-quality training in change leadership and implementation. So convinced were the Reckitt & Colman executive team about this that they put themselves through what they called a Transformation Leadership Workshop early in the big change programme, then rolled this out through the organization. The training was aimed at establishing change leadership as one of the fundamental principles of the transformation effort – and one of the central actions expected of people experiencing the workshops was to 'question the status quo: believe in change.'

Thinking back on his experience at Revenue Canada, Pierre Gravelle makes a different point – about encouraging sharing as a means to foster continuous learning at both the organizational and personal level. This kind of sharing need not merely be an aspiration or an exhortation to staff. It can be systematized, as Gravelle describes:

> Sharing exemplary service and organizational practices is an effective means for facilitating continuous service improvement. Successes in one area can often be adapted and applied in another. For employees, the sharing of best practices can engender a sense of pride in accomplishments and satisfaction in sharing and learning from colleagues.

In Word and in Deed

Words are easy and many, while great deeds are difficult and rare.

Winston Churchill, *Marlborough* (1933–8)

THE PURSUIT OF CONSTRUCTIVE INSTABILITY

We have now discussed the actions that will help an organization to extract maximum value from the exertions of transformation. But true mastery calls forth new endeavour. It calls forth change that goes beyond drawing value from the investment or raising the game within the new business logic – important as these objectives undoubtedly are. *Retaining a significant advantage or defensive capability will only be possible by energizing the internal capability of the organization in ways that allow it to destroy its old advantages and devise new ones.* I take no credit for this idea: Joseph Schumpeter in 1942 wrote of the need for 'creative destruction' by firms, if they were to retain any hope of holding their own against competitive action. It was clear to Schumpeter (and it is a lesson every executive should learn) that competition by its very nature is in a state of disequilibrium. It is never static. It changes – most usually in surprising, unexpected ways. This takes us back to leadership (Chapter 3) and my notion of *unpredictability* as one of the five essential elements of leadership behaviour. Leaders who take the market by surprise (by doing the unconventional and the non-traditional, by superseding or nullifying current strengths for new advantages) will always beat their conservative peers in other organizations. But they will do this only if they are also able to have taken their own organization by surprise – to have moved fast and decisively to build and then sustain a culture of challenge, change, improvement and innovation in pursuit of constructive instability.

Aggressively Investing in the Improvement of all Corporate Capabilities

The very great exertion demanded by transformation and the natural tendency of executives and employees to view it as a 'programme' or 'project' will inevitably mark big change as a single, once-and-for-all push that takes the organization to a new, sunny plateau. In this Nirvana, everything will be better. Things will settle. Uncertainties and pressures will stabilize. Expectations of this kind, once fulfilled (or more properly self-fulfilled) in the sense that the organization stops the transformation cycle to live off the fruits of its labours, are terribly dangerous. They begin to bed down as a culture that, in the current global context of competitive intensity, will rapidly make the firm as ponderous and ill-equipped to thrive (or even survive) as it may have been before big change. A new inertia will build up around the very things that have been changed. Employees will create bureaucracy as new procedures and rules, both formal and informal, replace the old. Only certain types of people will be recruited – in the image of those who recruit them. The information system will become hardwired to access and filter internal and external data in fixed ways that serve individual employees or coalitions but distort the true picture for decision makers. Victory will afford current strategy a mystical power, to be questioned by none until, ultimately, unexpected competitor action smashes the sacred edifice.

It is the role of leaders to recognize that transformation is not a one-off event (though it may last years) and does not end with consolidating gains and extracting maximum value. Nor should it mean the termination of investment in change, which to date will have been considerable – a good deal devoted to ramping up business capabilities across the value chain or even building new ones, acquiring or disposing of assets, in addition to streamlining and improving infrastructure, and not a little earmarked for upgrading skills necessary for the transformed business. Investment must continue. The higher level of mastery towards which firms should strive means sustained investment to ensure that the organization holds widespread, advanced and continually upgraded corporate capabilities. In Chapter 8, we described Level 1 and Level 2 capabilities. We said that Level 1 capabilities have to do with direction setting and decisions on where and how to compete, thus with actions that might involve needed changes in the business portfolio or in the way the organization approaches its markets. Level 2 capabilities have to do with how the organization operates, with those elements that provide the organization the wherewithal to shift towards selected new directions. The actions here, therefore, are to do with its structure and assets, systems and processes, technologies, its management talent, human resources (both people and practices) and the prevailing social–psychological ethos. Mastery seeks to invest in and upgrade these capabilities – *not to stabilize them within the new business logic*.

This necessitates ongoing change that is not the abstract, directionless executive plea for managers and employees to 'embrace change'. In place of regarding the elements of the corporate enterprise as fixed assets, systems or processes, this conception shifts executive thinking to view them as dynamic capabilities that must constantly be improved. Executives are then able to cascade responsibility for action to address each capability while retaining an overview of progress across the firm. This approach provides the management schema (agenda, objectives, measurement) for mastery of change; the motive power comes from the social–psychological dynamics of the organization – leadership, systemic innovation and conflict escalation.

Thus, an enterprise that can be regarded as having achieved mastery will habitually engage in activities which to conventional firms in the industry are disturbing and counterintuitive, but which nonetheless are provocations that stimulate meaningful change in corporate capabilities. A company might legitimize the off-the-wall, unconventional and 'difficult' thinkers and activists by rewarding and promoting them or by celebrating their ideas. Executives might establish and sustain budgets for innovative and entrepreneurial initiatives, budgets that are freely available to individuals to try out their ideas (under proper monitoring and review). The business might allow large salary or incentive discrepancies for successful internal entrepreneurs, treating them as if they were in business for themselves – i.e. paying people over the odds for actioning great ideas which deliver payback to the company. Just how many organizations believe that people are incentivized by working for the glory of seeing the organization make a great deal of money? Far too many. And so they lose good people – either to plodding, uninspired obedience inside the firm or to competitors who snap them up for their knowledge and skills. For firms attempting to compete globally, executives might deliberately and actively appoint an international mix of managers to senior teams, including the top team, breaking the widespread tradition of having an overwhelming concentration of home nationalities at the centre and elsewhere in authority. This is something that Nikko Securities, one of Japan's largest brokers, began to do in line with its global strategy – an unusual step for a Japanese enterprise. The same might also be true of general recruitment, encouraging a positive spiral of buying-in 'difference'.

St Luke's chairman Andy Law makes this comment: 'We decided that creativity is not enhanced by all the usual things you find in advertising agencies – habit-forming, bureaucracy, fear, hierarchy. We knew we must let people's values, aspirations and imagination flow freely.' Law and his colleagues worry about *ritual*, about those tendencies in life and work that become ingrained habits and that sap not only creativity but also interest in work. Consequently, they are dedicated to the unconventional and the unpredictable. At one stage, for example, Law brought in an art student to the agency's London offices and asked her to redecorate the place *every few days*. Law wanted to challenge his colleagues' thinking, but not in away-days and events that were disconnected from day-to-day experience. With that in mind, Natasha Rampley, the art student, set to work overnight, painting dozens of small mice along the skirting board, together with mouse holes with pieces of paper cheese, wrapping the office interior in bubble wrap, and pickling photographs of staff in large jars of glowing liquid and wiring them up to computers.

For St Luke's, this challenge (over one summer) to staff ritual and habit is but one example of the overall philosophy and detailed practice of the company. The commitment to change is everywhere evident: the virtually flat structure with few formal organizational arrangements, the participative decision making (even to setting their own salaries), upward and downward performance reviews, no secretaries 'owned' by directors and no offices, merely client rooms that clients can use in collaboration with St Luke's staff and where campaigns are initiated and run. Even the facilities, including personal computers, are shared so that a true collaborative ethos prevails. Change is likewise embodied in the design of the organization. It has evolved to accommodate and stimulate growth. So the company avoided what Andy Law calls the 'one big blob' problem and moved instead to 'creative cells' – bite-sized organizational chunks of up to 35 people – each of which operates as a group of owner–entrepreneurs, stimulating involvement, interest and intimacy with clients. Once a cell reaches 35 it must give up ten of its people to form a new cell.

These actions, and others like them, invite pressure, provocation and challenge. They are uncomfortable. They escalate conflict. They disturb the organizational equilibrium. But even by this standard, the disequilibrium of the competitive market will be more so: the world of *Faster, Faster* perhaps. Consequently, any pressure, provocation and challenge that upgrades corporate capabilities at a rate faster than competitors are able to match and new entrants are able to replicate or do differently will lead to breakthroughs. These breakthroughs, in turn, will lead to advantages and defensive capabilities that produce superior revenue growth, profitability and longer-term market value. With slightly different objectives in mind, the same is true in state and not-for-profit organizations. In 1995 in a speech in Washington, DC, on his eight years with Canada's Revenue Adminstration, much of that time engaged in its transformation, Pierre Gravelle commented:

> The challenge is to identify new, innovative ways of providing services rather than simply maintaining our traditional presence and current client services. . . . I have often characterized our vision for the future as requiring 'constructive damage' to the status quo, challenging our current service and compliance paradigm, and proceeding boldly and confidently.

It is sometimes argued that organizations are vulnerable to chance and circumstance, that superior performance is dependent on the peculiarities of the industry a firm occupies, the regulatory hurdles with which it must contend, regional variations, the size of firm ('small firms outperform their larger brethren'), the intensity of competition that blunts profitability and drives pressure to consolidate, and a host of other external factors. The research towards this book dismisses the vulnerability notion encapsulated here and supports a very different contention, one which is woven within Pierre Gravelle's comments above, notably that *superior performance grows out of leadership will, knowledge and capability.*

As I said in Chapter 3, the most effective leaders are both a stimulus for and a representation of the organization's collective will. Leaders, therefore, must trigger the organization's will to change and continue to change and at the same time demonstrate this in deed. The leader is thus both master and servant to organizational members. The sense of self-efficacy in the population of employees in a firm is in direct proportion to this dynamic quality of leadership. In other words, effective leadership produces conditions under which managers and staff feel able to make a difference, to have a real impact on the organizational environment. As such, the strength of leadership is a measure of the success a firm will have in its longer-term performance and in its capacity to transform.

Actively Seeking Exposure to External Pressures and
Competition

In the end, mastery must aim to build superior organizational
strength and capability as a matter of course. The best organizations will not wait for market discontinuities, external pressure,
threats and competitive action. They will seek them out. The
earlier they do this, the greater the headstart they will have to
execute properly in front of competitors. Stelios Haji-Ioannou,
who founded the UK-based cut-price airline EasyJet in 1995, did
exactly this when the European Union liberalized markets two
years later. New legislation allowed member states' airlines to
compete in all the EU's domestic markets. EasyJet set out plans
to establish new hubs in Amsterdam and Athens, boldly taking
the competitive battle direct to the Dutch KLM and the Greek
national airline Olympic Airways, and not from the security of
EasyJet's UK home base at Luton Airport but with hubs right
under the noses of KLM and Olympic – in the enemies' citadels,
as it were.

Failure to seek out discontinuities and pre-empt competitive
action may have devastating implications. Microsoft's failure,
oversight or inability to see the importance of the Internet left
Netscape to dominate the Web-browser market – *The Economist's* sampling of surveys (5 July 1997) estimated Netscape's
share at around 70% with Microsoft, despite all-out war to
recover lost ground and no expense spared, down at perhaps
30%. What longer-term effect this has, even on a firm as rich and
powerful as Microsoft, remains to be seen, but the consequences
as far as we can read them now have hurt Bill Gates' company.

The capability of the organization to perceive and act on
important market changes will be enhanced by the extent to
which it has developed and refined what we earlier called
'discontinuity search strategy' – systematic search for and early
detection of discontinuities in the business environment. Insight
into trends and needs will be most effectively leveraged by firms
that take action to access and integrate different knowledge
clusters worldwide and manage the inherent complexity. This in
itself will be facilitated by the firm's strength of links into either
geographical centres of excellence (e.g. locations such as Silicon
Valley and specific universities and research institutes) or
among local, focused networks (e.g. the firm's own employee
e-business networks, or those among suppliers or in related

industries). The aim in either case is to set a context that unavoidably and continuously brings together and manipulates knowledge that may produce forward-thinking ideas, new technologies and ways of working. There is clearly a cost to investing in this and a risk of provocation and disruption to the need for stability towards which organizations naturally gravitate. But both these things are foundation stones of mastery.

Furthermore, actively seeking exposure to external pressures and competition will eventually take organizations in most industries into the global sphere. It is shortsighted and dangerous nowadays to assume that your company has no role in the wider world, not least because you will require sound, well-thought-out strategic responses when your competitors pursue global expansion – or be left to scramble hastily behind. Moreover, the capital markets will be unrelenting in their punishment of companies that appear misdirected or, worse, confused in their global purpose. Apart from all this, there is a great prize to be gained from becoming a truly global company, as Percy Barnevik, chairman both of ABB and of Swedish investment group Investor, revealed in an interview with the *Financial Times* (8 October 1997, p.14):

> Globalisation is a long-lasting competitive advantage. If we build a new gas turbine, in 18 months our competitors also have one. But building a global company is not so easy to copy. . . . Building a multinational cadre of international managers is the key. It is one thing for a chief executive himself to be a global manager. It is quite another to persuade other executives to think and act globally.

Done properly and given time and investment, therefore, globalization of a firm is a powerful barrier to competitors and new entrants. Of course, determining a global strategy is not merely to operate on an international basis as a national company with dispersed overseas interests and markets (as Reckitt & Colman had for nearly two centuries) but to adopt a different business logic, one in which the firm transacts its business through the global integration of its operations. For organizations with global ambitions this is not a matter of choice. The *international* business model of old (as opposed to *global* model) proceeded from an assumption that the firm's own national culture would automatically determine the culture of the firm in its overseas operations. This view still predominates, particularly among American companies. Both the business logic and the culture of the global firm must change.

A truly global organization integrates its strengths across its worldwide operations, but is responsive to individual markets – 'think global, act local' as ABB put it. This requires a firm to establish itself in local markets, not simply to export to those markets. A case in point is Nikko Securities, one of the largest of the Japanese brokers. Anticipating the discontinuities that would arise from Japan's 'big bang' financial deregulation, its president, Masashi Kaneko, and his senior colleagues began to make changes to Nikko Securities that were radically different from the way traditional Japanese firms are run. First, non-Japanese managers were appointed to the most senior positions in its overseas offices. Second, Kaneko made the crucial decision to make London the hub of international operations – and not Tokyo – and seek out further international partners to help with the product areas where the firm was weakest. Moreover, Kaneko began to appoint non-Japanese to Nikko's board of directors. British Airways' aspiration to include increasing numbers of managers from multinational backgrounds, not only in customer service roles but also in key strategic positions, amounts to the same thing. In short, it escalates conflict and in so doing changes the way the organization thinks and behaves. International strength of management is therefore another sustainable competitive advantage for globalized firms.

Of course, there are great risks involved. Sometimes the only way to survive and prosper in a globalized market is to gain size through alliance, merger or acquisition. Worldcom, the telecommunications giant that rose in the USA from nothing to one of the major worldwide players in just over a decade, achieved this through aggressive acquisition and the bullish support of investors. Thus, access to capital (including everything that goes with this, such as assiduous management of investor relations) is in itself yet another of the elements that affords competitive advantage to firms with global aspirations. But business leaders must weigh the advantage of size and muscle, gained this way, with the potential disadvantages these actions may bring – most critically, the danger of shrinking from conflict, of becoming dependent on the apparent strengths of the other firms involved or becoming disinclined to upgrade one's own corporate capabilities or falling into a prolonged courtship and integration that distracts attention from the market, from competition and from innovation. Such things breed vulnerabilities in the firm, rapidly exploited by other better-adapted competitors.

But when it has sufficient size and strength to operate as a global player, the firm must establish the power of its brand or collection of brands on the international stage, cognizant of the perceptions of its potential customers: this is one of the first steps towards securing global primacy. The Ford Motor Company established the foundations of its globalized business on the back of technological advantages and the power of its brand, Coca-Cola primarily through excellent brand building and brand management. British Airways' second transformation was also aimed at exactly this: the corporate makeover involved 50 culturally diverse artistic designs expressing the company's new world identity, and were slapped on everything from aircraft tailfins to ticket wallets and airport lounges. In tandem with this, BA aimed to achieve an open and cosmopolitan style of service, finessed by a 'global, yet caring' tag. In Britain, accustomed to the airline's more sober livery and the success with which it had been associated, critics mocked. So did shareholders and some supporters. But on the international stage there were few complaints. And the company's customers and potential customers in far-flung corners of the world were the people who really counted.

Furthermore, beneath the fizz of colourful corporate image making, CEO Bob Ayling's ambition to turn the airline into the undisputed leader in world travel was not merely challenging and provocative but risky. It raised the stakes considerably: the airline would become more than just an airline; with all the implications of diversification into other world travel-related areas, BA was throwing down the gauntlet to powerful competitors in the well-established world travel business – organizations like American Express and Hogg Robinson. Certainly there were apparent synergies between flying all over the world and the related services of travel publications and guides, travel insurance, foreign exchange and travellers cheques, merchandise and photographic services. Yet these synergies are less important, in my view, than the net effect – amounting to deliberate exposure to external pressure and competition. Indeed, on another front, BA demonstrated that it was prepared to 'do unto itself what competitors might do to it' when, in late 1997, executives decided to launch a budget, no frills airline. This was to compete with the fledgling low-cost rivals in the European market such as Debonair, Ryanair and EasyJet. Only by striking out along these routes could BA continue to strengthen its capabilities and ensure longer-term value creation.

EPILOGUE . . . AND PROLOGUE

Chief executives, managers and employees who have taken on the challenge of big change – a few willingly, some unexpectedly, many without choice – and have come through the other side frequently make the same comment. 'It's hard to describe transformation,' they will say. 'You have to do it.' There is something in the nature of transformation that goes beyond the logical, rational, technical overlay of business and with which most commentators deal, and which has more to do with the *underground* work – the personal, the emotional, the unexplored and unacknowledged. Of course, this book has not been devoted to understanding the personal transformation of individuals, although this too has played its part. Rather, I have endeavoured to examine the economic, strategic and business challenge of organizational change, but from a deliberately social–psychological frame of reference. In this way I have attempted to bridge points of view or perhaps even schools of thought. This will not win everyone's support. Many managers and employees have a strongly rational cast to their world view. Mixing the rational and the psychological may be uncomfortable. It may not make sense. It may run counter to the apparent logic of business or the way some people prefer to compartmentalize the elements of working life or deal with the tasks, as they see it, that make up change. On the other hand, for some what I have had to say may be too rational, too systematic, ignoring the efforts of those who speak reverentially of change management and the utopia of learning organizations; it may be viewed as insisting overmuch that leaders lead, that they analyse and plan and take action. I hope for both reactions. If it is uncomfortable to my audience I will take a measure of cheer that it is: transformation, as I have reiterated through the book, *should* be uncomfortable. It should play at different levels of experience, or it will not work.

There are not many organizations across the world that have undertaken the kind of profound, all-embracing, tumultuous change that is transformation. Many have tried to change. Many are currently engulfed in change. And few enterprises, if any, have the luxury of choosing not to change. The old adage of *'when* not *if'* bears remembering. But how many of these will realize their aspirations? How many will even set out to create the right conditions for big change? How many will have developed leadership equal to the task? How many will be dismayed by the seemingly insurmountable difficulties of embedding systemic innovation or will recoil from the threat of conflict that is inherent to transformation? I choose to be optimistic. Big change can be threatening, but it can also be hugely energizing. This is the energy of aspiration and ambition, where the human spirit is lifted from slumber and the cocoon of workaday ritual, where being part of a great undertaking with all its risks and promises enables the ordinary to become extraordinary.

It is true also that big change is a cycle: in spite of the great effort and time we may devote, our yearning to seek a conclusion to things will be misplaced. To sustain competitive success, we must transform again. More than anything else, the current research has confirmed for me that senior executives and managers who understand the broader, cyclical sweep of change are rare and exceptional. The pressure of modern business life perhaps exacerbates this shortcoming: we see what is immediate and we react; the stakeholders who concern us – shareholders, lobby groups or this day's customers – exert a disproportionate influence. We struggle to see possibilities, how things might be, given time and dedicated effort. We cannot see the future so we decline to create it.

Transformation demands that we conceive the future. It tells us that when we have completed this day's transformation, there will be another. It tells us that there will always be change and that we can either lead it or be led by it. We end where we began. We begin where we have ended.

References

Alsop, A. (1996). Innovation and psychology: themes and research funding. In 'Innovation in organizations'. *European Journal of Work and Organizational Psychology*, **5** (1), 149–53.

Ansoff, H.I. (1987). *Corporate Strategy*. Penguin, London.

Bandura, A. (1977). *Social Learning Theory*. Prentice Hall, Englewood Cliffs, NJ.

Bennis, W. (1989). *On Becoming a Leader*. Century Business Books, London.

Business Week (8 July 1996). The globetrotters take over: the *Business Week* Global 100. 48–60.

Business Week (26 May 1997). IBM: The ultimate case for patient capital. 61.

Capers, R.S. (1994). NASA post Hubble: too little, too late? *Academy of Management*, May.

Carnoy, M. (1985). High technology and international labour markets. *International Labour Review*, **124** (6).

Carroll, P. (1993). *Big Blues: The Unmaking of IBM*. Orion, London.

Chaisson, E.J. (1994). *The Hubble Wars*. HarperPerennial, New York.

The 1996 Chatham House Forum Report (1996). *Unsettled Times: Three Stony Paths to 2015*. The Royal Institute of International Affairs, London.

Churchill, W. (1933–8). *Marlborough* (4 vols). Harrap, London.

Collins, J. and Porras, J. (1995). *Built to Last*. HarperCollins, London.

De Dreu, C. (1997). Productive conflict: the importance of conflict management and conflict issue. In De Dreu, C. and Van de Vliert, E. (eds), *Using Conflict in Organizations*. Sage, London.

The Economist (17 January 1998). The Lloyds money machine. 81–2.

The Economist (29 March 1997). Survey: Silicon Valley.

The Economist (5 July 1997). Why Netscape isn't dead. 74.

The Economist (27 September 1997). The clouds clear over Europe. 118–21.

Ekvall, G. (1996). Organizational climate for creativity and innovation. In 'Innovation in organizations'. *European Journal of Work and Organizational Psychology* (September–October), 134–47.

Financial Times (10 May 1996). ScottishPower sets sights on becoming 'Multi-utility'. By Simon Holberton.

Financial Times (13 May 1997). A new spirit is brought into the world. By Tony Jackson, 27.

Financial Times (26 June 1997). BA strike threatens to cloud Ayling's horizons. By Michael Skapinker, 9.

Financial Times (8 October 1997). Own words: Percy Barnevik, ABB and investor. Interviewed by Stefan Wagstyl, 14.

Flight International (15 November 1995). Dan dares – NASA. By Tim Furness, 32.

Forbes (2 June 1997). The Web and the workplace. By Joshua Levine, 178–80.

Fortune (29 April 1996). Big Blue is betting on big iron. 56–61.

Fortune (28 April 1997). Sears: the turnaround is ending; the revolution has begun. 106–18.

Gardner, H. (1995). *Leading Minds: An Anatomy of Leadership*. HarperCollins, London.

Gould, J.L. and Gould, C.J. (1982). The insect mind: physics or metaphysics? In Griffin, D.R. (ed.), *Animal Mind – Human Mind*. Springer-Verlag, Berlin.

Hamel, G. (1996). Strategy as revolution. *Harvard Business Review* (July–August), 69–82.

Hamel, G. and Prahalad, C.K. (1994). *Competing for the Future*. Harvard Business School Press, Boston.

Hamilton, P.F. (1995). *The Nano Flower*. Pan Books, London.

Handy, C. (1996). Finding sense in uncertainty. In Gibson, R. (ed.), *Rethinking the Future*. Nicholas Brealey Publishing, London.

Huntington, S.P. (1996). *The Clash of Civilizations and the Remaking of World Order*. Simon & Schuster, New York.

Imparato, N. and Harari, O. (1994). *Jumping the Curve: Innovation and Strategic Choice in an Age of Transition*. Jossey-Bass, San Francisco.

Janis, I.L. (1972). *Victims of Groupthink*. Houghton-Mifflin, Boston.

Kaplan, R.S. and Norton, D.P. (1993). Putting the balanced scorecard to work. *Harvard Business Review* (September–October), 134–47.

Kennedy, P. (1993). *Preparing for the Twenty-First Century*. HarperCollins, London.

Kotter, J.P. (1996). *Leading Change*. Harvard Business School Press, Boston.

Larkin, T.J. and Larkin, S. (1996). Reaching and changing frontline employees. *Harvard Business Review* (May–June), 95–104.

Lewin, K. (1947). Group decisions and social change. In Newcomb, T. and Hartley, E. (eds), *Readings in Social Psychology*. Holt, Rinehart & Winston, New York.

Mandela, N. (1994). *Long Walk to Freedom*. Little, Brown, London.

Merton, R. (1948). The self-fulfilling prophecy. *The Antioch Review* (Summer), 195–210.

Porter, M. (1990). *The Competitive Advantage of Nations*. Macmillan, London.

Robbins, S.P. (1974). *Managing Organizational Conflict: A Non-traditional Approach*. Prentice Hall, Englewood Cliffs, NJ.

Salk, J. and Salk, J. (1981). *World Population and Human Values: A New Reality*. HarperCollins, New York.

Schumpeter, J.A. (1942). *Capitalism, Socialism and Democracy*. Harper & Row, New York.

Seligman, M.E.P. (1975). *Helplessness*. W.H. Freeman, San Francisco.

Simmons, D. (1989). *Hyperion*. Headline Books, London.

Simmons, D. (1990). *The Fall of Hyperion*. Headline Books, London.

Stross, R.E. (1996). *The Microsoft Way*. Little, Brown & Company, London.

The Sunday Times (1 October 1995). Eco's pendulum of opinion. By Nicholas Fraser.

Taffinder, P. (1995). *The New Leaders: Achieving Corporate Transformation through Dynamic Leadership*. Kogan Page, London.

Time (13 January 1997). Hooray for Bill Gates . . . I guess. By Lance Morrow, 64.

Time (3 February 1997). Welcome to the wired world. By Joshua Cooper Ramo, 30–37.

Time (18 August 1997). Steve's job: restart Apple. By Cathy Booth, 34–43.

Time (18 August 1997). If you can't beat 'em . . . . By Michael Krantz, 41–3.

Turner, M.E. and Pratkanis, A.R. (1997). Mitigating groupthink by stimulating constructive conflict. In De Dreu, C. and Van de Vliert, E. (eds), *Using Conflict in Organizations*. Sage, London.

Van de Vliert, E. (1997). Enhancing performance by conflict-stimulating intervention. In De Dreu, C. and Van de Vliert, E. (eds), *Using Conflict in Organizations*. Sage, London.

Wallace, J. (1997). *Overdrive: Bill Gates and the Race to Control Cyberspace.* Wiley, New York.

Walton, R.E. (1969). *Interpersonal Peacemaking: Confrontations and Third-Party Consultation.* Addison-Wesley, Reading, MA.

Index

Note: Page numbers in *italics* refer to figures; those in **bold** refer to Tables

Index compiled by Annette Musker

REDEPLOYMENT takes readers to
the frontlines of the wars in Iraq, asking
us to understand what happened there,
and what happened to the soldiers
who returned.

Interwoven with themes of brutality and
faith, guilt and fear, helplessness and survival,
the characters in these stories struggle to make
meaning out of chaos. Written with a hard-
eyed realism andstunning emotional depth,
REDEPLOYMENT marks Phil Klay as one
of the most talented new voices
of his generation.

REDEPLOYMENT takes readers to
the frontlines of the wars in Iraq, asking
us to understand what happened there,
and what happened to the soldiers
who returned.

Interwoven with themes of brutality and
faith, guilt and fear, helplessness and survival,
the characters in these stories struggle to make
meaning out of chaos. Written with a hard-
eyed realism andstunning emotional depth,
REDEPLOYMENT marks Phil Klay as one
of the most talented new voices
of his generation.